Wealth Management in the New Economy

Investor Strategies for Growing, Protecting and Transferring Wealth

NORBERT M. MINDEL
SARAH E. SLEIGHT

WILEY

John Wiley & Sons, Inc.

Published by John Wiley & Sons, Inc., Hoboken, New Jersey.
Published simultaneously in Canada.

For general information on our other products and services or for technical support, please contact our Customer Care Department within the United States at (800) 762-2974, outside the United States at (317) 572-3993 or fax (317) 572-4002.

Wiley also publishes its books in a variety of electronic formats. Some content that appears in print may not be available in electronic books. For more information about Wiley products, visit our web site at www.wiley.com.

Library of Congress Cataloging-in-Publication Data:

Mindel, Norbert M., 1952–
  Wealth management in the new economy : investor strategies for growing, protecting and transferring wealth / Norbert M. Mindel and Sarah E. Sleight.
       p. cm.
  Includes bibliographical references and index.
  ISBN 978-0-470-48269-8 (cloth)
  1. Investments–Management.   2. Portfolio management.   3. Retirement income–Planning.   4. Estate planning.   I. Sleight, Sarah E.   II. Title.
  HG4521.M468 2010
  332.6–dc22

                                                           2009033772

Printed in the United States of America

10 9 8 7 6 5 4 3 2 1

To my wife,
Judy,
and my children,
Rachel, Ariel, Talia, and Zachary

Contents

Preface

It has taken me 30 years to write this book. I don't mean I have been working on this manuscript all that time, but it has taken me more than half a lifetime of experience to learn enough to be able to share my expertise as a wealth manager.

I have spent my career helping my clients grow, preserve, and protect their wealth. Over the years I have worked with hundreds of advisers and their clients as well as with my own clients. My story goes beyond my personal circle of experience; it is also the story of Terra Securities, the financial services firm I co-founded and which provided my laboratory for learning; and it is the story of my clients, my business partners, and the era I lived through. It is also the history of the financial planning industry, from the early days when financial plans were cranked out by the first primitive computers, until now, when a real financial plan has to integrate all aspects of wealth management.

What is the most important lesson I have learned? Growing and preserving wealth is not about picking investments, and still less is it about getting rich quickly through some stock tips. In fact, accumulating money is only a part of it. The single most important part of managing wealth is managing risk.

But managing risk does not mean *avoiding* risk; you will not be successful if you bury your head in the sand and your money in your mattress, even though that is what many clients want to do right now. Even after the disastrous down markets of 2008, I still believe that *not* staying in the market is the riskiest strategy of all. If you want to accumulate wealth, your long-term investment strategy has to accept risk and learn to manage it.

This message about the importance of managing risk is essential to the way I do business and the way I advise my clients, but it is not widely discussed in the popular media or even in the financial industry. Because many clients like to get their information from reading, I looked for a book I could recommend that would integrate all the aspects of wealth management with an overall understanding of managing risk—and could not find one. I knew then I would have to write my own, and talk about my own lifetime of experience.

I want to share with my readers the same kind of advice I share with the clients who sit in front of me in my office. My subject matter might surprise you the way it sometimes surprises my clients—I do not focus on finance and investments alone. I have known for a long time that accumulating and preserving wealth could not be accomplished through investments alone. This is truer now than it has ever been, despite the market debacle of 2008. However those markets affected you, you will still be able to accumulate assets, and protect and preserve them and pass them to the next generation, if you look beyond the investments alone and learn to understand risk.

My experience has been expensive. I made a lot of mistakes, but I wear them proudly because I made them with the best will in the world and while trying as hard as I knew how to do the right thing for my clients. I wish I had been able to avoid some of the mistakes I made; however, I am willing to share those mistakes because I think my readers can learn from them—and avoid the long years I spent in the wilderness. I believe my personal story can provide insight into an entire chapter of Wall Street history, and that reading about my efforts to help my clients can help other individuals better understand the astonishing period we have just lived through.

I tell my own story because it is what I know. But there is another important reason for including my own experience and stories about my clients in this book: Everyone loves stories. This kind of information can be dry when offered up in textbook fashion. I hope my own life experiences can bring the material to life and make it more interesting to read and easier to understand.

In this book I describe the failure of the people I call the Really Smart Guys (RSGs) on Wall Street, and why it was really only a matter of time before they collapsed. Books about the calamitous events of Wall Street's recent failures are going to pour out over the next 25 years, but that is not the purpose of this book. I am concerned above all with how the fallout from these gigantic system failures will affect the wealth strategies of my readers and clients going forward.

I explain why the notion of hiring so-called smart advisers to pick stocks is a waste of time. I tell you what the academics say about how markets really work and how I discovered a sustainable investment strategy. And I discuss how the system for delivering financial advice is broken and how clients need an independent, fee-based adviser who sits on the same side of the table as they do.

Managing wealth requires strategies to protect wealth from the risks of litigation, ill health, premature death, and taxes. It also requires you to plan for your retirement, when you will need a stream of income to maintain your standard of living for 30 or 40 or 50 years. I discuss the mysteries of the arcane world of life insurance and what you need to know before choosing a carrier and a policy. You also need to understand how to protect yourself from unnecessary estate taxes and devastating medical costs. Beyond that, when people accumulate wealth, they often have a decided perspective on how they want that wealth transferred to the next generation, and they need a basic understanding of how estate planning works.

None of this is easy or obvious. This is not a book about budgeting for credit cards or pricing a mortgage; this book is about managing and protecting your serious money for the rest of your life.

I believe that reading this book can help make you more knowledgeable in general about the topics of wealth management and will help make you a more informed investor and consumer of wealth management services. I hope you will be interested in the stories from my own practice and history. By the time you finish reading this book, I hope you will have a better understanding of risk and return and will be better able to manage both. You will also understand that although there is a great deal of the overall wealth management process that you can attend to yourself, depending on your own interests and lifestyle, you will have to consult specialists for at least some parts of the process—unless you are an estate-planning attorney or investment adviser yourself. Reading this book will give you a clearer vision of the strengths and capabilities such professionals should have.

So then, turning to the book itself, I divide the world of risk for individuals into four main categories:

1. *Investments and wealth accumulation.* How should you invest your money? Is your money safe? Will you receive a market rate of return? Is your money really invested the way you think it is?
2. *Retirement and retirement income.* Are you going to have enough money for all of your retirement? When you think about retirement, you have to take into consideration *longevity* risk, the risk of outliving your money; and *point-in-time* risk, the risk of retiring into a bear market. What is the most efficient way to turn your wealth into a stream of income to last the rest of your life, no matter when you retire or how long you live?
3. *Wealth and lifestyle protection.* What kind of insurance do you need, for all parts of your financial and economic life? Do you need permanent or term life insurance? What kinds of policies should you consider?
4. *Transferring your wealth.* How do you organize your entire estate so that you can enjoy your assets during your life but pass them on as you wish after your death? If you are part of a family business, you will have special concerns.

This book is divided into five main sections that correspond to these kinds of risk. Parts I and II address the investment part of the wealth management story. Part I relates my own experience in learning about managing wealth and the reasons the traditional methods did not work for my business, my clients, or me. Part Two introduces the investment philosophy I now endorse and use in my practice, but you will never encounter this kind of low-cost, passive, massively diversified strategy on Wall Street.

Part Three addresses income planning for retirement. Chapter 7 provides an introduction to the topic; Chapter 8 discusses the good and bad aspects of annuities; and Chapter 9 provides an introduction to the world of qualified plans. Make sure your IRA beneficiaries are up to date!

Part Four addresses an individual's need for various kinds of protection. Chapter 10 provides deep insight into the world of life insurance, and was written by my colleague Howard Kite, who has been working with—and trying to understand—insurance for most of his career. Chapter 11 provides an introduction to the need for long-term care insurance: why it is one of the most important elements in your entire estate plan, and why not having it can devastate all your otherwise well-laid plans.

Part Five addresses estate planning. An introduction to its most important principles will have to suffice, which I provide in Chapter 12. Chapter 13 is a look at the specialized circumstances of estate planning for family businesses. Entrepreneurs, especially those with family businesses, are some of my favorite clients, and this chapter is for them.

Finally, in the Epilogue I summarize some of the most important things I hope you will have learned by reading this book.

I suggest you take a step back and look at some of the important questions and issues you will read about in this book. By the time you have finished reading, I hope you will have a clearer view on all of these questions.

- The smart guys on Wall Street have long loved to offer the prospect of outsized returns in the form of hedge funds, gold and other commodities, structured products, derivatives, technical analysis, momentum investing, market timing, and more. Wall Street has always loved to gamble with *your* money. What do we understand now about these products? After generating billions of dollars in profits for themselves, in the end these smart guys failed their shareholders, their clients, and themselves.
- What can we learn from the demise of traditional Wall Street? Firms that had been in business for 150 years went bankrupt, sold themselves to other firms, or transformed themselves overnight from investment banking to commercial banking. Why is it important? The most ironic part of it all: Less than a year after their most abject failure, those guys are still around, ready to turn secure investments into structured products and talk the blather of Wall Street's golden years.

- Why is investment success so elusive for so many individuals? How do you recognize the right long-term investment strategy?
- How does the way you create wealth lead to predictable, identifiable mistakes when you try to protect and perpetuate it?
- What role has the financial media played in whipping up hype and investor frenzy to support Wall Street's casino mentality?
- Why are individuals so reluctant to take the steps necessary to protect themselves and their families from the dangers of litigation, ill health, and the IRS? Learn why the biggest threat to your portfolio is not a bear market but disability or a stay in a long-term-care facility—or your own inability to decide to protect yourself proactively.
- What types of insurance are cost-effective and necessary and what types are just expensive or even dangerous to your financial well-being? When do you need short-term insurance and why does long-term wealth transfer require permanent insurance?
- Have you ever met an annuity you could like? Today's annuities are not the same instruments your parents rightfully shunned, and you might need to use them to get to your long-term retirement goals.
- Why are individuals their own worst enemies when dealing with estate planning and inheritance?

My book is different because it is about the larger context of managing wealth. I am not going to tell an amazing story of techniques that only I can use; I do not depend on a secret sauce or a black box or a strategy so arcane it requires a PhD in physics to understand. In fact, I believe more strongly than ever that understandable, transparent investments are the only ones that individuals should use.

My principles of wealth management can—and should—be put into practice by anyone who wants to create and sustain wealth while managing risk. I hope my story will inspire others to work smarter while preparing for the future. Finally, despite all those other thousands of books you can consult, this is the only book that integrates all these topics together at a level of complexity that is understandable and actionable for normal people.

Acknowledgments

This book is about my experiences and lessons in becoming a better financial adviser. As with all life experiences, there were good times and bad, but through them all I had great teachers and friends along the way.

First, I thank both Dimensional Fund Advisors and Genworth Financial for generously allowing us to use some of their source material and research.

Turning to the important individuals in my life, who would ever have guessed that the guy who sat next to me in my law school tort class would be my friend for the rest of my life? Joseph B. Hudetz's coupon business helped subsidize our penniless law practice when we first started out in business together after law school, and 30 years later, he remains one of my closest friends. I will always be grateful to Joe.

Who would ever have guessed that the lunch Joe and I went to in 1979 with David S. Reedy would lead to an assignment to write legal documents for some real estate securities—and then to 30 more years in business together and a lifetime of friendship as well? Dave always brought optimism and cheer to get us through our most difficult times in business. Dave became a great business leader and I was smart enough to follow; he was president of Genworth Financial Securities when he retired. I also want to thank him for his help on this book. He had details and stories I could not believe he remembered which improved the book significantly.

I want to thank Brian T. Savage, CPA, PFS, CFP®, who taught me 30 years ago, when I was a young lawyer, not only how to deal with the IRS but also much of what I know about the U.S tax system. Along the way, he also taught me about the joy and history of the Irish, as well the fact that March 17 is a holy day. He has been my business partner, and one of my closest friends and confidants, ever since. His analytical skills are rare and helped us build a great business.

I cannot say enough good things about Marcus K. Heinrich, CFP, who has been my partner in two different firms. He burst onto the scene at Terra and brought so much enthusiasm and vitality that he energized our program and took it to a new level. He brought innovative thinking and a commitment to success that served Terra extremely well. Marcus was then brave enough to join me in founding a second firm, Forum Financial, and we took on the challenge of starting an advisory firm with few clients. I appreciate the contributions he made to this book. Marcus has taught hundreds of financial advisers how to be better advisers.

I want to thank Howard S. Kite, who loves to teach and mentor young advisers so they can become better advisers. When I was a young adviser, I had little knowledge of the insurance industry. Howard's unique gift is to be able to take the arcane words of an insurance policy and explain them so even I can understand. The chapters on insurance demonstrate his ability to make the complex understandable. Those chapters also make this book better.

I give special thanks to Susan Williams and Byron Faermark for their work on the estate planning sections and to Debra Carpenter for her contributions to the chapter on long-term care. This book is much better and more complete because of the contributions of these three individuals.

I am extremely grateful to Annette Bronkesh, an experienced PR professional with the world's most amazing Rolodex of contacts, for getting us over the finish line with our publishers. I very much appreciate her enthusiasm for this book.

Finally, I also thank the rest of my partners at Forum for their support during the time we were writing this book: John J. Adam, EA, CFP; Mary Pat Wesche, CPA, PFS, CFP; Joseph A. Spokas, CPA, PFS, CFP; Robert T. Methven; and Jack A. Folkerts, CPA, CFP. Even more important than my partners are the people who run the office and keep us organized. I want to thank Allison Tronnes, Debbie Manno, and Elise Milo for their diligence every day doing work I could never do (paperwork above all)—and for making us all better advisers.

I owe special thanks to the following people who helped to make this a better book: Thomas Mengel, CLU, ChFC, MSFS; Charles Surdyke, CFP; Thomas Murphy; and Mark Finke, CFP. I also owe special thanks to Alan Hambourger, CPA, CFP, PFS; David Strulowitz, JD, LLM; Raymond Sullivan Jr., CPA; Arvin Weindruch, CPA; Jacob I. Rosenberg, CPA, CFP, PFS; and James H. Bernath, CPA, CFP, PFS. I want to thank Michael J. McManamna, who understands how the numbers really work better than any of us, and Steven J. Sheehan, who has been a good friend throughout the whole odyssey of writing a book and finding a publisher. I thank Christopher Genzler for his 10 years of hard work as a colleague and a friend as we built the fee-based business post-Terra; I could not have asked for a better coworker through the thick and thin of those first years. Thanks also to Ted G. Stricker.

Sarah and I are both extremely grateful to Matt H. Miller, CFP, of Dimensional Fund Advisors, for volunteering to help us with this book and shepherding it through the permissions process with DFA. I thank my daughter

Rachel Mindel for taking on the challenge of designing the charts for this book.

I already knew that writing a book was very hard work, based on my earlier book. I did not realize, however, that it could also be a great adventure until I started working with Sarah Sleight. The fact of the matter is that knowing a lot about a subject is very different from being able to write about it, let alone write a book about it. Thank God I was lucky enough to find someone who could listen to my blathering and actually turn it into a book. She was able to take my lifetime of experience and add to it her own deep knowledge and understanding of the products and issues we address, thus allowing her to connect the dots that I left unconnected, fill in the background, and construct whole chapters. And then she applied her writing talents to turn the whole thing into a book that we hope people will want to read.

But when all is said and done, there is one person to whom I owe my life and who makes my life worth living. There are very few wives who would put up with the insanity and uncertainty of a husband who does not have a steady paycheck and keeps starting new businesses. I could never have gotten this far without Judy by my side, to tolerate all the days and nights I spent working, to do more than her share to raise the children and make a home for all of us. Because of her I have the American dream. I also thank my kids, Rachel, Ariel, Talia, and Zachary, for their ongoing love and support, although to this day I think they are not really sure what I do for a living. I know they always suspected that I did some kind of secret government work, but sorry, kids, the cat is out of the bag: I am not 007 or Spiderman (never mind that costume you found in the closet—talk to your mom about that).

Introduction

You might not expect the lonely, only child of Holocaust survivors to be telling you how to grow, protect, and transfer your wealth in any economy, let alone this one. I am often surprised by where I am today because my early years were so hard. My parents owned a kosher deli in Brooklyn and worked 80 hours a week. We never went out for dinner, never went on vacation, never owned a car. We never went anywhere. As an only child, my role was always and only to make do. I led a solitary existence. I made friends in school, but that was the limit of my social circle.

My father would close the deli only for the Jewish high holidays and Passover. My parents were not particularly religious, which might seem ironic to an outsider, given the Holocaust background. They kept the deli open seven days a week, trying to make a living. My dad was gregarious and engaging but not a particularly good businessman. He was the salesman while my mother was the bookkeeper, so I guess they made a decent team. They eked out their poor living without reaching the middle class.

We would get together with the rest of my family for Seder. These family occasions form some of my earliest recollections. The family did not talk about the war, but occasionally some black humor would seep out. We knew about the camps because my aunt had tattooed numbers on her arm, but survivors were reticent to go into detail.

My entire childhood had a dark, foreboding background that seemed the more ominous for being mostly unexpressed. I wonder if I would have felt differently if the stories had actually been told. But then, how could you tell that kind of story to a child without doing even more damage? So many children grow up with what I think of as a *Sesame Street* approach to life: Life is wonderful and beautiful. But I was surrounded by people who, although they seemed to be happy enough and were certainly functional, had lived through unimaginable horror. As a small child of five, six, seven years old, I gained a very dark impression of life that I have never lost. Is the glass half full or half empty? The answer for me is always the same. Against that horrific background, life is extremely fragile.

Growing up in New York City in the lower-middle class, surrounded by immense wealth, branded me with a starvation complex I have never

The Train Set

Jewish or not, when you live in New York City, you get caught up in the festivities of Christmas. For me, a high point of the year was my parents taking me to Manhattan to go to Radio City Music Hall and see the show and a movie. Then we would go to Macy's. One year I was transfixed by a train set I saw there. I had never seen anything like it and I wanted it. I stayed there for an hour and wanted to stay longer. I could tell that my parents were wishing they could get it for me. They looked at each other and my mother sighed and said, "Well, let me go see if I can put it on a credit card." I didn't know what that was, but the long and short of it was that we could not buy the train set.

When I look back at that time now from my current vantage point as a father, my heart breaks for the parents who wanted me to have a toy they could not afford. I was not asking for anything outlandish; it was the same kind of train set middle-class boys all over the country got for Christmas.

Even at that young age, that was a turning point in my life, and it later became an obsession. I never want to be in the position of not being able to afford the train set.

outgrown. Every day, my parents worked endless hours to make a poor living and we were always in danger of falling into outright poverty. I lived this way through my entire childhood and absorbed into my soul that fear of falling off the edge. We had no financial cushion. Even now, after all this time, I can find myself gripped by the irrational anxiety that I am going to be back there again, looking into a black hole of poverty. Of course it is irrational—that's the nature of anxiety: It attacks you at your emotional core like a nightmare, before your rational mind has a chance to come to the rescue. To this day, that starvation complex drives me relentlessly towards more work and more achievement. The further away I am from that place, the happier and more secure I feel.

Family Influences

I am probably no different from anyone else in saying how profoundly my life has been influenced by my family. But my family was not the *Ozzie and Harriet* American ideal. I got a sense of darkness and skepticism, as well as a perspective on the fragility of life, from my family of Holocaust survivors. Although I was an only child, other family members influenced my life so profoundly that I do not know who I would be today if I had not known them.

No one is quite sure how my father's son Sam managed to survive World War II. My father had been married before the war and most of that family was exterminated in the concentration camps. After Poland was divided between Germany and the Soviet Union at the beginning of the war, my father found himself in Siberia with his brother. He got separated from his family and wound up in the British army. Sam was the only other survivor from my father's first marriage.

Sam was 13 when the war started, and he forged papers to prove he was baptized as a Christian. He joined the underground during the war, and his work with the Jewish underground after the war ended with his nervous breakdown. Somehow he made it to the United States, got his plumbing license, and reconnected with my father before I was born. Sam was an intimidating individual who became enormously wealthy and successful doing plumbing construction in prominent Manhattan high-rises.

He was one of my most important role models. His amazing success, built out of a background of privation and personal suffering, demonstrated to me what can be achieved by focusing intently and maintaining discipline, despite obstacles that are literally incredible to us. Sam survived the Holocaust to become a rich and important citizen; I would never have to overcome anything remotely as challenging.

My mother was another driving force in my life and represented an intellectual pillar for me. My father was the outgoing one, whose gregarious nature provided a role model for whatever sales skills I have. But my mother, along with her four siblings, had received an elite education in prewar Poland and somehow survived the war. She spoke five languages and read books in French and German throughout her life. My mom was small physically but was one of the toughest, most resilient people I have ever met.

While my brother inspired awe for being able to struggle and fight for success against tremendous odds, my mother inspired intellectual curiosity and my rabid desire to accumulate knowledge. She passed down to me as well the Jewish tradition of learning, reading, and going to college. She taught me how important it is to study, study, study. This has been one of the most important influences in my life.

My mother had grown up in a wealthy, prestigious household, and then, through no fault of her own, lost her family, her friends, and the life they had led. Now she had to work very hard, 80- to 100-hour weeks, for such little profit that she could not afford to buy her son a toy train. You might expect such a person to be angry, bitter, and miserable. But she was not. She accepted the change in her life's circumstances very philosophically, no doubt because she was so profoundly happy to be alive. She never focused on money or material possessions. Her goal was to build inner toughness. She realized how fragile existence was and how little security anyone ever had. My mother never lost her intellectual curiosity and, at the same time, this diminutive person was never intimidated by anything.

The hard life my parents lived, set against the background of darkness that I was aware of but did not yet understand, underscored for me the importance of my mother's exhortations to get as much education as I could—which I did. However, it seems like tragic irony to me that, after all, her excellent education had not done much to improve the circumstances of my mother's life.

With rare exception, my mother did not talk about the war. She said that her father buried the family's wealth in the basement. There was always family lore about trying to go back and find the money they had put away, but only the children survived the war. It was not clear whether the siblings could even have located the family home.

High School Experiences and the Gypsy Cab

Beyond my family, my high school experiences were also formative. When I was finally old enough to go to high school, I passed a tough qualifying exam to be accepted into what was basically an engineering school filled with 6,000 male nerds and geeks. Brooklyn Technical High School specialized in engineering, math, and science, and I chose it because I thought I wanted to be an electrical engineer. That idea might be laughable now, but it is not that easy to figure out who you are or what you are going to be good at when you are 13.

Unfortunately, the school was located in the middle of one of the worst areas of Brooklyn. My friends got mugged. There was no way to stay after school for activities, and the idea of a football or basketball team or any kind of school spirit was laughable. The year after I graduated they allowed girls in; my timing was always impeccable.

It was an incredibly elite education because of the competition to get in. I met blazingly smart people who went on to fill the rolls of Harvard, MIT, and the other top universities, but it was not a place that helped anyone develop social skills or networks of friendship.

The summer before I went to college, my mom scraped together some money to get me a 1968 Ford Torino with an eight-track stereo player. I worked in New York City as a car service driver, a nice name for what is basically gypsy cab driving. That means that I drove a car for pay but did not have a taxi medallion or any kind of license making it legal for me to do so. I worked through a service. Only in New York would there be an established service provider for something that is essentially illegal!

I worked 10 hours a day and actually made a decent amount of money. Of course I met many weird, strange, crazy people. People used gypsy cabs for a reason, and the clientele included drug addicts and prostitutes. I would drive them to some of the most bizarre neighborhoods in New York. Yet it ended up being a pretty reasonable way to make money for college. At the end of the summer, the owner of the place actually called my mom to tell her what a great job I did, so I guess I can always have that job as a fallback position.

Higher Education

From high school to the gypsy cab to college, I kept growing up. I got a scholarship at the Illinois Institute of Technology (IIT) in Chicago. I did not want to stay in New York. I was aware that my family did not have money, and I knew that money opened doors. I didn't have much of a life there and I just wanted to get out. Even so, I still wanted to live in a city and for some reason IIT appealed to me. Then I arrived in Chicago only to discover that the Institute is in one of the worst areas of the city on the South Side of Chicago.

I registered for coursework in engineering. About three weeks into the engineering program, I was in a math class with a friend from Brooklyn. The instructor gave us a calculus problem about a lighthouse with a light that swept at a 30-degree arc, moving three times a minute; we had to give the equation for calculating the area of the light. My friend and I looked at each other, closed our math books, and walked out of the class: We were never going to be engineers. We both switched to business majors. I ended up attending the Stuart School of Business at IIT.

After graduating from IIT, I attended Chicago-Kent School of Law, the law school affiliated with IIT. I never had a tremendous passion for the law or for being a lawyer; I just wanted to have a career without working for someone else. I figured out early on that I was not suited for any kind of corporate-type environment.

My goal was to have my own business; I hoped that gaining a law degree and CPA certification would put me on the path to achieving that goal. My fellow freshman students in law school would talk about their passion for the law and how they had always wanted to be lawyers and litigators, to save children and trees and help the oppressed. When they turned to me, the only thing I could say was that I did not want to work for anyone. The irony is that, eventually, I worked for a while for one of the largest companies in the world. But even that experience could not transform me into a corporate man.

Gaining Credentials

While I was in law school, I became obsessed with the idea of gaining additional credentials, maybe partly due to the emphasis my mother placed on study and learning. I was motivated by the thought that credentials would make it easier for me to find a job, although 80 rejection letters were to prove how mistaken that idea was (more on that later). I thought that a Certified Public Accounting credential would make a powerful combination with a law degree, whether I worked for a firm or for myself. With an undergraduate degree in accounting, I had enough background to start working on my CPA.

I signed up for a CPA review class during my senior year of law school. These classes are as robust as college courses and require a tremendous amount of homework. Class was three or four hours twice a week; later we also had to attend on Saturday mornings.

Interestingly enough, the person sitting next to me in class was Joe Spokas, who eventually became a Terra Representative (much more to come on that topic) and then became one of my partners in the Forum. That was serendipity!

The review course was incredibly arduous. For a six-month period, I attended law school, worked as a law clerk and also attended the review course. I was disciplined and focused because I was determined that this was a one-shot deal since I was set to graduate from law school in another semester. The onerous CPA test has four parts, and we were allowed to pass two at one time and the other two at a later time. In those days, only about 18 to 20 percent of students passed all four parts the first time. I spent every spare minute studying. After taking the test, I went back to my life and anxiously waited for several tortured months to find out the results. In the meantime, I had to race back to catch up on my law studies. Yes, I passed.

I graduated from law school with both a law degree and a CPA accreditation. Next up was the bar exam. I took another review course, this time for law. Like my classmates, I was stressed out at the thought of not passing. Heaven knows what I would have done if I had not passed because there were no barista jobs available at that time.

There used to be a test called the Registry of Financial Planners, which was a competitor to the Certified Financial Planner (CFP®) designation. Given my law and accounting background, I was able to take one of the first tests for the Registry of Financial Planners and passed. Eventually the Registry merged with the CFP and that is how I became a CFP.

Being a CFP and also a CPA, I gained entrée to becoming a Personal Financial Specialist (PFS), which is a designation available only to CFPs who are also members of the American Institute of Certified Public Accountants (AICPA). Membership in the AICPA means a professional has agreed to a binding code of professional conduct, has a certain number of hours of financial planning business experience, and has passed a comprehensive and rigorous personal financial planning exam. This credential distinguishes CPAs who specialize in personal financial planning and demonstrates a higher level of skill and knowledge.

Much later, when I started working for a broker-dealer, I had to take the stockbroker's exams (Series 7 and 63). Because I was a principal in the firm, I also had to take the harder Series 24, and then needed an insurance license as well. Furthermore, at one point when I was a lawyer, we had developed a substantial niche in real estate, so I had to sit for my own real estate license and then taught real estate brokers about real estate closings and other aspects of real estate law.

Practicing Law and Teaching Accounting

Unfortunately for me, despite passing law school in the top 10 percent of my class, Chicago-Kent College of Law was not considered top tier. I applied for jobs but got rejected everywhere; I received those 80 rejection letters I mentioned earlier. I kept those letters for years afterwards as a negative motivator, because I was determined never to fail like that again.

Since no one wanted to hire me, and since I did not really want to join a corporate law firm anyway, my law school friend Joe Hudetz and I decided to open a law firm in Oakbrook, Illinois. I had no money and no particular prospects—and of course we had no clients. What value proposition can you have when you are selling law? We basically begged people to hire us because we said we would work faster and charge less than anyone else. Our only focus was on survival.

The first 90 days were one of the most difficult experiences of my life. I don't know how we made it through. Joe had a tiny bit of money on the side and I had nothing. Trying to get started, we spent more money on entertainment than we did on any other kind of overhead. The one saving grace was that Joe came from a very large, well-connected family in DuPage County, Illinois. His wide circle of acquaintanceship opened many doors for us to meet people, although getting paying business was another story. Joe fronted the money to start the firm so we could survive and I could eat and pay the rent. I will always be grateful to Joe for being our bank.

For the next few years, I sought out places to give talks. I was like a young comedian trying to break into show business in the Catskills—I accepted any kind of invitation. If I did not know the topic, I would learn it. Whether it was the church basement, the Rotary club or a real estate organization, I would get up in front of any group and try to get business. It was either do that or starve, and my starvation complex kept me going. This so-called starvation complex was really a fear of failure, and it has been a driving force for most of my business career.

However, in the long run, all that public speaking at such an early point in my career has served me extremely well throughout my entire career because I have never been intimidated by any audience. I know people who are paralyzed with fear at the idea of an audience, but I am not one of them.

Somehow, some of that began to work a little. I found real estate brokers and insurance agents who were willing to do business with me or who would serve as a center of influence to refer business to me. Both Joe and I had CPA certifications so we positioned ourselves mostly on the tax and real estate side of law. In 1978 and 1979, high taxes and high inflation created a boom in real estate and real estate tax shelters. We worked on real estate and corporate transactions and also wills and trusts—anything that did not involve going to court, since my exposure to the courtroom in law school was not a success: When doing mock trials, I lost cases with my own wife on the jury!

Like me, Joe's passion was never law. We did some legal work for his family's business and eventually Joe joined them as I moved to Terra. Joe has had a successful career and he and I remain close friends.

When I got out of law school and was starting up my practice with Joe, I wound up teaching at IIT as well as at Benedictine College as a lecturer in accounting. I needed the money because I was making next to nothing in my law practice.

I'm sorry that my big break the next year came when someone died. One of the professors at the Stuart School passed away and I got a job as lecturer of accounting, which meant I carried a full teaching load for accounting and cost accounting, including an evening course. During those first months of practicing law, three mornings a week I would drive to Chicago's South Side from my home in Woodridge (southeast suburban Chicago) and teach for an hour or two. Then I would go back to practice law at my start-up law firm with almost no clients. Two evenings a week, I had to go back to the South Side to teach a graduate program in accounting.

I did that for about six months, until I realized I was headed for a physical breakdown. At night I could barely talk because I was so exhausted. And then the next day I had to wake up and do the same thing all over again. It was not intellectually demanding but required a level of physical stamina I did not have. That was the closest I ever came to a nervous and physical breakdown. The college was paying me $20,000 a year, and in 1980 that was a whole lot of money for teaching three courses—nine hours of classes a week. But in the overall scheme of my life and work at that time, the load was too heavy.

The Trouble with Practicing Law

In these early years, I liked some aspects of practicing law. I enjoyed the creativity of writing estate plans and business sales, and I loved the complexity of designing a five-way, tax-deferred, real estate transaction. More than that, I loved meeting new clients. I have always been fascinated by observing how people create wealth and innovate businesses out of nothing, which I believe is unique to the United States. The rags-to-riches stories of many of the entrepreneurs I met through my law practice made me want to play a greater role in their lives beyond that of legal counsel alone.

The disadvantages included clients who demanded that I work 80 hours a week and get everything done yesterday, but would not pay me for 90 days. I was looking for a more creative business model that would allow me to expand the scope of my relationship with my clients so I could advise them on all aspects of their legal and financial lives. I was searching for a different way to be in business for myself.

The Person and the Professional

I wrote this Introduction to tell you about the most important influences on my life up until the point where the story of this book really begins. I have tried to offer a brief introduction to who I am and how I came to my beliefs. I have tried to distill the factors that have been most important to me.

I have spent my career trying to help my clients create and sustain wealth while being able to sleep at night myself, and I have traveled a long road to get here. In the life of an entrepreneur and a financial adviser, the personal is intertwined with the professional. The advice I give my clients about all aspects of managing their wealth stems from my years of personal and professional experience.

In my twenties and thirties, I defined success in terms of money and making a living. Many people starting out use that kind of definition. But like any person who has children and achieves some modicum of success, I started to climb Maslow's hierarchy. Soon enough, my top priority became making sure my children were well and happy, and I thought more about spiritual matters.

My definition of success certainly has evolved over the years in a way that is totally normal for a person who works and has children and is busy with life. Real success has to be a combination of financial success, physical well-being, and some self-actualization. It becomes much less about money and material success and much more about close relationships between and among families and friends. Having said that, having money doesn't hurt.

When I look back at my 30 years in this business, I wish I had not had to learn so many lessons the hard way. The financial and economic devastation of 2008 demonstrated to me that I am not yet finished with hard lessons. Even so, I want to share my story with you because I want to help others avoid the mistakes I made. While my story is personal, it is inseparable from the history of the investment industry over those years. My story provides ample illustration of the myths, errors, illusions, and delusions that other advisers, money managers, and investors also experienced during those years.

PART I

Evolution of a Wealth Manager: My History, World, Experience, Clients, and Company

CHAPTER 1

Starting Out

I n this chapter, I explain the first origins of the investment philosophy that now guides the way I advise my clients. Since investment philosophy in itself can be not only dry but abstract, I want to breathe life into that philosophy by offering it in the most personal way possible, as the story of my own education as a wealth manager. My story in this chapter and the next one will introduce the main concepts that I spend the rest of this book discussing. I hope that the personal context will make the concepts more easily understandable.

Inflation, Stagflation, and High Interest Rates

Before I begin this discussion, I think it is important for me to provide the briefest macroeconomic context for the period 1978–1982, when this story begins. In 1971, President Richard Nixon slapped wage and price controls on the economy in response to what was termed raging inflation (4.5 percent). That worked well enough in the very short term and backfired massively in the longer term, arguably resulting in both stagflation at the end of the 1970s and the inflationary cycle of the early 1980s. Remember stagflation? It is a macroeconomic term for a period of inflation combined with stagnation or slow economic growth and possibly even recession. Inflation was now really raging in a way it had not been previously—11.2 percent in 1979. Under President Jimmy Carter, the Federal Reserve enacted monetary policies to combat inflation, including raising interest rates significantly. The first effect was more pain, as inflation hit 13.6 percent in 1980. Meanwhile, economic growth had mostly ground to a standstill, and unemployment hit a high of 9.7 percent in 1982. Then the world economic system got a big jolt when OPEC first flexed its economic muscles and raised crude oil prices fourfold in 1973. We experienced some of the worst down markets in recent history in 1973 and 1974, with a mini cycle that ended in 1975.

Interest rates in the bond market tracked the rising inflation rate. The long bond yield hit a high of 15 percent in October 1982. Mortgage rates touched 18 percent in 1981. The housing market came to almost a complete standstill. There was little technology and no technology boom in those days; the Internet and electronic trading were still far in the future. The highest marginal tax rates were 70 percent or more and did not come down until the start of the Reagan administration. Those rates led to many investments that made little economic sense but sheltered income taxes. For affluent individuals, tax planning and investing were driven above all by this high tax bracket and trying to avoid taxes. It was a strange time.

Finding Partners

At the beginning of my career as a financial adviser, I never thought I was smart enough by myself to know how to invest for my clients, and I spent years looking for the Really Smart Guys who were going to teach me how to invest. I learned over time that, in fact, those guys were not really that smart—although they were certainly greedy—and never had the best interests of my clients at heart. They got paid their billions—some of them—and I did not. I don't know what happened to all of them, but I am still here.

I know that lives have turning points. You get up in the morning and have breakfast and walk out the door without knowing that, by the end of the day, the entire direction of your life will have changed. My life changed in that way at a lunch my partner Joe Hudetz and I had with Dave Reedy in 1979. I walked into the restaurant as a young attorney without a real direction, and when I left, I had found one of the individuals I would spend most of my business career in partnership with.

In the Introduction to this book, I mentioned the law business Joe and I had established in 1978. We specialized in networking lunches in our first year in business, as we struggled to get a toehold on enough business to sustain us. Joe knew Dave Reedy from high school and we solicited him and his partner Tom King for business.

The year 1979 was a bad year for us to start out in business; it was a terrible year for real estate businesses like Reedy-King. Stagflation and high interest rates were strangling the real estate market and traditional real estate firms were forced to reconsider how to stay in business. Dave and Tom had decided to branch out.

Dave and Tom asked if we had experience in real estate syndications and tax-deferred exchanges, both of which required a high degree of expertise in securities and income tax law. Dave hired me to write the offering memorandum for the first apartment building that he was going to offer as part of a limited partnership. Of course we assured him that I had the expertise this job required, and then spent weeks learning everything I could about real estate and securities law. The three of us quickly became fast friends.

As it turned out, this new business worked so well for them that they had to diversify beyond selling only their own deals, and this required a fundamental change in their business organization. You can sell your own limited partnerships privately but you have to get a securities license and belong to a broker-dealer to sell deals that you did not originate. In effect, at that point you are selling securities and you have become part of the highly regulated securities industry.

Dave and Tom also wanted to try financial planning. They believed the new fledgling industry called *financial planning* would become important. We all saw the limitations of focusing solely on real estate, and they wanted to expand their expertise and offer more services. Dave and Tom were already dealing with a wealthy, sophisticated client base that could use these services, although the International Association of Financial Planning (IAFP) had only just come into existence. No one really knew what a financial planning firm was, although I, too, was intrigued by the idea and imagined it could be a great business to meet successful people with vision and drive and be paid for one's expertise.

Founding Terra

For all these reasons, we decided to form a company. Dave and Tom founded Terra in 1981 and I soon joined as partner: Dave, Tom, and I were the original three partners. Dave used his Catholic education to come up with the name of Terra Securities, from the Latin word for earth or ground—a good name for a firm that began with real estate and was transitioning to securities.

At the beginning, we only wanted to find a larger broker-dealer with which to affiliate. Therefore, we attended the second conference of the IAFP held, ironically, in Las Vegas. There would be 20 or 30 brokerage firms at the convention and we thought they would all be interested in talking to us about our financial planning business and real estate partnerships.

Tax Shelter

Put simply, a tax shelter is a method to reduce taxes; taxpayers in general will always have more money left after taxes if they can increase the amount of tax deductions. In investment terms, a tax shelter makes money for the investor more from producing income tax deductions than from producing profit from the deal. If your income tax rate is approximately 35 percent—as it is likely to be at the time I write this book—then $1,000 of tax deductions will put approximately $300 in your pocket. If you look at the highest marginal tax rates at the time we are talking about—the late 1970s and early 1980s—then you can see that $1,000 of tax deductions could put on the order of $700 or more in your pocket (some deals gave $2 of losses for every $1 of investment). Then consider that it might be much easier to structure some investment so it can generate losses rather than profits. Now you have a tax shelter.

At that time, broker-dealers in our channel sold only tax shelters in the form of real estate limited partnerships, which basically consist of at least two persons: a general partner, who has unlimited liability, and a limited partner, whose liability is limited to the amount invested in the company. Limited partnerships are often used as a vehicle for raising capital, due to the limited liability for the limited partner. A real estate limited partnership would of course have been created for the purpose of investing in real estate.

The limited partnerships we saw at this conference went beyond real estate to include wacky tax shelters like gems, Christmas trees, oil, and lithographs. There were oil and gas drilling limited partnerships, movie deals, leasing deals, guns; I remember seeing the racks of guns. They were raising money for anything you could think of and creating big tax losses. It was one great sleazy group of people—way too sleazy for us. There was no way we would be able to join any of those organizations. As it turned out, most of those broker-dealers were eventually driven out of business for all the usual reasons, mostly bankruptcy. Even some of the financial planning on display was like something from an alien universe. No one was thinking about mutual funds or the stock market. There were just a few, barely perceptible signs of the first credible vendors and mutual funds that would play a significant role in building this industry.

It had not yet occurred to us that we should form our own introducing broker-dealer. At that time, you could form an introducing broker-dealer with only $5,000 in capital, but there would then be restrictions on the kind of business you could do. It turns out to have been an extremely fortuitous decision, but in fact we started it only so we could legally get into the financial planning business.

And yet, as we started up with Terra, our small group was captivated by the notion of changing clients' lives in a positive way. We were young; we thought we were smart; and we wanted to establish a good business and embrace the new world of financial planning so that we could help our clients in ways that had not been possible for us before.

As it turned out, founding our own company was exactly the right thing to do, but we did not realize then what a good decision it would turn out to be.

Creating a New Business Model

Acquiring new clients one by one is one way to establish a new business, but you get more leverage when you use centers of influence. From the inception of Terra Securities, Dave Reedy, Tom King and I were aware of the advantages of marketing through centers of influence such as tax professionals and other lawyers. The idea, obviously, is to woo them so they refer business to you. Accountants are preferable even to lawyers because they have a regular client base and are highly respected. Furthermore, they are perfectly placed to see when an individual has cash to invest or has made a bad investment or could use some investment advice. (I use the term *tax professional* rather than *accountant* or *CPA* because not every accountant is a CPA, but I am afraid that when using these terms casually, I—like most people—tend to use them interchangeably.)

So at first, Dave took referrals from accountants but he did not have a way to pay them aside from an annual bottle of J&B every Christmas. The securities laws made it illegal to pay them (because you had to be securities licensed to share in the commission), so it was not a lucrative arrangement for an accountant.

The governing body for accountants is the American Institute of Certified Public Accountants (AICPA). When Terra was first formed, the AICPA had a rule that its members could not be in the financial services business. Fortunately for us, just at the time we were getting started with that idea of working with accountants, the Federal Trade Commission (FTC) sued the AICPA and the latter had to change its rule. This was a transformative change.

Finally it occurred to us that we would still do the sale but the accountants we worked with should acquire the necessary licenses so they could get paid a portion of the commission or fee from securities transactions completed with their clients. It was not a matter of getting accountants to try to sell securities themselves; the central issue was our being able to share commissions legally with them. We thought we had really discovered a new business model! It was a novel idea to have them get licensed so that they could not only provide advice but also get paid if *we* provided the advice.

Building the Business Model

While we were figuring out the business model that was to carry us forward, my friend Brian Savage joined us in 1984. Brian was a CPA with a practice based mostly on tax preparation. We bought his business by making him a co-owner/partner of Terra Securities and moved him into the office with us. Since Terra had a value of basically zero, it was a good buy for us to trade part of our practice for his.

Like many accountants and tax professionals, Brian's tax business required him to work from 8:00 A.M. to 8:00 P.M. during tax time, and people just rolled through his office. Brian would finish his tax appointment, then walk that client into an adjoining office and say, "Talk to Dave." Dave would try to sell the client a mutual fund for an IRA or something. It was the easiest way to get new clients that we had ever experienced. Our epiphany was the realization that by affiliating more closely with more tax professionals, we could revolutionize the whole way we prospected and did business.

Although at the time tax professionals saw commissions as a huge conflict of interest, in1984 we brought in the very first outside accountant that we did not make a partner in the business. Our idea was so revolutionary that we then stopped looking for new clients and started looking for tax professionals who had 300 to 400 clients so that we could leverage their business. I could spend all my time building a book of business with my own 300 to 400 clients, or I could find one individual who already had those 300 to 400 clients and work with him on the securities business and split everything with him. That was the basic concept.

We realized that we had discovered a great business model because accountants were already in a position of trust with their clients and wanted to broaden and diversify those relationships. As time went on, we developed ways of talking to, educating, and serving our customer base.

Accountants are both risk-averse and analytical, which fit extremely well with our risk-averse, asset-allocation approach. The greatest risk an accountant faces is losing his or her clients. We found accountants to be a tough constituency: they wanted the right product at the right price for their clients, and that became a driving force in how we looked at money and investments.

Accountants are just not motivated by money: Their client is their most important asset, so they will not do anything to abuse that trust. Furthermore, an accountant already has a way of earning a living and generally will not push product sales to clients just to get some income.

Evolution of the Business Model

Working with a few of the pioneers was one thing. At some point, we realized that our doing the presentations for every accountant was not creating a scalable model for our business. It was just impossible for us to visit every accountant for every $2,000 IRA investment.

We decided that instead of trying to send out Terra principals for every sale, we would develop very robust marketing, training, and compliance so these accountants could do it on their own; that was what the model eventually evolved to. Here was our value proposition to accountants: *You* be the adviser, and we will give you everything you need to advise your clients about investments; we will give you the entire support structure. We will provide you with asset allocation models; we will do the due diligence; we will provide you with all the training and the compliance. *You* maintain the client relationship and provide your clients with investment recommendations that are truly in their best interests. We thus had two clients, both the accountant and the clients of the accountant.

Marcus Heinrich joined the firm as we were beginning to develop this business model and took the lead in recruiting accountants much more systematically than we had in the past, and then developing the Terra program to support and teach our accountants how to be registered representatives (meaning they were licensed to sell securities). Marcus immersed himself full-time in the business and brought an incredible energy to his recruiting and training efforts; he built out the company to the next level.

Brian Savage was both a CPA and a former IRS agent. Brian knew how accountants thought and he spoke the same language they did, thereby facilitating communication. Because of his IRS background, he was instrumental in helping Terra set up financial controls and became a leader in the compliance area; he really understood the regulatory environment. Small broker-dealers are notorious for getting into compliance trouble accidentally, but we never did, thanks to Brian. He was our financial principal—which was a big deal—and ensured that we kept a clean record: That was a credit to our products and our representatives, but above all a credit to Brian.

Howard Kite brought insurance knowledge and training skills. He had years of experience in the insurance industry; his special expertise in training came from his background as a business teacher and sales manager. We were babes in the woods in terms of insurance. Insurance products tend to be both extremely complex and arcane, but when we really needed to understand how a product worked, Howard would take it apart for us. He brought us to a new level in our ability to deal with insurance products.

Terry Gallagher brought banking and trust experience. He had had early exposure to the fee-based business through his trust background and he understood how the trust side worked—and could explain it to us.

Creating a New Value Proposition for Independent Broker-Dealers

We were also at the beginning of the development of the independent broker-dealer. Up until that time, most advisers or brokers or registered representatives were employees of the large wirehouse firms like Merrill Lynch or Smith Barney, which would dictate how they had to present products to clients and what they had to sell. (In case you are not familiar with the term *wirehouse*, it is an old name for these large, Wall-Street-type firms; it stems from the way the communication systems in that pre-electronic era linked the various branches and trading floors and enabled the sharing of financial information and prices.) The independent broker-dealer was not obligated to sell the products of a parent company, so the advisers who worked in this new kind of company were beholden first of all to their clients.

The regulatory authorities were used to the idea of wirehouse registered representatives who were all contained in one place. If we were going to have part-time representatives who were not even our employees, then we would have to demonstrate that they could function legally and ethically without a supervisor physically looking over their shoulder. Accountants were the perfect kind of person for this kind of independent existence.

I believe that the emergence of the independent broker-dealer was in the client's best interests. Beyond that, not only were our advisers independent, they had well-developed technical knowledge because they were accountants. They understood numbers and they really understood their clients; what they lacked was infrastructure. Our job was to provide the infrastructure they needed to be able to offer their clients investment solutions that were right for them. This was something new: truly doing the right thing for the client.

We started doing trade shows and other things to recruit. Our representatives joined us for different reasons. They could broaden and diversify their relationships with their clients while also diversifying their sources of revenue. In general, tax professionals are devoted to their clients, and most of them had seen some egregiously bad examples of financial service abuses. After the fact, the only thing the tax professional can do is report the loss on the tax return and say, "That was a really bad investment. I wish you had discussed it with me before you went into it." You hear that over and over when you talk to accountants: "I wish I could have helped but by the time I got involved it was too late."

Learning the Lessons of Tax Shelters and Limited Partnerships

In the first years of Terra, we were still heavily involved with limited partnerships and tax shelters. This experience in the early years of my career was a bitter lesson for me and transformed my understanding of risk. I began to understand that managing wealth means managing risk.

In my first years as an adviser, tax shelters (which took the form of limited partnerships) were a main focus of our business. Tax shelters are not even used anymore, but they were popular at that time because the tax structure was so different from the way it is now, and many investments were driven above all by the idea of saving on taxes. The extremely high tax rates meant that the potential tax deductions available from a limited partnership were worth far more in dollar terms than has ever been the case since, and the marketplace was filled with bogus opportunities. Clients primarily wanted to generate deductions; if along the way they also made money on the investment, that was a bonus.

We worked hard to find the deals with some underlying economic sense and stressed the value of the underlying real estate investment rather than the tax shield. I would sell and my clients would buy real estate and leasing partnerships that would save them one or two tax dollars for every dollar they invested. With the highest marginal tax rate at 70 percent, that seemed to be reasonable.

I believed the promoters of these deals, who claimed that they still made sense despite egregiously high fees charged to investors. I wanted to believe this was in the best interests of my clients. After all, my clients wanted to save on taxes, and if I did not sell them these products, I figured they would just go buy them elsewhere.

The people who sold these limited partnerships appeared to be smart, savvy, and sophisticated. Unlike many of the other broker-dealers at the time, we spent many hours doing our own due diligence[1] on the real estate partnerships we sold, visiting the actual real estate property and kicking the bricks, so to speak. By 1984, program sponsors were becoming increasingly shady and less competent and we found ourselves rejecting most deals. I learned the hard way that the promoter, meaning the general partner, always made money, whether clients did or not. This took me many years to realize. Even at the time, some of the people we wanted to do business with gave us a bad feeling. I remember going to California to meet the general partners of one of the leading syndicators doing historic rehabs. This kind of deal was in big demand because of its investment tax credits, and the deals sold out in days. Since the person I was supposed to meet with was an hour late, I had time to walk around the office by myself and talk to people. Although I admired the pretty pictures of their deals hanging on the office walls, I discovered that no one had been there longer than six months and no one knew much of anything about real estate. They did, however, produce some of the best marketing materials I had ever seen. We decided not to sell their deals, and within a year or so they were bankrupt, along with all their partnerships.

It was becoming glaringly obvious to us that there were too many syndicators who would buy property at any price, with all the profit front-end loaded[2] as fees, and we stopped selling real estate tax shelters in 1984. That decision was difficult because the commissions were large and investors wanted to buy them. However, it turned out to have been one of our best calls. In 1986, Congress changed the law on the passive losses[3] that generated the income tax deductions that made these deals profitable—and made the change retroactive. In the end, the vast majority of syndicators and limited partnerships, along with the independent broker-dealers working with those deals, went broke.

By contrast, we were well on our way by 1986 with mutual funds, insurance, and financial planning. We made plenty of mistakes along the way but we had dodged a big bullet, partly by putting our clients' interests ahead of our own. I still believe that most brokers and broker-dealers knew the deals they were selling were not in their clients' best interests, but they were making so much money they sold them anyway. This was not the finest hour of the financial services industry.

Many of these deals failed and some of my clients lost money, despite the thorough due diligence I thought I had done, as well as my good intentions. I was devastated. I lost clients and harmed my reputation. I should have tried to talk my clients out of buying those products. If they had insisted, I should have sent them elsewhere. It was a terribly hard lesson to learn because, for that client, you will never regain credibility. We had believed these were appropriate investments, but they weren't.

As a result, I promised myself that I would never fall into this trap again, that I would never sell products unless they were transparent. Apparently not everyone took this bitter lesson to heart the way I did.

But let me be clear on this: When I say we dodged that bullet, it was the bullet of business failure and bankruptcy. We stayed in business; we did not get sued; we did not get client complaints lodged against us with the regulatory authorities. We survived despite our naïveté about these deals.

But to this day, I am extremely wary of any so-called deal that does not have a sound, understandable economic basis. We realized relatively early on that if an investment is not liquid and transparent, it probably has some inherent problems. I am still wary when told that so-and-so is very smart and knows what he is doing and therefore I should just trust him.

In 2008, we saw not only the frauds and swindles—Bernie Madoff above all—but we also saw the results when individuals were sold investments that were fundamentally flawed. Unqualified people got mortgages; investors were sold derivatives and other securities that fell apart; high-flying hedge funds went out of business, taking their investors with them. I avoided all of it, both for myself and for my clients, because I had learned the hard way to invest only in transparent products that made fundamental economic sense.

Lesson 1

Avoid any investment you do not understand. If it is not liquid and transparent, walk away.

During the time that I have been writing this book, 2008 and 2009, I have congratulated myself a hundred times over that I learned this lesson so early on. It apparently was not possible to learn this essential lesson on Wall Street itself, where the Really Smart Guys were so busy spinning tales about the value and importance of the derivatives they were hawking that they apparently came to believe their own stories.

Evolution of Our Products

We set up our financial planning business model along the same lines we saw others using. A planner would charge $2,500 to write a financial plan for an individual. This seems counterintuitive to me now, but at that time the brand-new financial planning industry thought clients wanted such plans. We were not forging a new path; we were jumping on a bandwagon. That this kind of financial planning was not a brand-new idea could be seen by the amount of software that had already been created.

Although there were a number of different software packages to choose from, the software was primitive, and the output was voluminous and mostly boilerplate. Clients were required to supply large amounts of personal data about every aspect of their financial lives—data few individuals have at their fingertips. The plan with 80 or 90 pages was clumsy in the way it treated risk and did not really allow clients to interface with their advisers in the way they wanted. The client would turn pale at the sight of this massive document and say, "Just tell me what it says." Clients did not want to read the plan and absolutely did not want to pay $2,500.

Lesson 2

Clients want a prescription, like what they would get from a doctor. Assign them one task at a time

We realized very quickly that clients were not going to pay for that kind of advice and detail, and time has proven us right. What they wanted was a one-page summary. If you give a client six things to do, he will do nothing. You have to start by assigning only the first task. As we were to learn, clients want one-on-one communication, concise written plans, and access to an adviser when they need one. Clients also want wisdom, which means having the life experience to offer advice along with wide enough client experience to have seen what works and what doesn't.

Terra Introduces Mutual Funds

We also decided to start selling mutual funds. I cannot take credit for this decision but it was prescient. An interesting side note to this decision was the now-famous cover story *BusinessWeek* ran in 1981 proclaiming the death of equities after 20 years of dismal returns. This was one of my earliest experiences in seeing the disconnect between what the financial media trumpeted and what was really happening in the markets. This declaration was made at the very beginning of the greatest bull market the United States has ever seen. I was starting to understand that when the financial press declares which investments you should avoid, it is probably a good time to buy them. It also worked the other way: When the press tells you what to buy, run the other way.

Lesson 3

Take the advice of the financial press at your own risk.

Selling mutual funds was the new frontier. There was no Morningstar or any other popular or comprehensive place to go to do in-depth research on mutual funds, and not many mutual funds to choose from. In 1980, there were about 500 mutual funds in existence.[4] The Dow Jones Industrial Average broke through 1,000 in 1982 as the bull market began, and by 1983 there were 1,000 mutual funds.[5] Investors today will be surprised to learn that doing a mutual fund presentation at that time required first explaining what a stock was, then what a bond was and how it was different from a stock, and then what a mutual fund was.

At that time, you expected your client to buy one or two funds. The fund companies put out lackluster marketing materials that did not really help my clients understand what a mutual fund was nor why they should buy a mutual fund at all, or one rather than another. Today we would not recognize the mutual fund names used then, such as equity income, capital appreciation, large-blend, and growth and income. We looked for funds with long track records, and there were not many of those. Almost all mutual funds came with front-end sales loads; one of the most recognizable names was Templeton, which started in the 1950s and was well-known among brokers for its 8 percent load.[6]

The way we sold mutual funds was different then because clients had little access to current, in-depth information about investments in this pre-Internet world. We would say to our clients, "Buy this particular fund and don't worry about it for four or five years." Clients had little choice but to go along with that, since they did not want to change investments and have to pay another load. This proved to be relatively successful, since clients could not look on the Internet every night to determine if they were going to eat dog food or could go on vacation due to the change in value of their investment portfolio. In retrospect, I have realized that having too much information does not necessarily lead to being able to make better investment decisions.

Lesson 4

Unlimited information leads to analysis paralysis and emotional decision-making.

My goal for my clients was to grow their money as fast as possible. While we did not see ourselves as stockbrokers, especially the kind of stockbrokers who would call clients every week with a new investment idea, we assumed that the greatest value we brought to our clients was the return we could help them earn on their investments. Our challenging mission at that time was to get people to invest in mutual fund equities versus bank CDs. We were competing with the Wall Street wirehouses like Merrill Lynch and Smith Barney who said they were smarter and better than anyone else and were thus best positioned to make money for their clients. How could we compete with that? We were independent, but of course we wanted to make money for our clients. We wanted to pick good mutual funds and get a good return. We came to understand later that this was a misplaced value proposition because it did not account for the notion of risk, but that is what we believed in the early 1980s. Our value proposition as a company was searching for the smart people who would help our clients earn a high return on their investments.

As I mentioned in the Introduction, I was a Certified Financial Planner (CFP) and a Personal Financial Specialist (PFS). One of the ironies about being a financial adviser in the United States is that, legally, a securities license is all you need to provide investment advice to the public. Having a securities license means only that a person understands the most basic elements of financial products and regulation; it certainly does not mean that an individual is really and truly competent to offer investment advice. Given my growing interest in helping my clients and advising them in their financial and legal affairs, I always felt it was extremely important to gain all the real education, qualifications, and credentials possible. My personal value proposition was my commitment to obtain the knowledge and credentials necessary to be able to offer my clients the best advice available.

Introducing Asset Allocation

In 1984, I attended another IAFP conference. There were fewer weirdo tax shelters, a few more mutual fund representatives, and something that was really a new and unfamiliar idea at that time, both in the marketplace and to me: a presentation on asset allocation. As soon as you stopped to think about it, the idea of asset allocation made inherent, intuitive sense—it was as simple as not putting all your eggs in one basket, in case something happened to that one basket. For the first time, I was thinking about more than just the investment *return*. I was also thinking about how to protect that return and manage its *risk*. I thought that one way to do that was to divide the investment into several amounts that could be invested separately. That would be the equivalent of taking a dozen eggs and putting them into four or more different baskets, in order to protect the overall investment from risk. From an investment perspective, of course, there was much more involved.

Using asset allocation to manage risk is one of the overriding themes of my investment career. Later in this book, especially Chapters 5 and 6, I take up that topic at length. What follows here is the short explanation, for the sake of this narrative.

Using *asset allocation* means investing your money in different asset classes. An asset class is composed of a number of different securities that have the same risk/reward characteristics in the marketplace. Investing your money in several different securities that in fact belong to the same asset class—such as buying several different 10-year bonds, or several different large-cap stocks—does not accomplish the diversification you are seeking when you decide to use asset allocation.

There seemed to be a real science about it, and I was determined to use the new software to create the best allocations possible—to find the optimal way to combine assets to get the highest overall performance for the lowest risk. I was enthusiastic about the idea of asset allocation and diversification, but I had to figure out for myself how to implement these complex ideas. I bought one of the earliest asset allocation optimization programs and got started with an IBM PC 286, the one with the glowing green screen. The idea of asset allocation optimization, of course, is to find the *optimal* asset allocation.

The Importance of Risk

I was gradually starting to understand that the concept of risk is essential to any discussion about asset allocation, and that money management is concerned with risk as much as return. The commonsense understanding that it is risky to invest in only one or two securities, or even in only one or two asset classes, leads to the question of how many different kinds of investments should be combined together to create less risk for the client. What constitutes a different kind of investment? Does that mean two different stocks or two different mutual funds? We will come back to these questions.

I wanted to understand these issues so I could answer this kind of question for myself and for my clients. Each asset class has a set of characteristics as well as a history of performance. Performance is defined both by the potential increase in value, or *return*, and by the *risk* of the asset class. Defining market risk is one of those questions that has occupied market participants and academics alike for a long time. There are plenty of different kinds of risk that I can imagine but not quantify. The marketplace has come to define risk as *volatility*, because using a measure that is not totally satisfactory is better than not having any measure at all. Volatility in turn is measured by *standard deviation*, which is a statistical measure.

When I look back now at what I was trying to do, I marvel that I accomplished anything at all. In the rarefied air of the financial world, asset allocation is a very sophisticated concept. There are several generations of difference between the kind of analysis that can be run now and what I was doing with primitive software and a ridiculously underpowered IBM 286 to run it. But for us, it was pure revelation. It gave us a starting point for making an intelligent decision about asset allocation. We felt ourselves to be on the cutting edge of the financial world.

There was no training; I learned through trial and error how to make the asset allocation program run. Using my IBM 286, I had to plug in my own data manually. Each asset class required three all-important pieces of information: *historical return* (how the asset class had performed in the past), *expected return* (how I expected it to perform in the future), and *standard deviation* (as defined above, standard deviation represents the volatility of the asset class in the marketplace, and that volatility provides a measure of risk). I could get the historical return and standard deviation from industry data. Then the software asked me to provide the *expected return* of the asset class, the return that I thought the mutual fund or index would provide in the future. Asking me to predict the future return for the asset class was like asking me to look into a crystal ball; if I could predict future performance, I would spend my time investing my own money and making a fortune, not trying to manage other people's money. I ended up using historical return for expected return. It made sense to me that a particular asset class would continue to perform in the future in a way that was similar to how it had performed in the past, although you have all seen the warnings the regulatory authorities require on any prospectus or any discussion about a security: "Past performance is no guarantee of future results." But it can be a starting point or a proxy.

At that time, I had four or five different asset classes: U.S. large-capitalization stocks (U.S. large-cap), small-capitalization stocks (small-cap), bonds, a dash of international stocks, and some REITS.[7] I entered all my data, told the software to run, stared at the screen, and then realized it was going to take a really long time to produce an answer. I would go to lunch, go shopping, run some errands. At some point the program would stop and recommend an allocation or a series of allocations, each one depending on the amount of risk the investor wanted to take.

Implementing Asset Allocation

Meanwhile, while I was trying to develop asset allocation methodology, we at Terra were constantly searching for the best mutual funds for our clients. It was the same then as it is now. We would visit the fund companies and listen to the fund managers tell us why they thought they had a *model* (meaning a model investment strategy by which to manage investors' money) that would provide our clients with a good investment experience. We listened to some very smart people, but sometimes the actual investments just did not work out.

For example, take one of our early experiences with the managers of bond funds. In the early 1980s, the extraordinarily high level of interest rates resulted in unprecedentedly high bond returns. The bond managers assured us that the high interest rates on bonds meant that a retiree should be invested in almost all bonds. In general, the low volatility of shorter-term bonds can help reduce the overall volatility of most portfolios. But longer-term bonds, like 20- or 30-year bonds, in fact do have significant volatility, especially in that interest rate environment. The bond managers kept insisting that they knew how to manage volatility and tried to tell us that it was almost a free ride. They would say, "I can get you high yield on a long bond but don't worry about the volatility."

But I have real-life clients. How could I recommend a highly volatile investment to a retired person, despite the high yield that seemed attractive? I did not want to go with bonds only, and yet stocks are supposed to be even more volatile than bonds. How do you balance the risk of highly volatile long-term bonds with the normal risk of equities in a way that makes sense? I had been in the business for only a few years and I had no other reference point. This is where the software program came in, because I needed something analytical to provide some justification for the allocations we recommended. Working with a software program seemed like a very reasonable approach.

But now I had the opium of believing that if I just put everything into this black box—which is how I thought about the asset allocation software in my IBM 286, or maybe I was up to a 386 by now—it would give me the ultimate right answer about which mutual funds to buy to get my clients the best return and manage investment risk besides. I heard the word *optimize* and thought it must be idiot-proof, although I already knew that the software had flaws. You put in the correct data and got the correct allocation—presuming, of course, that there was such a thing as correct data and a correct allocation. To enter correct data meant to provide an *expected* return for each asset class—expected in the *future*. As I already mentioned, that meant I had to have an opinion about the asset class's future performance. I found that if I changed the expected return by even half of a percentage point, the resulting asset allocation would be totally different. In other words, expected return is only a guess, and changing a guess by a small amount seemed to skew the asset allocation significantly. We had to use mutual fund data to represent asset classes, because only mutual funds had data on past performance, both returns and standard deviation. Besides, what else could we use? The idea of an index fund was far in the future, and this asset allocation would certainly not work with individual stocks and bonds.

Once again, I was just going along with the mainstream, and it was better than nothing: I can see that I was dealing with the right issues and asking the right questions. Nevertheless, we were already seeing that there were flaws. I attended an Ibbotson conference in the late 1980s and learned that you had to use asset classes, not mutual funds, for this kind of asset allocation. (Roger Ibbotson founded Ibbotson Associates; he was one of the earliest proponents of asset allocation.) Normal mutual funds were *not* asset classes because they almost always combined more than one asset class.

Talk about an "aha!" moment for me! I realized that a balanced fund would hold both stocks and bonds. A large-cap manager would also buy mid-caps. An equity-income fund would buy stocks of any size as long as they paid dividends, and so on. What asset class did an equity income fund represent? You had to start with indexes such as the S&P 500 or international equities to figure out how much you needed of each asset class. Once you figured that out, then you had to figure out which mutual fund best represented that index or asset class.

CHAPTER 2

A Decade of Active Management

In Chapter 1, I related my earliest experiences with trying to find the best way to invest for my clients. I thought that optimization software would lead me to the optimal—the *best*—way to invest for my clients. I had become aware that risk was an important part of the overall picture. I was starting to become aware of the importance of asset classes in finding an overall investment strategy, but I still did not have a good understanding of asset class versus mutual fund investing. Now my story continues.

Working with Mutual Funds

Once again, I have to step back to provide context for the industry structure in those days. This was long before the technological innovations that would transform personal investing and allow discount brokerage and on-line trading. The kind of fee-based platform we use today, where the client pays one fee but can have a variety of different investments on one platform, did not exist then; the technology had to develop further before it would be possible.

The World of Mutual Funds

Mutual funds were mostly load funds sold by a registered representative. Only A shares were available—a mutual fund with a front-end load—with loads typically around 4 to 8 percent, which meant that if a client had $10,000 to invest, the load would be taken off the top. If the load was 5 percent, the client's net investment would be $9,500 and the $500 in load would be split between the rep and the rep's broker-dealer. We always had our clients buy mutual funds directly from the mutual fund company rather than use a brokerage platform (such as Pershing or Fidelity, two of the best known) that could hold individual securities as well as mutual funds from different mutual fund companies. We had a philosophical commitment to buying mutual funds and not picking stocks, so we did not need to ask our clients to pay more for the brokerage platform. I offer more information later about why we did not pick stocks.

Terra was like many broker-dealers in those days and restricted its mutual fund offerings to a few mutual fund companies because of mutual fund *breakpoints*. When a client had more than a certain amount invested with one mutual fund company, whether in one or more mutual funds, the percentage amount of the load would decrease as the dollars invested increased. For example, if a client had $50,000 to invest in one mutual fund company only, that 5 percent load might now be 4 percent, regardless of which funds in the family were chosen. We would of course want our client to get the benefit of the breakpoint and would make an effort to keep the client's funds all in one mutual fund company. A broker who did not take advantage of the breakpoint for his client would earn more, because it would be easy enough for a broker to split the amount of the investment across more than one fund family to keep the load—and therefore his cut of the load—at the highest possible amount. The National Association of Securities Dealers (NASD), our regulatory body at that time, frowned on this practice and we at Terra were scrupulous about observing breakpoints for our clients.

There was another reason each client basically had to marry one mutual fund company. If we took our client out of a mutual fund where he had recently paid a load, and then recommended a mutual fund from another fund company, the client would have to pay another load. This is called *switching* and is another practice the NASD frowned on. However, if we changed from one fund to another within a fund family, we could make the change for our client without incurring another load. It would be a bigger problem if the whole fund family went bad—which did happen—because the adviser would want to move all the money in one fund family to another fund family, and the NASD did not approve of that, either, even if the adviser had a good reason for it.

We used a broker-dealer model that was appropriate and ethical. In fact, one of the advantages was that when we told a client, "Buy this and don't look at it for some years because you paid a commission," the client was pretty much economically and compliance-wise forced to hold on to the fund, in good times and bad. Clients stayed invested and usually did very well. Clients who bought the Templeton growth fund would hold it for seven years because they had paid a very large 8 percent commission. Buy-and-hold has always been the best long-term strategy for individual investors; it was central to our investment philosophy and the loads encouraged it. Refer to Lesson 4, as stated in Chapter 1: Unlimited information leads to analysis paralysis and emotional decision-making. This was before the time that unlimited information was available everywhere to anyone who wanted to find it, and it was truly a simpler time in investing history.

Using Mutual Funds to Implement Asset Allocation Portfolios

As the 1980s went on, we made increasing use of portfolios that combined assets according to an asset allocation scheme, but our methodology for deciding which portfolio to use for which clients was primitive. I continued to work with the asset allocation software and my increasingly powerful computer, but sometimes it seemed that the decisions were really more of a judgment call, based on the bond allocation and a conversation with the client. Without an overall platform that allowed us to mix and match fund families, we were constrained in our ability to use asset allocation methodology anyway. We designed asset allocation models for each of the fund families, despite the fact that not every fund family had all the kinds of mutual funds we wanted to use. We had to compromise with every fund family, yet it was inappropriate to mix two families because of the commission breakpoint.

Of course we wanted to use credible fund companies. I worked closely with the other principals of Terra to choose our fund companies, looking for those that had been around for a long time and had demonstrated stability. We also wanted companies with good marketing and educational materials; although the sophistication of our clients was growing slowly, it was not insignificant if a fund family we wanted to work with did not have good materials because that would make it much harder for us to explain to our clients what the company was doing. Finally—obviously—we wanted to find good companies with good track records.

This business of having to work within a fund family was weird, and completely determined by the industry's domination by load funds and the regulations against switching, all of which was absolutely central to working with clients at that time. What tended to happen is that each rep would become extremely familiar with one or two fund families and then stay within those families. Unfortunately, not all of the fund families offered as many asset classes as we wanted, especially at that time in our economic history; I think fund families are much larger and more diversified now, even as we have been freed from the constraints of fund-family investing. We had to work within the limitations of what was available to us then.

One of the things I am proudest of is how early we recognized the value of international investing. Our data told us that overseas performance was not highly correlated to U.S. performance. It seems so obvious to me and everyone else now, but it was courageous and insightful at the time. Do you remember that the economic activities of Japan in the 1980s inspired great anguish in the marketplace because it seemed that Japan was going to take over the world?

We would not do what some of the other brokerage firms did, which was sell only a handful of top-performing funds—which actually all might represent one sector or asset class, most likely the large-cap growth stocks of the S&P 500 Index. We already knew how important it was to have a diversified portfolio that included a number of different asset classes. My value proposition was not "I am going to sell you the top five funds." My value proposition was that I was offering my client the opportunity to invest in a diversified portfolio. I learned that as a result of a lot of failure.

As I began to understand risk more clearly, I started to understand for myself that using asset allocation meant cutting off both the highs and the lows of marketplace performance, like a sine wave. My clients would never be subject to the greatest losses in the marketplace in any one year because they would never be fully invested in the asset class that incurred the losses. But, conversely, they could never be fully invested in the highest-performing asset class, either, so they could not get the highest return. I was starting to understand that my value proposition was using asset allocation to create a diversified portfolio that would get a good return for my clients for a certain level of risk.

Working with Mutual Fund Managers

My job still required those visits to New York, California, and all points in between to listen to fund managers. I knew they were very smart people and I still believed them and believed in them. And still we would find that, in practice, things just did not seem to work out the way they were supposed to. A fund that was large-cap when I chose it for the asset allocation mix might not be large-cap at the end of the year. In fact, one of the most prominent characteristics of mutual funds is something I have seen over my entire tenure in the business with virtually all mutual fund companies and their managers: Mutual fund managers will change their investment style to suit market conditions with little regard for remaining true to an asset class. This shifting of investment style is called *style drift* and it makes it very difficult to use mutual funds as part of an asset allocation scheme.

It was hard enough at the outset to figure out what asset class a mutual fund represented or what style the manager really had. Then it proved to be extremely difficult to monitor the funds to see if they maintained their style. At the end of the year, fund managers are looking for their bonuses or comparing their results against those of their peers, and they decide to add a little of this or a little of that to perk up the fund performance. Of course, that is in a fund manager's best self-interest. You can even argue that it is in the best interests of his shareholders, because the manager is trying to get the best return he can for those who have invested in his fund. In addition, there were even more issues: What if a fund manager left and was replaced? Would the new fund manager continue with the same style as the previous manager? Would a fund's track record have any meaning at all in that case? How do you define what a good fund is?

But I had a different problem. If I wanted a large-cap fund to fill the large-cap slot in my asset allocation scheme, I wanted it to be a large cap at the beginning of the year and I also wanted it to be a large cap at the end of the year. I began to see that this was going to be a problem. The mutual fund managers would pick stocks so that the fund's style would drift away from what it had been. We also, of course, tried to pick the funds that had the best track records, because we wanted our clients to get the best returns. But we also found that even managers with great track records would just fail at some point. There would be a misstep, or a manager would get fired, or he would pick the wrong stocks or the wrong sectors, and all that track record would disappear. The idea of a track record was quickly losing its credibility. Funds with supposedly great track records seemed to mysteriously fade away and not be able to provide in the second five years the same kind of results they achieved in the prior five years. Having said that, it was much easier to manage client expectations in the 1980s.

Here is what we did: We came up with an asset allocation model that we thought would work. It would ask for certain proportions of the different asset classes: small cap, large cap, international, bond, and so on. Then we would look at the various mutual fund families we worked with, to see if we could figure out which of their mutual funds could represent each of these asset classes. We read mutual fund prospectuses and often found them to be nonsensical. The mandate for the manager would be so broad that the fund would be unusable for our purposes (called colloquially a *go-anywhere* fund). Asset allocation defines asset classes clearly: large cap, small company, international, bonds. Then we would try to pick funds to match the asset classes we needed. But the mutual fund names, such as equity income, balanced, growth and income, capital appreciation, and so forth, did not tie in to the way we were supposed to allocate assets.

We wanted two things from each mutual fund:

1. We wanted it to represent one specific asset class.
2. We wanted it to be an exceptional fund with a great track record and high alpha.

Alpha is a sophisticated financial concept and calculation that is actually widely used quite colloquially to refer to a level of performance return that is higher than expected for a particular asset class in a particular period.[1] We wanted every asset allocation category to be filled but we wanted a great performer in each category.

We did not realize at the time that we were asking for the impossible: a manager to produce alpha by staying in a defined style category. It became evident quickly enough that the broad mandates in the prospectus, coupled with the manager's desire to capture alpha or make a bonus by beating a benchmark or to go in for some end-of-year window dressing, or any other motive, meant that the manager was almost certain to drift out of the assigned style. We came to realize that it was okay not to capture alpha, because we wanted a large-cap fund to perform like a large-cap fund, and that would mean, sometimes, not showing great performance in a given year. The greater sin, as far as we were concerned, was that, in trying to capture alpha, a mutual fund manager would often stop being style-consistent, for the basic reason that it was impossible for a manager to capture alpha consistently while staying within the style constraints. Then the style drift would ruin the asset allocation model.

If it was going to be impossible to get a large-cap manager (or a manager for any asset class) who produced positive alpha, then we would give up the idea of positive alpha and look for managers who would stay with their style. So instead of a manager who tried to outperform and committed two sins—underperformance and style drift—we looked for just the one fault: Get an average return but stay true to your stated style. Eventually we realized that even that was going to be very hard to find.

And yet we continued to work with asset allocation—despite the fact that its practical application compromised the theoretical methodology—and it continued to prove its value. As it turned out, clients were the least harmed by it, which was the initial goal. We continued to try to figure out the best way to use it to get our clients the most return for the least risk. Our accountant reps loved the asset allocation methodology we promoted because it made their job so much easier. At that time it was very typical for reps anywhere in the industry to become familiar with a couple of funds and to sell only those. Our reps at least had to enlarge that body of knowledge to a whole family of mutual funds, so they would be able to talk fluently about the different asset classes represented by the different funds in a fund family.

Then as now, the wholesalers for the different mutual fund companies would visit our offices, touting the virtues of the funds and fund families they represented. The whole mutual fund industry was organized around the hot fund of the day. The wholesalers would walk into a brokerage firm and say to the reps there, "This is our hot new fund. Here are the reasons it is a good buy. Now call your client and sell it." Since many registered reps in the industry lacked sophistication, knowledge, experience, or their own ideas, they would do whatever the wholesaler recommended, because they wanted to make sales. What inevitably happened was that the hot fund of today would end up being mediocre (or worse) the next year.

Understanding Wholesalers

A wholesaler is a representative of a mutual fund company who visits the broker-dealers that sell the company's mutual funds. Typically a wholesaler will not only present a mutual fund and its results to the registered reps of a broker-dealer, but will work with individual registered reps to teach them sales techniques or improve their market knowledge.

Why is it important for you to be familiar with the concept of wholesalers? Because you should know that every single load mutual fund company in the world has a highly paid flock of professionals charged with the single goal of getting your adviser or registered representative to sell more of that company's funds. Wholesalers buy a lot of lunches for the registered reps they sell to! The term comes from the fact that the wholesaler represents the mutual fund company, in effect the wholesale part of the financial markets, whereas the registered reps talk to individual retail clients.

In the end, our asset allocation methodology saved us an incredible amount of time and aggravation over 25 years. It kept us out of trouble in 1987, 1991, and during the Internet bubble. If you look at the entire history of the firm, our idea of asset allocation made *hot fund* a meaningless concept. Although we were not the only brokerage firm working with asset allocation, we were clearly early adopters.

Making Asset Allocation Work

As time went on, we found three significant problems with the way we were developing and using our asset allocation.

The First Problem

The first problem was with the optimization calculation itself. The goal of optimization is to provide the investor with the greatest return for the lowest risk. The problem, especially in those early days and especially if you used the software blindly, was that the program would want you to get the greatest return by calculating a very large allocation to the asset class that had the largest recent historical return, which was never large cap or bonds or something quite normal. Instead, the software would look at the recent high return of REITs (discussed in Chapter 1) and decide you could get the best return on your portfolio by putting 50 percent of your investment dollars into REITs. This is what you could get if you let the program do whatever it wanted to do mathematically; it just searched for the highest return.

If you wanted to avoid that and you wanted the software to tell you the future right, secret way to allocate, you had to figure out—using your crystal ball, presumably—what the *future* return of REITs would be and put that number into the program. We would end up having to constrain the software as far as how much could go into certain asset classes, which means we had to specify that no more than, say, 10 percent of the portfolio could go into REITs—which made us wonder what the point of the software was at all, if it needed so many manual adjustments. This was long before there were other asset classes of the high-risk, high-reward kind, like emerging markets or micro caps, that could also make the software a little crazy. Those would come later.

So even though we would get this tremendous allocation to REITs, even if we wanted to go with it, in many cases we had no way to implement it in mutual funds. I think maybe only one or two of the mutual fund families we used even had a mutual fund relevant to REITs, and yet our software wanted us to put big allocations into it. We had a separate set of asset allocation pie charts for each mutual fund family, according to the asset classes that its mutual funds represented. I think we substituted small cap for REITs, just to have somewhere to put the money.

The Second Problem

The second problem I have mentioned before: trying to match the mutual fund classification nomenclature with the asset classes we needed for our calculations. Our asset allocation was done using the S&P 500 Index (for U.S. large-cap stocks), the Russell 2000 Index (for U.S. small-cap stocks), the EAFE Index (for international stocks), and bonds. Mutual fund names—equity income, balanced, capital appreciation, growth and income versus income and growth—did not match asset classes. We did the best we could to try to understand what a mutual fund manager owned. The data we could get was always old because we did not have the Internet to look up current holdings. Using prospectuses meant the information was always out of date. Even the early stage of Morningstar was a breakthrough because we could finally get all the information we needed about a mutual fund in one sheet. Morningstar gave us enough information so we could finally figure out what funds we could look at.

We ourselves had to learn what asset classes were by looking at the way the academics used asset allocation. They never used the terms the mutual funds used; instead, they looked at a universe of large companies or small companies, Treasuries (short-term fixed income), and overseas investments. The researchers and consultants at Ibbotson, as mentioned earlier, were still the leaders in showing the industry how to use asset classes and in giving clarity on how to go about doing it.

Even so, we still wanted to use good funds run by managers with great track records. When a fund did not do well—which happened all the time—we could not easily move the investment to another fund family, as I have explained. And then the worst part of it was the style drift, which was just horrific. If you're an asset allocator, you can tolerate that a fund is down. If you buy an S&P 500 fund that is supposedly a growth fund, then it represents the asset class of large-cap stocks and is supposed to go down when the S&P 500 goes down. Not only is that acceptable, but that is actually the way it is supposed to work. But when the fund manager decides to save the day by becoming a mid-cap manager, it just does not work for the asset allocation framework.

The Third Problem

Finally, you are always, inevitably, headed toward a crash and burn because there is no way, in my opinion, that any amount of research can help you identify a manager who is going to do really well in the future. Great managers with great track records would always go astray at some point.

Summary of the Issues

So, to summarize my issues with asset allocation methodology itself and implementing it using mutual funds and mutual fund families:

- If we left the optimization wide open, we wound up with bizarre results, like 50 percent allocations to certain asset classes, usually a specialized or esoteric one like REITS or micro-cap.
- We had a hard time finding mutual funds that would represent the asset classes we needed in our scheme, and it was hard to match up mutual fund names with asset classes.
- Mutual fund managers would change styles whenever it suited them; style drift was a huge problem.
- Even the best managers inevitably disappointed.

These were not insignificant issues. At that time, I believed my value proposition for my clients was that I was going to help them find the great funds to buy. As it turned out, that was a bad value proposition that I was not able to live up to.

I wish I could say this was an epiphany. It wasn't. This was the result of my value proposition and my methods not working over a decade. In the early 1980s, when I was starting out as an adviser, I was not smart enough or experienced enough to understand what the problems were. I had to spend 10 frustrating years of my life before I realized that the methods I was using were not working. That does not mean that clients were not doing well; many of them were doing fine, but I was not satisfied that I had found a satisfactory way to advise clients. My expectations about my ability to pick great managers and manage risk were misplaced. Great funds became mediocre funds. Even mediocre funds would drift away out of their supposed style.

The Value of an Adviser: Black Monday, 1987

We got an early indication of both the value of the adviser and the importance of managing client expectations when Black Monday occurred in 1987, when the market dropped almost 23 percent in one day. Fidelity's switchboards *collapsed* because of all the retail investors who called in to redeem their mutual fund investments. On Black Monday[2], those people just wanted to get out. At Terra, we got so few phone calls it was eerie.

The calls we got were from clients who wanted what I later came to call a *financial hug*. They wanted to know that everything was okay. I remember one of my clients called me to say, "I'm calling you because I need to have this conversation. You're just going to tell me to ignore all this stuff, because I'm in this for the long run, right?" I said, "Right." He said, "I wanted you to tell me that again." I said, "That's right; just hold on." And that was that.

As a young adviser, I did not have any great intellectual insight. I was as nervous as everyone else, but I had no other choice for what to tell my clients. Although I understood that my job was to be the calming influence, I had the same emotional trauma they did, but I was not going to get on the phone and start feeding off the emotions put out by everyone else. My job was to say, "Let's just relax, let's not make any precipitous decisions." And as history tells us, within three months everything was fine. We had sold the program correctly and our clients understood that they were invested for the long term, despite periods of volatility, even large drops.

As one of the principals of a broker-dealer, I had my own clients, but the accountant reps who were part of Terra also had their own clients. (As I have explained before, Terra had two layers of clients: our accountant representatives who sold mutual funds and other investments, and the retail clients of our representatives.) Our accountants would call us and say their clients had called, so we would call *their* clients, too. Since we were more experienced with clients than our reps were, I think we were able to sound calmer and more reassuring when delivering the "stay calm, everything is fine" message.

Lesson 5

It is essential to manage client expectations up front.

But we learned an important lesson from this experience. You might even say it was our first hit on the head about volatility and market turbulence. We learned how incredibly, unbelievably important it was to manage client expectations up front so that clients understood that major market events were certainly going to occur. We used asset allocation to try to lower the impact of the volatility on an individual's portfolio. Then when events like Black Monday occurred, our clients could weather the storm without demanding to sell out. Contrast that to the Fidelity experience with retail clients and an 800 number, where there was no one available to offer calming and reassuring words to clients. The person on the phone was basically an order taker, and retail clients just wanted out. I think this is some of the clearest early evidence we got about the value of the adviser.

Lesson 6

An adviser can help individual investors stay invested for the long term.

In those days before the Internet and cable TV, individuals got their financial news from the newspaper or their adviser. We certainly worked with our clients to help them see four or five years into the future and not react to day-to-day markets. We set expectations when we talked about investing. We were not traders and we did not pick stocks, and we tried our best to make sure our clients knew what to expect.

I have learned that many people can accept risk if they have some understanding of what it is and how it can be managed. In my view, entrepreneurs are one of the best examples of the kind of people who can understand risk. They know risk inherently and will understand the financial and investing risk if you explain it to them up front.

The Terra business was filled with entrepreneurs. *We* were entrepreneurs. Somehow we connected with that portion of the investing world and then our client base of entrepreneurs just kept growing. After all, who has money to invest, anyway? Entrepreneurs or retired people. Although we did have some corporate executives as clients, our worldview was based in the world of entrepreneurship. We knew and understood the risk, motivations, and desires of entrepreneurs to make a difference in their lives and the lives of their families. Many were dedicated to their employees and the community they all were part of. This is not taking anything away from corporate executives who, in many ways, want the same things, but large corporations limit the amount of scope for action or change that one individual can have. We were an advisory firm in the suburbs and our business was centered on small businesses, plus some retirees.

By the end of 1987, the market was actually up on the year, although it did not match the highs of 1987 for two more years. At year-end, who was better off? Those who had called Fidelity on Black Monday and sold out at the market lows? Or those who just stuck with their investments? It was meaningless to have been invested in the greatest fund in the world if you bailed out at the market low. So what was more important, ultimately? Getting fund returns or managing client expectations? Here is where it hits you between the eyes: My value proposition was not managing money, it was managing clients and their expectations.

Specialized Approaches

We got through 1987 and our models got better. We were still trying to figure out how to get more and different asset classes, although it was becoming more evident that there were problems with the funds and with the way fund managers picked stocks. During the next years, we tried a number of different approaches that always at first seemed promising.

Timing the Market

We decided to try something else that was much discussed at the time, a timing service that would tell an investor when to buy a certain kind of fund and when to sell it. The service would tell you to buy large caps when they were going to go up. After they reached some peak value, the service would tell you to sell them and go into cash while the market corrected. Later on, the service would tell you to buy bonds, because interest rates were going to go down, or to buy funds that were invested in international stocks, or to sell them, and so on.

The timing service used a *black box*—that is actually what they called it. That should have been a clue to us that it depended more on something mysterious than on real financial insight. As always, we thought we should at least try it. The individuals representing this service would show you how, by applying their algorithms and formulas to past events, they would have made you more money because the box would have told you when to buy and when to sell. This was hindsight and backtracking, not actual performance, but they produced very credible evidence.

We did try it and found out, quickly enough, that it did not work the way we had been told it would work. We know now that it is theoretically impossible for such an approach to work, but years ago we were totally intrigued with this incredible tool. What if it had worked? We were willing to experiment with different techniques if we thought they would help our clients. So here is yet another lesson: Black boxes do not work. Today there are more and more sophisticated black boxes but they all end up having significant flaws, foremost among them the fact that you should not trust something you cannot see or understand, which is almost the definition of a black box. The timers were smart people and a fair amount of money had been invested with them, but they just missed the signals: The timing did not work.

Lesson 7

Do not trust your money to a black box. Timing does not work.

Lesson 8

There will always be new people with new, improved black boxes. Don't trust them, either.

Technical Analysis

Because I was young and had an open mind, and because I was still search- ing for the smart people who would manage money for my clients, my next experiment was with *technical analysis*, also called *stochastic analysis* or *charting*. In the late 1980s, I went for a week's training with a well-known company that sold this kind of software.

Technical analysis is an attempt to predict the performance of a security or commodity by looking for patterns in price movements. In its earliest, crudest form, it involved keeping records by hand, using a pencil to draw lines on chart paper (hence the name *charting*) for daily price movements of whatever you were trading. Of course as computer technology became available it was quickly adapted, since drawing charts by hand was time-consuming and inflexible. The patterns formed on the charts provided trend lines that were supposed to provide powerful indicators for trading activity. Some of the best-known terms of technical analysis are *head-and-shoulders formation, resistance levels* (where we expected selling to take place), and *support levels* (where we expected to see buying). The chartist would analyze market action by studying price movement, moving averages, volume, open interest, other kinds of formations, and other technical indicators.

Technical analysts use judgment gained from experience to decide which pattern a particular instrument reflects at a given time and what the interpretation of that pattern should be. Technical analysts may disagree among themselves over the interpretation of a given chart. How many of you remember the Elliott wave principle? It was named after an accountant who developed the concept in the 1930s. He proposed that market prices would follow a specific pattern, the so-called Elliott waves.

We thought it could be important for us to understand a technique and a theory about the mathematical relationships found in markets; it was much discussed at that time. I went to the training and learned everything about moving averages, stochastics, head-and-shoulders formations, breaks in the formation, and so on—all the signals that were supposed to let you look at the chart and say, right there was where I should have sold. However, as I quickly realized, the problem was that I could do it looking backwards but not going forward.

Even now there are many people who believe in this. The market is oversold, the market is undersold; here is a support level; here is a resistance level. It just looks like voodoo. Soon enough, we realized that the problem was what I just stated: It is 100 percent clear in hindsight; the hard part is taking that data and using it going forward.

We did have a little flirtation with technical analysis, but just never got anywhere with it. There were actually mutual funds based on using these black boxes. The only thing we really concluded was that any money manager who proposed using technical analysis was probably someone we did not want to work with. For a while, there was a great argument in the marketplace between fundamental investing and technical investing, but the great dichotomy of the 1980s was part of a different era.

Lesson 9

If someone tells you that he uses technical analysis, walk away.

Star Wars

In the early 1990s, Morningstar information on mutual funds was becoming much more readily available. In addition to providing comprehensive fact sheets on mutual funds, Morningstar awarded star ratings on mutual funds. I cannot overemphasize the popularizing effect Morningstar had on mutual funds, for two main reasons:

1. So much information was now available about mutual funds that individual investors for the first time believed they could see and understand what mutual funds were all about.
2. It seemed possible to select and buy a good mutual fund as easily as you selected a restaurant. Morningstar seemed to demystify mutual funds.

Thus, mutual fund investing became star wars. How many stars do your funds have? Advisers were excited to think that the choice of which funds to use was solved. Everyone was going to sell only five-star funds. Why would anyone settle for a two-star fund? Our clients walked in with copies of the tear sheets from Morningstar, asking about particular funds. Sometimes our clients demanded that we sell them the no-load funds they found in Morningstar but we did not have a platform that allowed us to do that.

There was disillusionment in this as well. For one thing, no matter how great a mutual fund had been—and there was more than one way to evaluate this—that old compliance disclaimer that we have been putting on our materials for years is quite literally true: Past performance does not predict future performance. We all were really hoping that we finally did have a way to know which funds were going to be great. But it just did not work the way we wanted it to.

Morningstar

Is there any investor in the world who does not recognize the name of Morningstar, Inc.? In 1984, Morningstar published its first edition of *The Mutual Fund Sourcebook*, which collected performance data, portfolio holdings, and other information on 400 mutual funds in a format that changed the way investors approached mutual funds. The quarterly publication quickly became the industry standard for mutual fund reporting.

But we had a second problem: When Morningstar first came out with its star awards, it lumped all U.S. stock funds together and ranked them within one big group. Stars were supposed to be awarded according to risk-adjusted performance, but it worked out so that the mutual funds that invested in the best-performing asset classes in the marketplace were the ones that got the stars. For example, in mid-2000, "Three-quarters of all funds that invested mostly in large, fast-growing companies garnered four or five stars. At the same time, only six of the 123 funds that specialized in small, bargain-priced stocks earned four or five stars."[3] But those stars had power: "In a study, Financial Research Corp. in Boston found that of the 25 top-selling portfolios in 1998, 22 had a four- or five-star rating."[4] (As a footnote to this story, Morningstar very significantly revamped its star ranking system in 2002 and instituted 48 different categories for mutual funds. Stars are now awarded for performance within a given category.)

So here was our problem. We chose mutual funds for asset alloca- tion. The mutual funds representing the asset classes that were out of favor in the marketplace would have fewer than four or five stars; they might have only one or two stars. A fund might be a poor performer with few stars because its asset class was not doing well. If small caps were doing badly, no small-cap mutual fund could get four or five stars, even the best small-cap manager. And then we had to persuade our clients that buying a small-cap fund with only two stars was the right thing to do. As you can see from the statistic quoted previously, the money poured into the four- and five-star funds while the others languished. Clients became indig- nant: "How dare you try to sell me a two-star fund?" We had a constant battle with our now-informed clients as we tried to justify buying two- and three-star funds for the asset allocation. Our clients also battled us for a kind of mutual fund that we saw as exceptionally high risk, the four- and five-star sector funds issued by some no-load companies. Our mission was to get our clients more and more diversification, and these focused sector funds were going completely in the wrong direction. Sector funds would own only health stocks or financial stocks or one country (Japanese funds were one well-known example) and were extremely popular at one time.

Advising our clients became much easier in 1995 when we set up our fee-based platform, discussed in the next section.

Why I Did Not Pick Stocks—and Why I Would Never Pick Stocks

I think we recognized early on that no one at Terra had the qualifications or skill set for picking stocks. If the really smart people, the Wall Street people and mutual fund managers, were not very successful at picking stocks, I did not have a big enough ego to think that I could do it. Rather, it was my job to look for the smart people—the Really Smart Guys, as I called them—who would be able to manage money for my clients. And then, as we watched those large funds not do very well at picking stocks, it would have taken extreme hubris to think we could do it better. It was hard enough trying to pick mutual funds.

We took the position that the people who picked stocks were smarter than we were and we thought—incorrectly, it turns out—that our job was to find the best ones to manage money for our clients. You could recognize the really smart people because they would have a track record. Money managers came in two basic flavors:

1. "We're a top-down manager. We look at macroeconomics and look for opportunities in the various industries. When we have identified the top growth industries, we will find the best players in those specific industries."
2. "We're a bottom-up manager. We look for those companies that have great growth opportunities in the future."

I would listen to these presentations and say to myself, this is great, they're buying good companies; I don't want my clients in bad companies. The money managers came in; they showed us the data. And I was wondering how I could possibly compete with the resources they had: 20 analysts, libraries of information, international offices, computer technology I could only dream about. But I never had any desire to pick stocks. I figured there were smarter people with better resources who could do this. At that time, I believed my value proposition was that I was going to find the great fund companies and the great fund managers. I had no interest in trying to pick individual stocks. Our value proposition at Terra became finding the smart people and designing a diversified portfolio that would obtain the highest return for a given amount of risk.

But there are even more reasons why we never tried to pick stocks. This was not fun money; this was client money. Furthermore, imagine I think I have a great idea about picking a certain stock. Am I going to execute that idea using client money to play around in the stock market to see if it really works? I did not see any upside for me in this. What would be the point? So that I could make a $100 commission selling the stock? My greatest concern was loss aversion.

Occasionally a client would ask us to pick stocks and we would say that we just did not do that. This was not our value proposition and it never intrigued us. If the client insisted that I help him buy a stock, I would send him across the street to a discount broker, saying, "Go ahead and do that with your play money. Then come back when you want to talk about your serious money." We even used only mutual funds to buy the fixed-income portion of the asset allocation, because even fixed-income securities need to be managed. As we know in hindsight, today's AA or AAA corporate bond is tomorrow's junk bond.

Becoming a Fee-Based Adviser

After the big crash of 1987, there was less drama in investing for a few years. During this time, technology was changing the way people invested. For one thing, technology had created the personal computers that everyone was using and the Internet that everyone was accessing. All of a sudden, it seemed, individual investors had access to boatloads of detailed information about individual companies and their stocks, mutual funds, and every other investment you can think of. Individuals began to realize the kind of hefty fees brokers and mutual funds charged and sought out no-load mutual funds. Online trading got its start during the 1990s: something brand-new in the investment world.

Understanding Mutual Fund Fees

Charles Schwab did not invent 12(b)-1 fees, which had been in existence for some time, but brought them to a new level of prominence. Named for the section of the Securities and Exchange Commission (SEC) regulation that allows this kind of fee to be charged, it is a fee paid by a mutual fund to the broker-dealer who maintains the customer account with the mutual fund, such as, for example, Charles Schwab. The fees might or might not be shared with the registered rep who sold the mutual funds. The amount of a 12(b)-1 fee might be an annual 15 to 50 basis points of the assets under management, paid quarterly. The original intent of 12(b)-1 fees was to compensate broker-dealers for maintaining ongoing contact with customers, answering questions, and sending account statements. Some mutual fund companies use these fees to pay for aggressive advertising and marketing programs. The fee is in effect a direct deduction from the customer's return. But for some perspective on how large this feature has become, the February 18–22, 2008, issue of *Investment News* (vol. 12, no. 7, p. 16) cites SEC Chairman Christopher Cox as stating that Rule 12(b)-1 "has allowed mutual funds to spend about $12 billion of fund assets a year to pay brokers to distribute their products."

Basis Points and Percentage Points

A financial text intended for the public can get itself all wound up in terminology. If you learn the meaning of basis point (bp), the discussion about market performance and percentage returns can be simplified. A basis point is one one-hundredth of a percentage point. In the financial markets, it would be cumbersome to talk about the difference between, for example, 6.00 percent and 6.06 percent as being six one-hundredths of a percentage point. Saying that the difference is six basis points (bps) is much easier. It is even easier to say 150 basis points than it is to say one and a half percentage points. Ten bps is equal to one-tenth of a percentage point and 100 bps equals one percentage point.

Finally, you have to note the difference between percentage points and percent when talking about returns. If I compare one security that yields 10 percent with another security that yields 12 percent, the difference between the two is *not* 2 percent but two percentage points. If I compare the number 10 with the number 12, I say that 12 is larger than 10 by 2, which is 20 percent. This confusion happens all the time in the financial world and I at least want to be clear on the terminology. So 12 percent is 20 percent more than 10 percent, or two percentage points higher.

The First Supermarket for Mutual Funds

Technology also made it possible to change the way we as advisers were offering investment solutions to our clients. In 1990, discount broker Charles Schwab introduced one of the most important technological innovations of the century, a *mutual fund supermarket*, so called because a retail investor could select from hundreds (later thousands) of different mutual funds. This supermarket offered clients the ability to select mutual funds from different fund families but have them all combined into one account that had one consolidated statement.

This resulted in an innovation in the way fees were charged. Although the funds were offered as no-loads that retail investors bought without the up-front loads of A shares, all the mutual funds had a fee built into them called a 12(b)-1 fee, which the fund paid to Schwab for the privilege of being on their platform. The new Schwab platform initiated a restructuring of the way the financial industry got paid, forcing full-service brokerage firms to move away from commissions and towards fees based on assets under management. How your broker or adviser gets paid has a profound influence on his actions.

While individual clients could use the Schwab supermarket, it also provided advisers with a platform for selecting mutual funds from different companies and then charging a fee for advisory services. A client who worked with an adviser could have access to certain *institutional funds* (meaning they were created to be sold in million-dollar increments to institutions, not in thousand-dollar increments to retail clients) that were not available to the public directly. Institutional funds tended to have lower costs as well as a certain cachet due to limited accessibility. Schwab technology streamlined fee collection and payment, quarterly reporting, and back office support.

This technological shift allowed us to envision liberation from the prison of only one mutual fund family for each client. This was extremely important for us! Being able to offer independent financial advice was at the heart of our value proposition, and yet we had been so tightly bound for so long to individual mutual fund companies—and the different limitations inherent in each—that it took us a while to understand how important this innovation could be for us and our business and our ability to be truly independent.

The Terra partners sat down to try to figure out how we could offer a fee-based program that went beyond the limitations of the commission-based business we had been conducting for so long. For those who are not fully aware of the industry terminology, we had been selling mutual fund A shares with front-end loads. As I explained at the beginning of this chapter, a client's $10,000 investment in a mutual fund with a front-end load would mean that only $9,500 would get invested and $500 in front-end load would be paid in commissions to the rep and the broker-dealer to which the rep belonged. In the normal world of wirehouse brokerage firms, it was very normal for the rep to invest the client's money, get paid the one-time front-end load, and then more or less disappear unless the client had more money or the rep had a better idea of how to move the money around to get paid again.

A fee-based adviser works differently. There is no front-end load; the adviser uses no-load mutual funds. Instead, the client pays the adviser an ongoing fee of something like 150 basis points annually. The adviser has a *fiduciary obligation* to meet with the client at least twice a year and, basically, to stay in touch. The adviser can recommend investments without worrying about loads because the client pays the same amount whether there is activity in the account or not. Most importantly, it creates a relationship based on providing the client with ongoing advice that is not based on a series of transactions that might or might not have an economic basis. It opens up the relationship with the client to include all aspects of wealth management, including financial and estate planning, insurance and other kinds of lifestyle protection, and the all-important retirement income planning.

Up until now, we at Terra, along with our accountant representatives, had been registered representatives, meaning we had passed the Series 7 exam, worked for commissions, and were part of a broker-dealer. Our standard of care to our clients was called *suitability*, meaning the investment basically had to be *suitable* to the client's circumstances (no selling high-risk stocks to orphans and widows, etc.). But when one became an Investment Adviser Representative (IAR)—a fee-based adviser—one's standard of care became *fiduciary*, meaning that one has to put the best interests of the client above one's own. Investment adviser representatives (IARs) are regulated by the states and the SEC rather than by the Financial Industry Regulatory Authority (FINRA), but generally the adviser has to pass what is called the Series 65 exam. He would then be affiliated with a registered investment adviser (RIA) rather than with a broker-dealer. The idea of working on a fee basis started gaining traction in the late 1980s and early 1990s, although the wealthy had long had access to fee-based advice through places like the Northern Trust Bank.

Finally we would be able to offer our clients real asset allocation investing using the fiduciary standard of care we believed in. This new electronic platform would allow us to charge an advisory fee and use no-load mutual funds as the investments. In fact, it seemed to us that we might also get access to some of the most famous institutional money managers that did not offer mutual funds or had minimum investments that were far too high for most individual investors.

A Final Note on the Terra Years

From the very beginning, we at Terra understood the importance of service. We recruited the first representatives who joined the company and we knew what it took to get them in the door. We also knew what it took to keep them, and sometimes that was harder. We retained our representatives because we really understood our customers—both the representatives and their clients. We even had some who left for greener pastures and then found out that ours was really the greenest—and came back.

I look back over the past 25 years and see one Wall Street problem after another. We were able to escape the corporate mandate and put the client and the client's needs at the center of our business. We were part of something that was really new in the investment world. Part of our evolution was introducing our fee-based products and having our advisers become fee-based advisers. The standard of care in the broker-dealer, commission-based world is suitability, which, as we well know, can easily lend itself to a variety of abuses. As soon as one crosses over to the fee-based world, the standard of care for the client shifts to putting the client first.

Above all, and most importantly, from the beginning we believed we were on a mission; we believed we were the good guys. We believed with all our hearts that we were going to do the right thing for both our representatives and their clients. When I look back through the haze of time, it seems to me now that we, the Terra partners, were the seven musketeers. We were a diverse group dedicated to helping people through the maze of financial choices and to providing independent financial advice. We were independent of large name-brand brokerage firms or proprietary products like mutual funds. Furthermore, our accountant representatives were independent because they were not our employees and valued their relationships with their clients above all else. They would not put themselves in the position of losing a client over a sale of any financial product because the relationship was far more important than any money generated by any single sale. We believed we had created the perfect balance of independence and competency.

My story has now reached a breaking point. Before I continue with my story, I think it is time to talk about *you*, those who are reading this book: individual investors.

CHAPTER 3

Working with Individual Investors

I have shown you how, in my career as a financial adviser, I made every mistake in the book. So maybe individual investors do not need financial advisers—they can learn on their own the same way I did. Maybe individuals are able to tap into all the financial information around them to learn what they need to be able to take care of their own investing.

Before I continue the story of how my investment strategy evolved while I worked at Terra, I want to take a look at investors and investor behavior. Understanding how individuals approach investing is extremely important, both to me as a professional and to you in understanding your own predispositions to investing.

The Emotions of Investing

Throughout my career, people have told me amazing stories of their investment prowess—to the point, sometimes, that I wondered how anyone but me was still working. Plenty of individual investors got confused during the great tech bubble and thought their investment success was driven by their great skill rather than by the fact that a giant bull market was in progress. I do not hear many stories like that at the moment, unfortunately. But even when investors still had stories to tell, and even if they were mostly telling the truth about their success, there is still a big difference between hitting it big on one or a few stocks, and making enough correct investment decisions to take care of your entire financial and economic future.

People are not rational about money. There's big news. Yet the academicians who theorized about efficient markets started with the idea that investors behave rationally. Even at the outset of my career, I could see that people are not rational about money. It did not take many years of experience as an adviser to realize just how irrational they are—and how swayed by great tides of emotion.

TABLE 3.1   Individual Investors Do Not Earn Market Returns

Type of Performance	Return
S&P 500 Index	8.4%
Average equity investor	1.9%
Inflation	2.8%

This table shows investment results for the 20 years ending
12/31/08. In this case, the S&P 500 Index is used as a proxy for
performance of the broader market.
Source: Dalbar Quantitative Analysis of Investor Behavior 2008.

Table 3.1 shows a study done by a company called Dalbar. They wanted
to look at the investment returns individual investors actually earned rather
than at the financial results achieved by securities in the marketplace, and
they do that by examining investment flows in and out of mutual funds.
Dalbar first introduced the results of this study in 1995, and the results were
shocking to the investment industry. The 2008 results are similar to what
they have always been. The results of the study showed that average equity
investors earned 1.9 percent on their investments, compared to the results
of the S&P 500 Index, which increased 8.4 percent during that period, while
the inflation rate was 2.8 percent. This result would appear even more
shocking if you saw a graph representing those investment returns. The
average individual investor does not manage to achieve even the inflation
rate! A return of 1.9 percent means that an investor's money doubles in
approximately 35 years. A return of 8.4 percent means that an investor's
money doubles for the first time in approximately eight and a half years,
and then doubles again eight and a half years after that.

Dalbar does not look at the performance of a mutual fund itself. Rather,
it looks at how individuals invest. For example, when a mutual fund is going
up, investors pour money into it, so many of them invest not at the low
point, against which the performance is measured, but somewhere near
the top. Then the mutual fund cannot sustain the high performance, or
perhaps too much money has flowed into it to be invested effectively, and
some of the recent investors decide to take their money out and invest
elsewhere. They jump from one fund to another, buying what was hot *last*
year and therefore missing out on that upside, and then selling the stock
or mutual fund once it has gone down. This is not the same as having had
your money in the fund over a period of years.

Every client I meet wants to beat the market. The evidence from
Dalbar says that, on the whole, when individuals invest for themselves,
they underperform the market by 6.5 percentage points per year! Our emotions can be so destructive that not only do we not beat the market, we
cannot even get close to doing as well as the market.

What can explain this poor result? Twenty years ago, investors held mutual funds for 10 to 12 years. Today, that holding period is down to less than two years. Why? Chasing investment returns and hot managers is one part of the answer, which demonstrates that developing and sticking to a sustainable strategy is more important than figuring out which fund or stock is currently the best in the marketplace. Individual investors are emotional and they let those emotions drive their investments.

Discount brokerage accounts and no-load mutual funds allowed individuals to have self-directed brokerage accounts and to manage their own investments more directly. They could move their investments around—buy and sell mutual funds and stocks—without talking to an adviser or broker. It is true that some parts of the financial services industry had been charging excessive fees for years, and stock commissions were an embarrassment before deregulation in 1975. I have also mentioned the unconscionably high loads and fees charged by load mutual funds. It was, overall, an excellent thing for investors to be able to buy no-load funds and index funds for themselves using their discount brokerage accounts.

But on their own, investors have traded even more emotionally than we would have guessed. They did not call up the discount brokerage and buy an index fund and then refrain from calling again for five years, which would be a pretty good investment strategy. Instead, being able to execute their own trades has been exciting for some people—and like a narcotic for others.

Online Trading Will Make You Rich

The introduction of online investing was the real breach with the past. The first versions were primitive but still allowed individuals to trade as much as they wanted to. It was not even all that cheap at the beginning, but I never heard anyone complain about trading costs. The cost of trades decreased throughout the 1990s as the technology got better and competition heated up, and newcomers like E-Trade gave the old financial firms a run for their money. Still, it was not unusual to hear that someone was trading one or two dozen times a day, and even a $9.99 cost per trade adds up quickly at that rate. As the decade wore on, if you were into online trading, you could progress beyond your own computer and a modem. There were organizations that offered day-trading facilities so you could trade even more. In my opinion, an online trading addiction looks just like a gambling addiction.

How much money did anyone make? We now have some hard facts to measure the performance of those first avid day traders.

Terrance Odean, currently a professor of business at the University of California, has been studying investor behavior for years, particularly online trading. He has done studies using tens of thousands of online trading records from an online trading firm.[1] The same technology that enables online trading also enables this kind of extensive and intensive data analysis.

Odean and Brad Barber did a study that tracked the investment results of 1,600 investors who began trading online when it was first offered, investors who had earned "exceptional" results before going online. When they first went online, *they dramatically increased their trading activity, but also underperformed the market,* due to excessive trading.[2] The authors of this study speculate that the investors may not understand transaction costs, or may have acquired a greatly enhanced illusion of knowledge from online sources. Or perhaps the illusion of control from doing their own trading may have fed the kind of overconfidence that drives excessive trading. The important thing to note is that these investors had been able to create good results when using that old trading tool, the telephone, but lost control once they went online and could trade as much as they wanted to.

Barber and Odean also wrote a paper titled "Trading Is Hazardous to Your Wealth: The Common Stock Investment Performance of Individual Investors." I think their abstract statement, in their own words, deserves to be quoted here in its entirety:

> *Individual investors who hold common stocks directly pay a tremendous performance penalty for active trading. Of 66,465 households with accounts at a large discount broker during 1991 to 1996, those that trade most earn an annual return of 11.4%, while the market returns 17.9%. The average household earns an annual return of 16.4%, tilts its common stock investment toward high-beta, small, value stocks, and turns over 75% of its portfolio annually. Overconfidence can explain high trading levels and the resulting poor performance of individual investors. Our central message is that trading is hazardous to your wealth.[3]*

Information Overload

Many things changed during the 1990s. Do you remember how we were all going to get rich? The so-called experts told us that each day—in fact, they still do. There was an explosion in the amount of financial information that was available. You could turn on the TV or go online 24/7 to get advice about which stocks or mutual funds to pick. It was impossible not to get caught up in this market noise. Stocks were doubling and tripling in value, neighbors and friends were making thousands of dollars by buying and selling, and you were dying to take part in it yourself.

This is in stark contrast to the 1980s. At that time, if a client of mine wanted to change from one mutual fund to another, he would have to get some information first. The introduction of Morningstar tear sheets greatly increased the amount of information a person could get about a bunch of different mutual funds (rather than having to find and examine a prospectus for each mutual fund one was interested in), but those sheets were not available at home. An investor would have to come into my office or go to a library to research what mutual fund he wanted to change to.

There was a whole process of change that happened more or less simultaneously. As soon as some of the early adopters reported making lots of money in their investments, everyone else wanted to do that, too. Discount brokerage firms would let you use their information sources if you came into the office, but the Internet itself was taking off, and there was information available online. And then suddenly there was an explosion in the magazines devoted to individual investing, and we got cable news—both investment and not—around the clock. Frenzy ensued. If you were not making a fortune in trading stocks, then you *were* left behind, because all your neighbors and friends and families were making fortunes—or that's what they told you.

Figure 3.1 shows graphically how investor flows of money lag the market. When the market is going up, the money pours in. In Figure 3.1, market performance is represented by the trend line. Flows of funds are represented by the vertical bars. You can see how the funds continue to pour in after the market has hit a peak—although no one can know when that is, of course—and then when the market starts down again, the money starts to

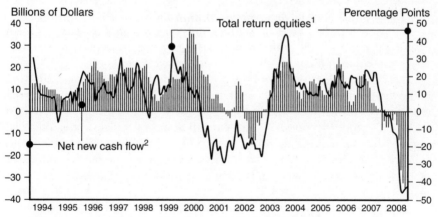

[1]The total return on equities is measured as the year-over-year change in the MSCI All Country World Total Return Stock Index
[2]Net new cash flow to equity funds is plotted as a six-month moving average.

FIGURE 3.1   Flows to Equity Funds Related to Global Stock Price Performance 1994–2008

Source: Investment Company Institute and Morgan Stanley Capital International.

dry up. We can see that only when the market starts to increase again do investors again start to invest. The lagged flows of funds from 1999 to 2004 provide a textbook illustration of this principle, otherwise known as buying high and selling low. As it turns out, behavioral finance has some theories about this behavior, which I discuss later in this chapter.

When You Love Your Stock

One of the main themes of this book is the importance of diversifying your investments as a way of managing your overall risk. Diversification is one of the central themes of my investment philosophy and I discuss it at length in Chapters 4, 5, and 6. Concentrated positions in any security represent potential investment disaster. If you did not learn that in 2002, you had another opportunity to learn it in 2008, when so many former blue-chip companies simply went out of business. My investment strategy involves investing in the entire market worldwide—something like 10,000 securities—so that while the failure of any one company is of course regrettable, it is minuscule in the overall portfolio.

What about the investor who holds a concentrated position for emotional reasons? This comes in two flavors. One is the investor who holds on to some stock for a personal, emotional reason. The second is the executive or other employee who holds a concentrated position in his own company because he loves the company, knows the stock, and believes so strongly in its future. Sometimes the company itself strongly encourages its employees to hold large portions of their wealth in its stock.

Consider the first kind of investor, the one who holds a stock for an emotional reason. You could have read many sad examples in the *Wall Street Journal* over the past few years, but I have experienced it myself many times. For example, I once worked with an elderly widow whose husband had owned only Phillip Morris stock that had done extremely well for them over the years. Now she had to figure out what to do for herself. I advised and then argued strenuously that she sell some of it. The other financial person she was talking to was a stockbroker, and he advised her not to sell—but she did. Six months later, the stock plunged by 60 percent when the first tobacco suits were introduced. As an adviser, I live for moments like this.

I have seen this so many times over the years. A wife holds a stock because her husband had bought it in the early years of their marriage—and then the widow takes offense when the adviser suggests selling some of it. Sons and daughters hang on to stocks just because their parents had bought them—that is the sentimental reason—or because the children figured that their parents were the investing experts. I just do not understand how people get so emotionally attached to a *security*. And you just cannot talk them out of it. Frame a picture of your parents; frame a copy of a stock certificate; take a picture of the local bank: Just do not confuse the love you had for your spouse or your parents with the cold reality of the stock market.

Over the years, I have had in my office executives from every one of the well-known, Chicago-based corporations: Sears, Lucent, Motorola, Allstate, Sara Lee—you name it. Almost all of them have been in love with their company and in love with its stock. For successful executives, the stock represents pride of ownership in a company that represents their own success. It has also been a profitable investment over the years. They want to stay on the train because they think it will go on forever. Occasionally I see an executive whose position in the company is high enough that he is required to own a certain amount of company stock; in that case, I recommend trying to satisfy that requirement through options.

In the past—which was very different from today—there were circumstances where stock grants over a long career resulted in a prosperous retirement. I have heard of millionaires created by 30 years of stock or option grants from Quaker Oats or Sears. Of course, these days, everyone imagines becoming a Microsoft or Google millionaire.

But compare those situations with the employees of Enron. They were so convinced of the ultimate value of their company that they kept buying it in large quantities as its value fell to zero. In the end, what they had was zero. I have read that the management of Bear Stearns always encouraged employees to hold large amounts of company stock; the managers held large stock positions as well. They were left with virtually zero. Lehman Brothers? Down to zero. AIG? Available for the price of a postage stamp. And so on. This was the litany of 2008. You can add to this list all the tech companies that disappeared during the dot-com bubble. Employees just do not think this is going to apply to them.

I have seen this so many times that I know how real it is. It has been interesting for me to find out that the field of behavioral finance backs this up. Employees do not understand the risk/return profile of owning company stock in general, and a study found that half of those surveyed think that owning company stock is less risky than owning a money market fund.[4] Individuals are overconfident, ignorant of the principles of finance, or just think that bad things will not happen to them. It's human nature.

I have seen many individuals with concentrated stock positions—and I don't recall ever seeing a situation where the concentrated position was more profitable in the long term than holding a diversified portfolio would have been. You have to look at the big picture of your financial situation. The company that employs you already represents a gigantic part of your overall prosperity. Do not put yourself further at risk by holding large amounts of company stock.

If you have inherited a concentrated stock position, please try to remember that it represents the securities market, not your mother's love. Get in touch with a financial adviser as quickly as you can, to figure out how to start selling out of it.

Wealth Creation and Investment Style

Thousands of words have been written about investor types and the psychology of investing, how emotions influence an investor's attitudes about money, and how and why investors behave as they do. In my experience, the best way to figure out how an individual is going to invest his or her wealth is to find out how that wealth was created. The circumstances of wealth creation also determine the biggest challenges the person is going to face when investing, and that includes the emotional traps that various types of professions fall into.

There is a huge divide in the world of investors between wealth that is created and wealth that is inherited. There are many different kinds of wealth creators: professionals such as lawyers, doctors, or CPAs; entrepreneurs or business owners; company executives; people with pensions; and finally steady Eddie, the rare person who actually saves enough. Inherited wealth, by contrast, can all seem much the same, regardless of its source. I talk about that later in this chapter.

Whether you are the business owner who is looking for enough equity to be able to retire on, or the professional who is paid well but needs to accumulate wealth, or the person who has inherited wealth and has a legacy to transfer, or the executive who needs to diversify—all these issues are difficult for an individual to grasp and manage. This is where the adviser has to be unbiased and maybe the devil's advocate, to have some very difficult discussions with clients about things they are uncomfortable dealing with or even talking about.

Wealth Creators

In this section, I discuss the various ways in which wealth is created.

PROFESSIONAL While the kind of professional I am talking about here—doctor, lawyer, CPA—has his own business and is clearly an entrepreneur, this person is likely to be a sole proprietor or a partner. Although the business might also employ an assistant or receptionist, it does not employ many employees or manufacture anything. That is how I distinguish the *professional* from the *business owner*, discussed next.

The first thing you notice about professionals is that they are paid a large amount of money over their working years, but the residual value of a doctor's or lawyer's or CPA's business is minimal. Their challenge, then, is to turn that income into wealth over their lifetime, so they can continue to support themselves in retirement. Although of course there are exceptions, many of these individuals get used to having a certain kind of affluent lifestyle, all based on income. Although they may save money through their pension plan or qualified account, in order to turn the income they are used to into enough wealth to keep supplying that kind of income, they have to accumulate an enormous amount of money.

Later in this book we discuss the fact that, to make your portfolio last for the rest of your life, a 4 percent annual withdrawal rate is most likely to ensure that you never run out of money, no matter how long you live. While $100,000 annually hardly represents great affluence, you need to have a $2.5 million portfolio to get that much. Even with a relatively high lifetime income, it is not that easy to save enough to build a multimillion-dollar portfolio. If our professional is used to spending $200,000 annually, the required portfolio would double to $5 million.

My observation of these individuals is that they need planners and advisers to help them understand how much they need to save to get to that retirement amount and also to counsel them realistically about the low residual value of their practice. However, that tough-love kind of advice can also lead those individuals to reckless investing habits since growing that large a portfolio based on reasonable, conservative rates of return, such as 7 to 9 percent, will just not get them to where they need to be. In other words, these professionals may believe they have to take inordinate risks in order to compensate for the difficulty or their inability to accumulate wealth.

You have to be highly intelligent to get the kind of qualifications these professionals have. But it is only human for them to assume that they will also be highly successful in investing. They do not consider that, although it took them years to qualify for their profession, they never put the same amount of time and energy into studying investing. Investing should be easy, right? And that belief leads to very poor decision-making. In fact, I have found that because many professionals are so successful in their professional lives, they start to believe that no one can tell them anything about other important aspects of their lives. This can be very serious!

They also tend to invest in herds with their peer groups. So, for example, if one lawyer or doctor tells his friends what he is investing in, those friends will believe that the first one has done the appropriate due diligence and will jump right in. These very busy people need an adviser to help them with this essential aspect of their lives. Their assumption that their intelligence and success in their respective profession automatically transfers to investing has unfortunately proven to be incorrect time and again. This has led to very many situations where I found myself dealing with successful professionals in their fifties or sixties, having some very hard talks about truly saving and investing quite large amounts of money in order for them to have any kind of dignified retirement.

ENTREPRENEUR OR BUSINESS OWNER   Business owners are some of my favorite clients. They live the true American dream. Whatever their educational background, through hard work, true grit, opportunity or luck, they have been able to build thriving businesses with employees who rely on them. Many business owners are extremely dedicated to their employees and believe they have a moral obligation to help the people who work for them.

From an investment perspective, the business clearly represents a disproportionate amount of the asset allocation of their net worth, so one part of the challenge is trying to diversify them away from the business, which means accumulating wealth beyond the business. The other part of the challenge is figuring out how to help the business owner cash out his or her equity.

There's an old joke about a man who owned a business and worked long, arduous hours. He would come home every night and complain about unions, employees, clients, collecting money, and all the problems of a business, and then would look at his son and say, "Someday this is all going to be yours." Figuring out how to transfer a business is the main challenge. Business owners have only about three or four scenarios for cashing out their equity. Their situation is likely to be only a little better than the professional's.

If the business owner dies, the business might have to be liquidated because the skills are not transferable. The business owner might try to sell to the next generation, who might or might not have the skills necessary to run the business. Or the owner might try to sell the business to the employees or to a competitor. For many business owners, the optimal scenario would be to have their children come into the business, but in many instances—based on that old joke—the kids have no desire to take it on.

The adviser's challenge is to try to get the business owner to accumulate wealth outside of the business and to diversify away from it—which means, of course, not keeping every cent in the business and instead investing in pension and qualified plans. Then there is another dilemma. Imagine that the business owner is able to put savings away independent of the value of the business and has really hedged himself personally. Now he wants to retire. If he sells to his children or employees, he ends up acting as the banker, in effect lending the money to the buyers to buy the business. You have to think about the quality of the note the business owner is taking back from his children or employees, meaning that there is a lot of risk associated with that sale. What if his kids decide to stop paying him? The consequences will be different than if a bank held the note.

My goal for my business-owning clients is to get them invested so that the sale of the business can be just gravy on top of a solid retirement plan. I love working with business owners because they truly understand risk and they understand my investment philosophy about managing risk.

Business owners have a much better understanding than the average person of what it takes to make money. However, they sometimes want to invest too aggressively because that's their style in business. The challenge for an adviser is to guide them towards moderation. You say to the business owner, "Of course you want to have growth in an outside portfolio, but you take risks every day when you go to work, so let's ensure that we have a portfolio that actually has a little more constraint on the risk and return—just because of what you have to do on a day-to-day basis."

Succession planning is also important to business owners. Business owners are certainly motivated to try to get some of their equity out of the business for their own retirement, but a large part of their motivation for succession planning usually includes taking care of employees. We discuss later what happens when the children are not suitable owners, along with some other strategies for succession planning in the context of the owner's wish to make sure the business survives for the sake of the employees.

COMMODITY TRADERS: ONE OF A KIND   The commodity traders who used to work in the pits at the Board of Trade were always a unique breed. A young man from the Midwest could make a fortune in a very nontraditional way. Commodity traders in general were just smart—some of them so street-smart it was scary. But the gold traders from the last great gold market—the end of the 1970s and the beginning of the 1980s—were a breed apart.

The gold traders in the pit would make on the order of 10,000 to 20,000 trades in a year, and maybe a half a dozen of those trades would actually make their profit for the year. Whether or not they understood the complexities of the overall economy, they knew how to read other people as well as the activity and interactions in the pit, which was the center of the universe for them. They knew how to integrate what was going on in the pit with what was going on in the general market. They were true risk-takers, the ultimate risk-takers. Watching these traders, I could not decide if I was more awestruck or aghast—probably equally both.

There were stories of people, not my clients, who lost $100 million in a day, and that was back when $100 million was a lot of money. They were very smart people who knew how to take and manage risk. But the real genius of this group was that, when gold started to lose its luster during the early 1980s, they took their chips off the table. They walked away with a lot of money to use for the next stage of their lives. As the song says, they knew when to hold 'em and knew when to fold 'em.

COMPANY EXECUTIVES   I mentioned company executives earlier as being people who might fall in love with their stocks. Such people can be a challenge. Many of them are passionate and dedicated to the company they work for, and their job, status, and standing in the community depend on continuing to work for that company. Keeping all their wealth tied up in the stock of the company they already depend on for a job is a strategy that might have worked well enough 50 years ago, but we have learned the hard way from the experience of the 1990s and up until today that many of them simply own too much stock in the company they work for.

As an incentive, mid- to high-level executives are often granted stock options or restricted stock in their company, and it is extremely challenging to get them to diversify. I have worked with executives from at least two dozen of the Fortune 500 companies located in the Chicago area. When their company stock was doing great, they clearly did not want to sell it because the company was on a roll and they also did not want to pay taxes on the accumulated capital gains. Then when the stock was not doing well, or the company was in a turnaround situation, they would be waiting for it to come back to their high-water mark.

I remember being at a swim meet some years ago, talking to an executive from Lucent. This individual was passionate about his company, as you would expect. I introduced myself as a financial adviser and we started talking about stocks. I explained that I did not pick stocks at all, and yet here was an individual who had invested his entire portfolio in one stock, Lucent.

He said he intended to hold on to his Lucent stock. I suggested that he sell half of it. He said he wanted to wait until it passed $75. I asked him what made him think that it was going to go to $80. The only answer was his personal conviction, an artificial line he had drawn in his head. He was not even in the kind of executive position where he could have had real insight into the company's fortunes. We all know the rest of that story. The stock never got to $80 and he, along with thousands of other unfortunate employees at Lucent, rode the stock down to $4 a share.

This is an extreme but not uncommon example. It starkly illustrates the dilemma that executives face. Some companies require executives at the highest corporate levels to own a certain amount of stock because it represents their commitment to the company, and, as I said, some of those executives are helped with this commitment through stock options and restricted stock. However, the vast majority of executives are not required to own large amounts of company stock and are certainly not required to keep a large proportion of their wealth in that stock. The challenge for the adviser is to try to persuade the executive to keep the proportion of that stock to a more reasonable allocation; in my view, it should be no more than about 15 to 20 percent of the executive's overall portfolio.

The executive has to diversify away from company stock through his 401(k) account or an outside portfolio. It is essential for the executive to realize that this is not an act of disloyalty but reflects the reality of self-protection through diversification. In fact, since the executive depends on the company for his job and income stream as well, owning too much company stock represents one of the most extreme examples of the danger of a concentrated position.

STEADY EDDIE　I used to see this kind of person much more than I do now. This type was probably best recounted in the book *The Millionaire Next Door*.[5] Steady Eddie lives rather modestly and saves his money year after year—after year after year. He lives in a modest home that was paid off a long time ago and he has $1 million or $2 million in CDs, stocks, and mutual funds. These people typically had lives touched by the Great Depression; whether they were born in, grew up in, or went to college during the Depression, it marked their lives. The members of this group scrimped and saved, lived very modestly, and really did not enjoy spending money—and, as a result, accumulated significant wealth. Boomers do not have this kind of approach to life or spending money, although I find the occasional exception. These preboomer, saver personalities are now in old age.

And here's the ironic, maybe even sad, part of this story: I will sit down with these steady Eddies to talk about their wills and estate plans for money they have been saving for 40, 50, 60 years. More often than not, the heirs are boomers who are eager to be able to spend their inheritance.

PERSON WITH A PENSION　The last type of investor is becoming more and more rare. The practice of working long enough for a company to earn a robust pension was somewhat rare in the 1950s and 1960s but is in danger of becoming extinct in our time. In 2007, only 21 percent of full-time employees had an old-fashioned pension plan, compared to 54 percent in 2004, according to Transamerica Center for Retirement Studies (a nonprofit corporation funded by Aegon NV's Transamerica Life Insurance Co.).[6] I remember doing presentations while the Internet bubble was in full swing. My audience would be people who had retired and rolled over their money and were significantly overinvested in technology stocks. I would have a whole series of frustrating discussions with such clients about diversifying out of stocks and getting an asset allocation that was more diversified and reasonable. Of course that was the time when it was tech, tech, tech all the way. I know many of them ultimately lost a very large amount of their savings, due to their failure to diversify.

In contrast to the struggle of this kind of retirees, then I sat down with a couple who were both retired school teachers. They each had a rather robust pension; together they received around $140,000 annually. If you look at that amount in light of the 4 percent withdrawal rule,[7] it was as though they had saved $3.5 million over the course of their working lives—which would be an incredible achievement for schoolteachers. They had only about $100,000 in savings in CDs.

They said to me, "What do you think?" I looked at them and said, "I don't think you need a financial planner, except to get some wills and trusts and long-term-care insurance." These people never made a lot of money in their working lives and certainly never saved very much, but they were really much better off than the vast majority of people I talk to every day who have to deal with the emotional trauma of how to invest their portfolios and manage their resources for the rest of their lives—and overall do a rather poor job.

We might look back ironically at the old paternalistic days when workers spent their entire careers in the service of one company and were provided a pension after that, and think that we have been liberated to manage our own money through 401(k) plans and IRAs, but I think managing their own money is difficult and stressful for most people. The majority of companies have moved away from pensions because they are expensive—and more expensive than ever in this era when lifetimes have lengthened so much. Whether the current system works as well (or at all) and whether Social Security is going to be there for us are discussions for another day. But the fact is, for those rare individuals who have this steady income rolling in, it looks like they have really figured it out, whether intentionally or not.

There are two main risks faced by those with pensions:

1. *Inflation.* If the pension is a rather low amount or if it does not have an escalation clause to adjust for inflation, the person who is living well at 65 might be living poorly by 80, when the cost of living has doubled. For a person with only $100,000 in savings, it is going to be a problem.
2. *Company risk.* Companies go bankrupt or find it expedient to cut back on pension payouts—not only companies but government entities can and have done this. While the Pension Benefit Guaranty Corporation (PBGC)[8] offers some protection to those with pensions, it does not guarantee the entire amount of a pension and certainly cannot guarantee that any given pension and set of benefits will not be affected in cases where a plan terminates.

After the devastating markets of 2008 and 2009, the topic of retirement savings is on the mind of almost everyone age 55 and older. We have seen Citicorp, Merrill Lynch, General Motors, Freddie Mac, Wachovia, and Ford post write-downs and losses in the billions of dollars—that is *billion* with a B. In the face of that, how can the employees and pensioners from those companies expect not to face cuts in benefits?

Sure enough, buried in a press release titled "GM Statement on Additional Cost Cuts," we find this statement:

> *In addition, health care coverage for U.S. salaried retirees over 65 will be eliminated, effective January 1, 2009. Affected retirees and surviving spouses will receive a pension increase from GM's overfunded U.S. salaried plan to help offset costs of Medicare and supplemental coverage. And there will be no new base compensation increases for U.S. and Canadian salaried employees for the remainder of 2008 and 2009.[9]*

As an article in the online *Wall Street Journal* notes,

> *GM's announcement Tuesday that it would cease medical coverage for its salaried retirees age 65 and above signals that a new era of ever-shrinking benefits has arrived. . . . Retirement-benefit experts have for some time been recommending that all workers—even those close to retiring and who've "earned" full retiree benefits—should assume that those benefits will likely be eliminated, either before or during their retirement, and start planning and saving for it.[10]*

While this particular announcement concerns health-care benefits only, in fact this kind of reduction in one part of a company's pension benefits is only the first shot across the bow. We will certainly see actual cuts in pension amounts in some circumstances.

INHERITED WEALTH   Finally we come to those who have inherited wealth. Almost everyone else in the world looks longingly at the rich, no matter how they got their money. Before the mass media of our age, the average Joe just did not know that much about really rich people. The rich hid behind their wealth and the rest of us went about our business without having a point of comparison to those who do not have to work. All that has changed, thanks to *People* magazine and its imitators, as well as to a myriad of programs on TV that make the point that the rich are rich and we aren't. Now the great masses still manage their money badly but have become so desperate for money they plow what little they have into lottery tickets.

And yet wealth does not create happiness. There is a reason that is such a well-known cliché: because it is too often true.

In my role as an estate-planning attorney for 25 years, I have spent a great deal of time trying to help my clients preserve and transfer wealth, and yet I am sad to say that the transfer of wealth to the next generation is not necessarily a good thing. This might sound like the title of a book (or maybe be an idea for a reality program on television), but individuals who are just handed a large amount of wealth often have a very difficult time finding a purpose for their lives; in fact, they sometimes cannot figure out a purpose for waking up each day. Foisting that amount of wealth onto the next generation may not be doing your family a favor.

Of course some people who have inherited wealth do become very successful wealth owners in their own right, but more often we find that the succeeding generations do not have the talent of their parents or grandparents. Furthermore, they tend to make poor decisions because they have all this wealth and think accumulating money is easy because it was given to them. They do not have to reach for a business background and they have not been challenged with risk and the force of necessity. In fact, they do not have to reach for anything. By my observation, more often than not, those who inherit wealth end up living off the interest of their trust accounts—which is unlikely to be what their parents or grandparents had in mind for them and for the resources represented by that wealth—or they wind up sadly eroding away, via poor decisions, whatever wealth they received.

The challenge for an adviser is to help these inheritors put together a basic core strategy so that they are at least able to take care of their children and the children's college education. For many of them, it is a challenge to find a profession or job where they feel a sense of purpose. While I believe that the challenges of my own life have provided me with some insight about these issues, an adviser can go only so far in advising the wealthy generation about the likely or possible results of the wealth transfer. At the very least I want to help make these individuals aware of how wealth can in its own way corrupt or erode the quality of life for their children or grandchildren. Those are funny words to use in these circumstances—*corrupt* and *erode*—but wealth can really have that effect. Transferring wealth is not necessarily doing the next generation a favor.

Sometimes the wealthy parents or grandparents want to transfer wealth downstream through philanthropy or the creation of foundations. This is not a moneymaking scheme for the succeeding generations but it can provide a purpose for them in getting them involved in the community and in the board of directors for this type of charity. Laymen are often convinced that this is merely a device to allow the kids to make a big pile of money off some kind of tax scheme, but in this case the laymen would be very much mistaken: The tax law is very vigilant on this kind of scheme. Instead, this type of venture is driven by the parents' or grandparents' recognition that sometimes it is more important to give something back to the community rather than transfer great wealth to the next generation.

The bottom line is that, for the succeeding generations, one of the best tools a family can have is a strong wealth adviser who is willing to be frank about the use of money. Even so, the family has to be willing to listen.

Behavioral Finance

Anyone who has been in business as long as I have would be able to tell the same stories about the mistakes we see individual investors making on their own. Sometimes I think I've seen it all. Behavioral finance takes that behavior as its subject matter; it is a huge and growing field. Furthermore, the same progress in technology that has enabled online trading also enables academicians to study the online behavior of 10,000 or 60,000 investors over a period of time. I wish I had space to cover these principles in depth, but I am just going to mention some of the most important ideas. I highly recommend that you seek out more information for yourself. I am fascinated by how closely much of this field of study tracks my own observations about clients and investors.

The Professors of Behavioral Finance: Kahneman, Tversky, Thaler

The work of behavioral finance has been studying investor behavior for 40 years, starting with two Israeli professors, Daniel Kahneman and Amos Tversky, who published their seminal article in 1979: "Prospect Theory: An Analysis of Decision under Risk." That article laid the foundations for the field; Daniel Kahneman went on to win the Nobel Memorial Prize in Economics in 2002 (unfortunately, Tversky died in 1996). While the first paper is highly statistical and was intended above all to cast doubt on expected utility theory, the theory that individuals act rationally and in their own best interests, later elaboration by the authors and others is more accessible. Richard H. Thaler is the third pioneer, cited by Kahneman as a major factor in his receiving the Nobel Prize. He believes that people do not act rationally and in their own best interests. They usually know what is best, healthiest, or most productive for them, but they have a hard time doing it.

Source: Daniel Kahneman and Amos Tversky, "Prospect Theory: An Analysis of Decision under Risk," *Econometrica* Vol 47, no. 2 (March 1979): 263–292. As you would expect, it is full of survey data and mathematics. It has graphs of things like probability functions and probability weighting functions. It is not popular science.

However, behavioral finance has had plenty of detractors, given its basis in psychology. The world of finance and economics is based on the idea of the rational investor, after all, and demonstrations of how irrational investors really are have not been met with enthusiasm in some parts of the financial world.

I have one caveat. My whole investment philosophy is founded on the idea that markets are both efficient and random—which is not the same thing as saying that the markets, or market participants, are rational. It is true that great waves of irrationality seem to grip the market at times, and markets react with exuberance or despair. But even though behavioral finance can predict with some consistency that investors will behave irrationally, that does not change my view that the markets are efficient and random. The market is gargantuan; total market capitalization of the U.S. market alone might be on the order of $11 trillion, even after the bear markets of 2008–2009. Even if Joe Investor wins the lottery and then stays up all night trading in a frenzy online, his activities are negligible in light of overall market size.

Prospect Theory

Daniel Kahneman and Amos Tversky named their theory *prospect theory*, because it looks at the alternative prospects an investor faces and tries to determine how investors really make decisions. Until the time their seminal paper was published, the financial world believed investors would rationally weigh both gains and losses and make rational choices according to expected utility. They found that people responded to situations according to the way they are framed, and are much more sensitive to losses than they are to gains. There can be a 30 to 40 percent shift in preferences depending on how a problem is worded.[11] People tend to think in segments and we do not look at a gain or loss in the context of our entire economic picture. The fact that we have gained or lost, and how we feel about it, is more important than the amount of money at stake.[12]

Furthermore, people tend to underweight outcomes that are merely probable in comparison with outcomes that are more certain, leading to risk aversion in choices involving sure gains and to risk seeking in choices involving sure losses. One of their most important findings is that investors do not weight losses and gains equally; in fact, a person finds a loss about two and a half times more painful than he finds a gain pleasurable. Investors will work harder to avoid a loss than they will to seek a gain.

We call this *loss aversion*, and it can be troublesome for advisers. An investor might have a positive overall financial outcome, but will focus in narrowly on the one part of the portfolio that has a loss, thus losing sight of the big picture. An investor might thus insist on getting out of one part of an asset allocation program. This is surely one of the explanations for the fact that investors hate to sell out losing positions, because it then makes the loss real rather than theoretical; they want to hold on until it comes back. On the other hand, sensitivity to losses also contributes to panic selling when the market starts to go down.

You can put this into a bigger picture and say that fear is twice as strong as greed.

Narrow Framing, Narrow Temporal Framing

Investors often make decisions based on too narrow a point of reference. This relates back to loss aversion as well, when a person focuses on the one losing part of a portfolio rather than on the big picture. Investors are more likely to agree to something new if it is described as having a 50 percent success rate rather than having a 50 percent failure rate.[13]

Most people focus more on short-term rather than long-term results. This, of course, is not a good thing for an individual who wants to achieve long-term success in markets where everyday volatility is a fact of life. The way information is presented to investors affects the frame investors use for their own decision making. A very significant study showed what we knew anyway, that investors are led astray by being bombarded daily by too much information.

Disposition Effect

The disposition effect says that investors are predisposed to hold losing investments too long and to sell winning investments too early. As the researchers said: "Individual investors demonstrate a significant preference for selling winners and holding losers... and it leads to lower returns, particularly so for taxable accounts."[14]

Optimism and Overconfidence

Go into any room full of people and ask how many are above-average drivers. Most people will say they are—which is statistically impossible. Overconfidence is a trait of human nature. People attribute successes—with investments or in other things—to their own abilities, but failures are always due to something else, bad luck or even victimization. And overconfidence builds fast. Studies have shown that merely a few successful trades can convince a person that he is a talented investor.[15] People have an illusion of control and believe they actually have more power over events than they really do.

Overconfident investors trade excessively, and men are more overconfident than women. Overconfident investors (which includes most people) trade more than rational investors and it results in lower investment performance.[16] Men trade more than women and thus reduce their returns more. Individuals may turn over their investments around 70 percent annually, yet the ones who trade the most earn the lowest returns.[17]

To summarize: To be overconfident is to be human. In the investment world, when we are feeling overconfident, we are more likely to act on our beliefs. That leads to more active trading. And the more actively an investor trades, the more money he loses.

Naïve Diversification

One of Thaler's greatest insights into investor behavior particularly concerns 401(k) accounts, although it also applies to other kinds of investing. Many or even most of the individuals who manage their own 401(k) have little or no knowledge about investing, so they use a simple rule of thumb: They divide their investments evenly over the number of mutual funds available. One of the more amusing aspects of this is that the famous Harry Markowitz, founder of modern portfolio theory, admitted that he invested this way with his own retirement money.[18]

A related principle is insufficient diversification, meaning that most individual investors have no real understanding of diversification. They buy five mutual funds for diversification, and all five have more or less the same investment philosophy. Or they simply do not understand what real diversification means.

Persuasion Effect

People are more likely to be persuaded by a perceived credible source than by a credible argument.[19] People do not investigate a money manager as much as they look to see who else invests with that manager. As I mentioned earlier, professionals like doctors are particularly prone to using this investment approach. This was one of the tragedies of the gigantic Bernie Madoff fraud, the Wall Street legend who defrauded investors of more than $50 billion.

The Bottom Line

After reading this chapter, you have to wonder how it is possible for anyone ever to make a rational decision about investments! And this is only the most cursory overview of a huge and growing field of study. I left out more than I had space to include.

The bottom line is that most people have no more business trading stocks than they have fixing the brakes on their own cars. If you have the time and inclination and you find it relaxing to work on your own car, then go for it. But if you need your car to get to work and have not had specific training, you should take your car to an expert.

Why do individuals think that managing their finances in a way that will provide for them for the rest of their lives is easier than fixing their cars? Institutional money managers with all the resources in the world on average achieve approximately market returns minus transaction costs. What possible amount of reading *Money* magazine in your spare time—or even *Smart Money* magazine—do you think is going to prepare you to succeed where full-time professionals cannot?

Beyond that, it is almost impossible for most of us to escape the pull of emotions when managing our own money. Some of those emotions are built into our DNA for good reasons; they just do not work very well in an investment context. Furthermore, a financial adviser works full-time with investments and will have insight that is difficult to come by when you do it for yourself part-time.

Managing your money is serious and important business. Let a full-time professional help you. If it amuses and entertains you to trade online, allocate the same amount of money for your online trading entertainment that you would allocate for a trip to Las Vegas. No matter what you think you know—no matter how confident you are—you are pretty much doomed to fail.

PART II

Investments and Managing Risk

CHAPTER 4

The Futility of Active Management

So far in this book, I have told the story of my search to find a sustainable investment strategy that would work for my clients over the long term. I found a great many tactics and approaches that did not work, such as trying to time the market or use a black box or engage in the voodoo of technical analysis. I thought I was on the right track with asset allocation, but I was finding two main challenges. First, the optimization programs I could use on my PC gave weird results that varied according to how I entered the data. My great hope had been to find an optimization program that did not require me to guess about the future. Second, I could not find mutual funds that would act like asset classes. Mutual fund managers always seemed to follow their own inner drummer rather than the prospectus.

And yet I still believed that there were Really Smart Guys on Wall Street and in the great institutions of money management. I really believed that the problem was *my* failure to find the right managers or the right funds.

Up until now, this book has been organized mostly chronologically, as I have been relating the experiences I had at Terra that taught me about what did not work. In the preceding chapter, I took a break from that chronology to talk about the issues of individual investors who are ruled by emotion in so many different ways. In this chapter, too, I break with the chronology, and in a big way. When I originally planned this book, the topic of *futility of active management* called mostly for performance results presented along with the fees of active managers. But 2008 and 2009 so far have been years for the record books. There has been a clear break with the past: trillions of dollars lost, billions of dollars of rescue funds, and so on.

In this chapter, then, I talk first about some of the Wall Street failures we have seen over the markets of 2007 to 2009 and what that means for the development of my investment strategy. I review that performance in light of how the 24/7 media pumps bad news into our faces. Then I give a few of the statistics about the expense and failure of active management, along with statistics showing why timing the market can never work. That should about finish the topic of what does *not* work—although I could write much more! This is to prepare us for Chapter 5, where I introduce the investment strategy that I believe *does* work.

The Demise of Wall Street

The fall of Bear Stearns in March 2008 was not a wake-up call—it was an earthquake. As the spring and summer went by, the news brought one blow after another to the large financial firms: the final fall of Lehman; government bailout of Fannie Mae, Freddie Mac, and AIG; Goldman Sachs and Morgan Stanley turning themselves into commercial banks; Merrill Lynch selling itself to Bank of America; and the markets going down and down and then down some more. Just when you thought the year could not bring any more pain, we found out that Bernie Madoff, long a well-respected name on Wall Street and a former NASDAQ stock market chairman, had somehow managed to defraud his investors of some $50 billion. The wildest ride in Wall Street's history happened as the era ended. I already wished I had not had to learn so many lessons the hard way, but now it seemed that I was going to have to learn some more.

In my early days I had always thought of those Wall Street investment bankers and money managers as the Really Smart Guys (RSGs), a term I use throughout this book. However, I never thought of myself as one of *them*. I thought it was my job to sit at the feet of the experts to learn. If you went to New York, who could fail to be impressed? The biggest and most beautiful buildings; the biggest and most impressive trading rooms; the prominent names and the long histories; the guys with the multiple degrees from Harvard and Princeton and MIT. . . I thought I could learn from them how to do the best for my clients; I thought that is what they wanted to teach me.

The firms on Wall Street had the best sources and resources of information in the world, meaning they had both instantaneous electronic communications and whole systems of old-boy networks. They had the smartest people money can buy and sophisticated technology that NASA would envy. They had pay and power and clout. They had had access to billions of dollars for capital and money management, from individuals, other corporations, and sovereign governments.

As it turned out, the greatest indictment of the Wall Street culture and the most damning evidence of the way things had gotten out of hand was the fact that, in the end, these largest and most sophisticated investment and financial firms in the world *could not save themselves!* How could anyone take advice from them when their own best counsel led them off a cliff? As they fell, they almost brought down the entire United States and maybe even the global economy with them. Throughout my career, I railed at clients, partners, and anyone who would listen about the inherently flawed system for providing financial advice. My worst fears were realized in 2008.

Traditional Wall Street died in 2008. All the challenges in the marketplace have of course created extraordinary challenges for advisers like me who were trying to implement sustainable strategies for their clients in the midst of the greatest market turbulence since the Great Depression. What did we learn in 2008 and how will those lessons affect our ability to manage our assets—and to help our clients manage their assets—for the rest of our lives?

Moral Hazard: The Painful Lessons of 2008

Moral hazard is a funny term. The dictionary definition does not explain the way the term is really used. You might think the term is quite generic and refers generally to moral issues in the marketplace—but that is not correct. We need a philosopher to elucidate the term and give it a grounding so we all understand it the same way.

Lacking that, I will just have to attempt to describe what it means and why I think it is important in this context. Moral hazard has a specific meaning to the Wall Street community. It means essentially that someone else takes the risk for you and that your actions are unlikely to carry consequences for you. The meaning comes back to the Wall Street context of making money. You will behave differently if you think that your attempts to engage in Wall Street ways of making money are insulated from some of the risk. You are exposed to moral hazard if you or your company is unlikely to bear the full consequences of your actions and therefore you may take more risks or otherwise act less carefully than you would if you thought it would all come back to you. You have one kind of behavior if you think you will be fully accountable for what you do; there is another kind of behavior if you think someone else will have to take some or all of the responsibility for the consequences of those actions. Whether our advice proved right or wrong over time, as an adviser, I always had to pay the consequences with my client—if he stayed a client. I think it was different on Wall Street.

For example, the traditional way Wall Street traders have been paid exhibits a kind of moral hazard. Bond traders on Wall Street make millions of dollars in bonus money for years when they make a lot of money for the firm. If they lose a lot of money, nothing much happens, or they get fired. But there is not a consistent relationship between

(continued)

(*Continued*)

winning and losing. If I make money; I get paid a lot. If I lose money, I don't have to give anything back and/or nothing much happens.

Imagine how this encourages risk taking. If I am a trader and take some extremely aggressive risk that puts company capital on the line, and it pays off, I get a huge payday. If it does not pay off, well, too bad, I probably do not get a bonus, and maybe I keep my job or maybe I do not, but I surely will not have to make up the company capital that has been lost or account for the fact that I put the company at risk. This has been standard operating procedure on Wall Street for a long time, although the scale of bonuses has climbed steadily. For all the fuss about a couple of hundred million dollars for AIG bonuses, Merrill Lynch paid out about $4 billion in bonus dollars to its employees in December 2008 after it was acquired by Bank of America. You can just imagine how the idea of millions of dollars of bonus money kept Wall Street traders awake at night, trying to figure out new ways to take risks.

The Heartbreak of Hedge Funds

Merely receiving a market return was not sufficient for Wall Street. The RSGs had to come up with new products to sell. It is my belief that the main purpose of Wall Street research is and has been to sell new and creative products. That's what pays the bills. When markets are flat they need to come up with new ways to generate fees. So if traditional mutual funds could not beat the market, the RSGs had to find new ways to do that. One of these was the hedge fund.

What on earth is a hedge fund? I cannot tell you the number of times I have been asked that. Hedge funds are basically mutual funds for rich people who have to demonstrate, before putting their money into a hedge fund, that they can afford to lose the money. The regulators who try to protect ordinary investors have given hedge funds pretty much an open field to make any kind of investments or market bets that they want.

Hedge funds have two interesting and unique components:

1. A hedge fund can basically buy or sell anything. It does not have to actually own something in order to sell it; that is called *short-selling*.
2. Hedge fund managers are paid in a way that encourages both risk-taking in the first place and then fund liquidation if the risk strategy does not work out.

They got the name *hedge* because originally they used sophisticated hedging techniques—like protecting their assets from falling markets by selling calls or buying puts on the securities the fund contained—but they soon soared far beyond such basic techniques by buying and selling anything under the sun. A hedge fund can buy or sell—meaning go long or short—anything from coffee futures to currency forwards to derivative structures that require a PhD in math to understand. They are allowed to function freely and with basically no regulation because, as I said, you have to demonstrate that you have a lot of money in order to invest in one of them; you have to be a *qualified buyer* with a certain amount of assets or income to invest in a hedge fund. A few of the early hedge funds demonstrated spectacular results, and the fix was in.

The second interesting component is the hedge funds' unusual structure of fees for paying the managers. In this new iteration of appeal to our greed we give a super RSG money to invest for us and agree to pay him or her (losing money is not gender-specific) on the order of 200 basis points a year for managing the money *plus 20 to 30 percent of the profits generated.* This is a new feature of money management. That means if the hedge fund managers take $1,000,000 from you (that is to say, you invest $1,000,000 with one of them), off the top you pay $20,000 to them for the privilege of having them invest your money for you. (And there are no breakpoints, so you pay $20,000 per million for as many millions as you can afford.) Then if they do a good job with your money, and say it goes up 25 percent in one year, you pay them an additional $75,000. But you are happy, right, because you are still up 15.5 percent for the year. Meanwhile, the managers have just generated an infinite return for themselves because they did it on zero outlay of their own funds; they are making money only with your money.

Additionally, hedge fund investors can usually withdraw their money only once a year at a specific time and only if the manager of the fund has the cash to liquidate. It gets better. The investors may not know how the managers are investing the money and what securities the manager is buying or selling. The pitch is that, because of his ability to buy anything and to go long or short, this super RSG will make money in any environment regardless of market conditions. After all, look at the incentive we have provided to the manager: He gets to keep 20 percent or 30 percent of the upside.

What about downside participation of the hedge fund managers? Do they bear any of the losses? These are super RSGs—*really* smart guys. That means they do not have to bear the losses. If they did, they would not be that smart and you would not want to hire them. Most active mutual funds could not beat the market (as represented by some index) with internal charges of 200 or 300 basis points, but now hedge funds have to do this while taking 20 to 30 percent of your upside. Imagine the risk they would have to take to overcome the drag of these fees on performance.

It is all so logical. They risk your money in creative, complicated new ways that only nuclear physicists can understand (yes, they sometimes hire those guys to design strategies), then take a good part of the profits and none of the losses. Brilliant!

So do they work? Well, some do, for a while, but about a third close every year. Everyone has heard about the few with spectacular results, and those few have drawn in thousands of investors with billions of dollars. The success of a few hedge funds was like hearing your neighbor talk about making $100,000 on AOL stock during the tech boom. Both things draw other investors like a narcotic. The point of hedge funds originally was to profit by taking advantage of market inefficiencies, but in general they could not do it.

Now say the hedge fund has a bad year. The way the accounting works is that a hedge fund manager does not get paid his performance bonus if the hedge fund goes down in value; that makes sense. But if the fund goes down and then goes up again, he does not get paid his performance bonus until the fund gets above its earlier high-water mark. The way to deal with that is to dissolve the current, underwater fund and start a new one; the new one starts at zero with performance fees from the first tick up.

This whole investment structure makes no investment sense. It does make complete Wall Street sense because it generates huge profits for the hedge fund managers.

Now let us loop back to the subject of moral hazard. If a hedge fund does really well, it draws in billions of dollars and makes hundreds of millions for its managers. The person with the largest payday ever on Wall Street got a billion dollars in one year. Imagine that! Ask yourself what one person could possibly do in one year that would fundamentally be worth a billion dollars. Ask yourself where that billion dollars came from. The answer is, it came from his investors. And whatever value he did or did not return to his investors, he walked away with a billion dollars for one year's worth of work.

This is the same kind of moral hazard I mentioned earlier in terms of Wall Street traders. If I do well, I get a huge pay check; if I do badly, I lose your money. What kind of incentive is there to take care of the client? There is *no* incentive, and that is the problem.

These are not people I want to trust with my clients' money.

The Media and the Market

But the financial services industry consists of more than wirehouses and banks. There is a whole financial media, of which financial magazines represent one part. They promulgate the message that you do not need to pay for a financial adviser; all you have to do is read this magazine and you will be able to master investing on your own. Their single agenda is to sell more magazines using flashy headlines like "Buy These Funds and Get Rich for Retirement." Every magazine, every month, has a new top fund or top stock to buy, mixed in with the articles about planning for vacations and finding the best places in the United States to live. Lesson 3 in Chapter 1 said not to trust media predictions. That *BusinessWeek* cover predicting the end of equities at the beginning of what proved to be a huge bull market is only one small example of how the media operate.

It is the glory of our free press that we have magazines that offer that kind of advice—because an adviser is not allowed to say that kind of thing. Ironically enough, the adviser is going to know a great deal more about the situation of an individual investor than a magazine can know about any of its readers, and yet advisers are strictly limited in how they communicate with a client; they can never predict outsized returns or make such blatant *promissory* statements (as the compliance people call them).

The free press makes flamboyant and exaggerated statements—makes the kind of statements the regulators would fine me for if I made them. Financial magazines end up encouraging poor performance because the constant agitation of advice and interest in this month's top fund encourages the kind of active buying and selling that individual investors, working on their own, tend to do too much of anyway.

Every new issue of *Money* magazine tells you the top funds to buy. For the price of the magazine—a couple of dollars—they will tell you how to make a zillion dollars. If their methods really worked, do you think those journalists would be writing for a magazine, or do you think they would be managing their own money and making a fortune? I spent many years trying to figure out how to beat the market and I gave up because it is impossible—but then, I do not have to sell magazines every month.

So every month, readers are encouraged to buy this month's top fund and maybe to sell last month's. The real truth about investing—that investors are most likely to succeed by buying and holding a widely diversified portfolio—is boring and has no entertainment value. Can you see the cover page of *Money* magazine in succeeding months? January: "Buy and Hold, the Best Way to Accumulate Wealth." February: "Buy and Hold a Diversified Portfolio, Still the Best Way to Accumulate Wealth." March: "Still Holding That Same Diversified Portfolio." April: "Diversified Portfolio Needs No Changes," and so on.

Beyond the print media, the financial channels available on cable are part of the entertainment industry (main goal: get viewers, sell advertising) and have to provide you with something new to buy or react to every half hour. I saw this myself when we were part of GE Financial and I used to appear on CNBC to provide a financial planning perspective. This was during the late 1990s when Internet stocks were soaring. I did not talk about Internet stocks or any stocks because my subject matter was financial planning. For a while I would have a slot maybe once a quarter, but finally the word came down that CNBC programming was eliminating all planners because they realized that the ratings basically depended on someone talking about stocks.

This comes back to what I call *financial pornography*; I did not invent that terminology but I find it accurate. Those TV programs provide the salacious information about stocks that makes viewers want to see the programs. Their agenda is to create excitement to get people to watch talking heads talking about stocks—that is how they sell to their advertisers. And what is the underlying message? You can get rich quick if you follow this advice. This is no longer about investing and is maybe a half step away from buying a lottery ticket.

The Internet is yet another channel in the financial services industry. You could argue that the Internet is independent, but it is much more accurate to say that it gives a soapbox to every nutcase in the world, without any kind of filtering system. Anyone can and does say anything about any subject. You—or anyone—are allowed to talk about anything, and viewers have to filter the information for themselves.

There are many, many examples of the kinds of crazy things the media promulgates. I used to have to explain this at length and provide examples, but I think most people now are familiar with how it works. Jim Cramer by himself is an excellent example and just the latest of the financial commentators who are better viewed as entertainment rather than as investment advisers. Cramer is famous for reassuring his television audience that Bear Stearns was in fine shape, days before it collapsed in March 2008. It is possible to go online and read lengthy analyses of his stock picks, which are probably as good or as bad as those of any media person. However, note that he made 800 recommendations from October through December 2008. That is entertainment. What good to an investor are 800 recommendations in a three-month period? That in itself is as good as random.

The Futility of Active Management

What further evidence do you need of the futility of active management than the demise of Wall Street in 2008? If the Wall Street gurus were really so smart, don't you think they could have done better than having *none* of the old Wall Street firms still in existence in classic Wall Street organizations by the end of 2008?

Look at your own experience. How successful have your mutual funds or money managers been over the long term? How many times have you bought stock in a great company and lost money? I am sure that you, like me, have been disappointed by results that range from uneven to disastrous. You bought a great mutual fund with a 10-year track record, only to have the manager tank the year you bought it. Maybe you think, as I used to, that the problem was that you had just never found the right RSGs to deliver the investment return you needed. As we will point out elsewhere in this book, a track record for an active manager is meaningless. And yet this is used by the media and most financial magazines and rating services as the key indicator of the future success of any and every manager.

Here is the answer to that conundrum of trying to find the right Really Smart Guys: Active management does not work.

I am about to use a couple of academic studies plus some information on the cost of active management to reinforce an argument that should be compelling based on your personal experience. First let me clarify what I mean by *active management*. Active management is an approach based on stock picking and market timing. Active managers choose to buy a stock based on judgment, opinion, research, and stock analysis. Passive management is a buy-and-hold strategy that seeks to provide broad asset class or market exposure and market-consistent returns. It does not include or exclude a stock based on research, judgment, or opinion.

Before I start to give you the statistical evidence, probably the first place you are going to go for information is your own experience. Have you ever been invested with any kind of money manager—whether a mutual fund or separate account or a regular brokerage account—and seen your results beat any kind of benchmark, consistently, over the years?

Table 4.1 shows that, over a 15-year period, average mutual fund performance trailed that of the most important market indexes by 85 and 83 basis points—almost a full percentage point.

Most managed mutual funds, when compared to their appropriate indexes, fail to achieve superior performance.

TABLE 4.1   U.S. Large Cap Returns 1994–2008, Indexes versus Mutual Funds

	Annualized Compound Return
S&P 500 Index	6.46%
CRSP 1-10 Index	6.44%
Average performance for mutual funds as reported by Morningstar	5.61%

This table shows the performance of more than 400 U.S. large-cap mutual funds that were in existence for the entire 15-year period.
Source: Dimensional Fund Advisors.

TABLE 4.2   Percentage of Active Funds That Failed to Outperform Their
Benchmarks over Market Cycles

Fund Category	Benchmark Index	2004–2008	1999–2003
All domestic funds	S&P Composite 1500	66.2%	50.8%
All large-cap funds	S&P 500	71.9%	53.4%
All mid-cap funds	S&P MidCap 400	79.1%	91.4%
All small-cap funds	S&P SmallCap 600	85.5%	69.4%

"Standard & Poor's Indices versus Active Funds Scorecard, Year-End 2008," published April
20, 2009, and freely available on the S&P web site. Analysis is done using data from CRSP
Survivor-Bias-Free U.S. Mutual Fund Database.
Source: Standard & Poor's, www.spiva.standardandpoors.com.

Standard & Poor's analyzes the performance of mutual funds compared
to the performance of the various benchmarks used by the mutual funds.
Their analysis covers far more kinds of mutual funds than only large-cap
funds although unfortunately it covers only five years. (See Table 4.2.)
Because some people claim that active managers are more valuable under
circumstances of a bear market than when the markets are trending up, S&P
also looked at the percentage of mutual funds that failed to outperform their
benchmark during the last bear market.

Just so you understand what this chart is telling you, between 50 percent
and 85 percent of all mutual funds failed to achieve a higher rate of return
than the market benchmark they are being compared to. This S&P analysis
shows similar results for non-U.S. equity funds.

These funds that were outperformed by the benchmark pay their managers millions of dollars in fees and yet they fail to provide you, the investor,
with a consistent market return. As we discuss later, you would have been
far better off buying an index fund. So you might ask, why not just buy
the ones that did perform well over the past 15 years? Because track record
is meaningless! There is no statistical probability that the winners for the
past 1, 5, 10, or 15 years will be the winners in the future. That's why on
the prospectus in bold print it states: "Past performance is no guarantee of
future results." The problem is that so many advisers and investors refuse
to believe this.

We are all looking for the next Warren Buffett. (Please note that there is
only *one* Warren Buffett, not even a half dozen great investors.) Sure, someone always gets it right for some period of time, but everyone inevitably
fails—just like Wall Street.

Did you read about the legendary Bill Miller's results in 2008? Bill Miller's
Legg Mason Value Trust had outperformed the broad market (and the S&P
500 Index) every year from 1991 to 2005, something no other manager had

been able to do. But thanks to his buys of Wachovia, AIG, Bear Stearns, and Freddie Mac in 2008, his fund lost 58 percent in 2008, making his fund the worst-performing in its class in the 1-, 3-, 5-, and 10-year periods, according to Morningstar.[1] Everybody has a bad year now and then, right? And I am not trying to pick on Bill Miller. What I am saying is that it is impossible to outperform the market. The investors in Bill Miller's fund were doing much better than the market, and now they are doing worse. Furthermore, *Forbes* magazine calculates that investors paid Miller and his management team $2 billion to *destroy* wealth.[2]

The best any investor can hope to achieve over time is the market rate of return. If you use active managers, the best you can hope to achieve is the market rate of return minus the fees you pay those managers.

We hope they (meaning more than one) are out there, but we will not know who they are until they have managed money for a very long time. So we spend our time futilely looking for the next RSG, we spend lots of money on fees and commissions, our portfolios perform poorly, and we are surprised.

Showing this comparative data on mutual funds is one of the most powerful tools I have for demonstrating the ineffectiveness of active management, but this is not the only place you can see this kind of information. I have shown it to clients for years. The fact that I have used updated data for so long demonstrates the evergreen argument. By that I mean that year after year, I update the data for the most recent year, and while the data change, the truth remains the same, that active management does not work.

What I was beginning to realize about the failure of active managers in the mid-1990s was not news to the academic world, where a large number of studies have shown that it is pretty much impossible to beat the market on a consistent basis, although I have to say that I do not need a study to confirm what I myself have learned over the years. But in addition to the current evidence I can offer, here is the evidence of a few of those studies. The truth about money management and its fees and costs has been known for a long time.

In Chapter 5, I tell the story of how modern portfolio theory was developed in the academic world. Gene Fama, one of the key players, relied on a study done in 1969 by Michael Jensen, covering the performance of 115 mutual funds from 1955 to 1964. The results showed that investors who held mutual funds for 10 years would have been worth 15 percent less than if they had invested in a broadly diversified portfolio of common stocks with similar risk. In Jensen's study, only 26 out of 115 funds performed better than the market.[3]

In 1975, Charles Ellis published one of the seminal articles of modern finance. In "The Loser's Game," he said, "The investment management business (it should be a profession but is not) is built upon a simple and basic belief: Professional money managers can beat the market. That premise appears to be false."[4] He then proceeded to provide an analysis of the cost structure of money management that is actually still reasonable today, saying that a manager's fees and transaction costs are about 200 basis points annually.

From a study published in 2006 in the *Journal of Financial Planning*:

> *During the study period, most actively managed large- and mid-cap mutual funds underperformed their respective passive strategies. While every period under review had mutual funds that outperformed the passive strategy, few funds did so consistently.*[5]

Fama and French have recently been working on a study about luck versus skill. This is their conclusion:

> *The aggregate portfolio of U.S. equity mutual funds is close to the market portfolio, but the high costs of active management show up intact as lower returns to investors. Bootstrap simulations produce no evidence that any managers have enough skill to cover the costs they impose on investors.... We cannot reject the hypothesis that no fund managers have skill that enhances expected returns.*[6]

This is what Zero Alpha Group (ZAG) concludes:

> *Even though they are paying for brokers to assist them, investors in load-carrying mutual funds end up making significantly worse timing decisions than investors in no-load funds, underperforming their own funds' reported returns by three times as much as no-load fund investors.*[7]

I could go on and on with this, but will offer a few concluding thoughts: 2008 saw the worst stock market performance since 1931. Don't you think that all that Wall Street talent, all the research departments and the fast computers and analysis, could have softened the blow for investors? Apparently not. *Forbes* says that the "average active stock fund lost 40.5 percent, versus a 37 percent loss for the market-tracking Vanguard S&P 500 Index, according to Morningstar."[8] Furthermore, if you look at a longer time frame, "According to Standard & Poor's, 69 percent of actively run large-company funds, 76 percent of funds buying midsize companies and 79 percent of funds buying small companies underperformed their indexes in the five years through last June."[9]

Active management does not work.

Timing the Market

After all that, maybe you are thinking that, while active management itself does not work, at least you—or some professional you hire—can time when to be in the market and when to be out of it? Maybe you wish your money had sat in cash over the second half of 2008, but somehow you are going to buy into the equity markets when they start to go up again.

Part of what individual investors think they can do is time the market—buy in when prices are low and sell out when prices are high. And they are going to know when to do this even though no institutional investor has ever figured it out. In actuality, they do just the opposite. Somehow they think that some market commentator—whose prediction or advice is heard simultaneously by millions of people—is going to provide them alone with what they need to do. You can imagine what happens when several million people attempt to follow this advice the next day. If you remember my stories from Chapter 2, in the 1980s—when investing was not yet as big a business as it is now—I tried hiring market timers who had all kinds of black boxes (of various sorts) and they all failed miserably. Oh, it all looked like such a good idea when they showed you the hypothetical past and the places they would have advised you to buy or sell, but somehow it just never worked out that way going forward.

Timing the market is a fallacy from another point of view, because the market mostly does nothing, except for the occasional day that shows most of the market change. If the major market moves come out of nowhere and happen in one day, it means it is literally impossible to catch the upward movement in the markets by waiting until they start to go up. The most important market motion starts and happens in one day only, as illustrated in Table 4.3.

Jason Zweig updated some of these numbers in January 2009 in his "The Intelligent Investor" column in the *Wall Street Journal*. He cited research from 1900 to 2008 (*109 years!*), showing that if you

> *...took away the 10 best days in all that time, two-thirds of the cumulative gains produced by the Dow over the past 109 years would disappear. Conversely, had you sidestepped the market's 10 worst days, you would have tripled the actual return of the Dow.... The moments that made all the difference were just 20 days out of 29,694.*[10]

Wow—all we have to do to be successful investors is pick which 0.07 percent of days will be the ones on which we should have been invested. Put another way, you need to be able to pick the one day every four years on which you have to be in the market. Beating those odds would have nothing to do with knowledgeable investing and everything to do with

TABLE 4.3   Staying Invested Is Important for Long-term Results; Market Timing Does Not Work; Growth of $1,000

	Total Period	Missed 1 Best Day	Missed 5 Best Days	Missed 15 Best Days	Missed 25 Best Days	One-month T-bills
Total amount at end of period	$34,310	$30,749	$22,402	$13,365	$8,593	$9,167
Annualized compound return	9.49%	9.18%	8.30%	6.87%	5.67%	5.85%
Percentage less than staying fully invested	NA	−10.4%	−34.7%	−61.0%	−75.0	−73.3%

This table uses daily data for 39 years and calculates the effect on performance of being out of the market on the various best days.

Sources: Dimensional Fund Advisors using performance data for January 1970 to December 31, 2008, provided by Bloomberg; S&P data provided by Standard & Poor's Index Services Group; CRSP data provided by the Center for Research in Security Prices, University of Chicago.

winning the lottery. The real message of this chart is clear: Stay invested for the long term, because you cannot predict, ever, which are going to be the most important up or down days.

You can also look at this another way. During the years of the tech bubble, there were people around who recognized that it was a bubble or had some thought that it would not go on forever. These people thought, however, that they were good enough investors that they could stay in the market until the exact day they needed to get out. Do you know of anyone who was able to do that?

CHAPTER 5

The Academic Background

In most of this book so far, I have been talking about investment strategies that do not work. Now it is finally time to talk about the investment strategy that I believe in, the strategy that *does* work. In this chapter, I want to make the case for why I believe in it. I know this is a long chapter, but I hope you will invest the effort to understand these very important concepts. I have tried to make these complex ideas a little more approachable by including some of the personal stories of the individuals who first proposed them. I highlight the individuals and ideas that are most relevant to the kind of investing I now use and endorse. The development of these theories required a great many individuals in supporting roles. I have had to be very disciplined about which of this group to present because all of the stories are interesting. For those who are interested in reading the complete story, I highly recommend Peter L. Bernstein's book, *Capital Ideas: The Improbable Origins of Modern Wall Street* (New York: Free Press, 1992).

Background to the Story

As I have said so many times, the entire financial services industry has long been dominated by the idea of picking winners, whether stocks and mutual funds, or structured products and hedge funds (which are the latest and arguably most egregious examples of ways to extract the highest fees possible from investors). As I related in Chapters 1 and 2, I was under the same spell, the idea that I should be looking for the Really Smart Guys who were going to help my clients get winning performance for their portfolios. Not only Wall Street but the whole giant financial services industry has been telling us for years that we should invest in the winners that we can buy or learn about (in order to buy) from them. The industry includes not only the famous Wall Street investment firms that have so recently come to a bad end, but discount brokerage firms, massive mutual fund complexes, money managers of all stripes, and members of the investment media, including magazine and book publishing,

But there is another whole world out there of people who do not work on Wall Street and who have studied the market more objectively than any investment firm or salesperson at an investment firm ever could. I finally bumped into this world myself when I stumbled into Dimensional Fund Advisors. That was my wake-up call.

There is a robust body of academic research that most people have never heard of. It is not hard to find this research and many of its principles are widely used in institutional investing. And yet so many individuals, even those who have spent their lives working in the financial services industry, have never come into contact with it. It is not simple, and certainly not as simple as "invest with us and we'll get you winners." Part of the reason for its relative obscurity is that it is counter to the interests of the combined Wall Street industries. Once you have learned about these academic theories, you will stop paying Wall Street's exorbitant fees and use a low-cost, passive, highly diversified investment style that is more suited for your long-term investments and best interests than anything a broker recommends. Furthermore, these academic principles will help you gain perspective as the dramatic events from the markets of 2008 continue to ripple through the wider economy.

This investment philosophy comes from the academic world centered on the University of Chicago, and is based on more than 80 years of investment results, not on what happened last year or even over the past few

Center for Research in Security Prices

The Center for Research in Security Prices (CRSP) is a research center at the University of Chicago Booth School of Business and has been an integral part of the academic and commercial world of financial and economic research since the early 1960s. Academicians whose research and publications must withstand rigorous analysis for accuracy rely on CRSP's portfolio of stock, indexes, mutual fund, Treasury, and REIT market databases. Quantitative analysts in the commercial market depend on CRSP's historical depth and unrivaled quality in order to perform back-testing and modeling calculations. The data series first developed at CRSP have a characteristic that makes them instantly recognizable: They start in 1926. Any time you see a data series that begins with 1926 or 1927, somehow it originated with CRSP and the academics and practitioners who have developed and worked with that data.

investment cycles, which is the longest time frame a money manager will have. This philosophy of investing was not developed by modern product managers or traders or wirehouses in an attempt to get you to place more business with them. Although many of the academic personnel involved have gone on to work with and consult for financial firms, that came after the studies that informed the investment philosophy.

Markowitz Introduces the Idea of Risk

Harry M. Markowitz invented modern portfolio theory one afternoon in 1950 in the University of Chicago library while working on the assigned reading for his doctoral thesis. The essence of modern portfolio theory states that investments should be considered in terms of risk as well as reward. I know it is hard to believe now, but that idea fundamentally changed our understanding of investing. Peter Bernstein calls it "the most famous insight in the history of modern finance and investment."[1]

Markowitz's idea was first published in a 14-page article in March 1952 in the *Journal of Finance* while he was still a University of Chicago graduate student, although he went on to develop these ideas more fully in his PhD thesis. As he later said, "Everybody knows you are not supposed to put all your eggs in one basket. At that point, it was obvious that people diversified because they are interested in avoiding risk as well as earning return."[2]

To back up a couple of years, Markowitz's high school standings did not get him admitted to the University of Chicago, but he was allowed to take the entrance test—and did so well that he got himself exempted from the survey course for physical sciences because he had already learned as much as they would teach in the course! In other words, he was clearly a prodigy. He did both undergraduate and then graduate work in economics.

We humans take comfort in the idea of destiny, that some events are straight lines from cause to effect. We might like to believe that once Harry Markowitz gained entrance to the University of Chicago, it was a straight line to his revolutionary PhD thesis. In fact, his choice of dissertation topic was accidental. One day, as Markowitz was waiting to see his adviser, another person happened to be there who was a stockbroker and who suggested Markowitz do a dissertation on the stock market. One of Markowitz's later biographers suggested that was the best tip Markowitz ever received from a stockbroker.

On that famous afternoon in the library, Markowitz was thinking that people diversify because they are interested in avoiding risk as much as in gaining return. He had two factors, so he drew a graph with two axes, one for risk and one for return, and thought up the idea of the *efficient frontier*, a line that would demonstrate the relationship between the various levels of risk and reward. The idea of using standard deviation or variance as a measure of risk just popped into his head, as he says, because he knew it was widely used in statistics. His epiphany ended with the thought that the riskiness of the portfolio depends on covariances, meaning how much the behavior of one security resembles the behavior of another security in the marketplace. He drew an efficient frontier that represented combinations of risk and return that you could obtain as an investor. If the efficient frontier is new to you, there is much more on this topic later in the chapter. I later show a more sophisticated version of the simple line curve that Markowitz drew which demonstrates how he plotted standard deviation (risk) on the y-axis against return on the x-axis. The most important point of the graph is that it shows that risk and return are related.

Being concerned about risk as well as return—how obvious it is to us. But it was a new idea in 1952, and it was Markowitz's key insight. It won him a Nobel Prize in 1990.

At that time, the science of finance was seen as a branch of economics and not as a separate subject. Markowitz's undergraduate degree therefore

Defining Risk

It is impossible to talk about performance without also considering risk. For example, so many investors are willing to accept rock-bottom returns on Treasury bills or bank CDs because the risk is essentially zero, and there is a whole world of investors who consider zero market risk to be the most important attribute of an investment.

We now have to revisit some concepts introduced in Chapter 1. To be able to manage risk, you have to be able to measure it. A full discussion of all the issues surrounding risk measurement is beyond the scope of this book. We will simply state again that volatility is the definition most often used for risk—how often the security price goes up and down and how wide the swings are—expressed in terms of standard deviation, a statistical term that provides a good indication of volatility.

Standard deviation is a relative measure of how much actual results varied from the average rate of return for a given historical time period. The larger the difference between the actual return of a security and its average return (or expected return), the higher the standard deviation will be. The larger the standard deviation, the greater the volatility, and the greater the risk of the market.

had to be in economics and he wrote his PhD thesis as a student of the economics department. When he went to defend his thesis, one of the members of the examination committee was Milton Friedman, the influential, Nobel-Prize-winning economist considered the leader of the Chicago school of economics. Markowitz tells the story of thinking he knew his subject so well that not even Milton Friedman could give him a hard time. But about five minutes into the meeting, as Markowitz tells the story,

> *Friedman says, well Harry, I've read this. I don't find any mistakes in the math, but this is not a dissertation in economics and we cannot give you a PhD in economics for a dissertation that is not in economics. He kept repeating that for the next hour and a half. My palms began to sweat. At one point he says, you have a problem.*
>
> *It's not economics, it's not mathematics, it's not business administration, and Professor Marshak said, "It's not literature." So after about an hour and a half of that, they send me out to the hall.[3]*

Let history show that Markowitz did in fact receive his doctorate. Only five minutes after Markowitz had left the room, his adviser Professor Jacob Marshak came out and congratulated *Dr*. Markowitz.

I think that is how it happens when you are a pioneer.

Modern Portfolio Theory

Markowitz's ideas about the importance of return *and* risk and the importance of diversification within the context of an overall portfolio seem completely obvious to us now because those ideas have become so firmly entrenched in our financial and economic thinking. But they did not exist before Markowitz.

Markowitz's ideas together are referred to as modern portfolio theory, although I think we ought to call them something like "proven portfolio management practice." The phrase *modern portfolio theory* suggests that diversifying your investments will both reduce risk and increase return over the long run. Markowitz contended that appropriate diversification was not so much a matter of how *many* securities were included in a portfolio but, rather, the *relationship of each* to the other. When you add a security to your portfolio, you evaluate how the addition of the asset to the portfolio changes the *portfolio's* characteristics; it is much less important to evaluate the asset in itself. You can add a security that is itself highly risky but complements the portfolio so that adding it to the portfolio reduces the overall portfolio risk.

Covariance Is Like an Engine

All securities change value according to external or marketplace events or factors—or according to factors that affect individual companies. In an ideal situation, the securities in a portfolio complement each other so that when one decreases in value, others increase. This averaging effect reduces the volatility of the portfolio and permits more consistent and predictable returns, and also reduces the risk that your overall portfolio will decrease in value. Since there is less overall risk, the risk-adjusted return (the amount of return an investor receives adjusted for the amount of risk taken) will be higher than that for an undiversified portfolio. In some cases, the actual returns (not just risk-adjusted returns) could be greater than those for an undiversified, poorly diversified, or concentrated portfolio, depending on the asset mix. I demonstrate this in Chapter 6 when we take a look at some actual portfolios.

My simplistic analogy, for readers who like cars as much as I do, is to think of an eight-cylinder engine. Each cylinder is a different asset class. At any point in time in an engine's cycle, half the cylinders are down and half of them are up. This powers the car and also powers the portfolio. If the pistons move up only, you will not go anywhere. If *all* the cylinders went up *or* down at the same time, what would happen to the engine? It would stall. The same thing is true of your portfolio.

What happens if all the asset classes move in the same direction at the same time? If you are in that situation, one of two things is happening: We are in a big bull market and everything is going up and you are very happy. If all asset classes are moving down, then there is a big bear market and everyone is unhappy. But either situation should make you reexamine your asset allocation strategy because you are not diversified properly. In the case of everything going up at once, you are setting yourself up for a big fall at some point in the near future. To have forward progress, all the pistons—all the asset classes—must move up and down in an appropriate and sustainable sequence. Some asset classes should always be moving down at any point in time, although of course we all wish for investments that move only up.

You might think that buying 20 different stocks will automatically give you a diversified portfolio, but it will not be diversified at all if the stocks are energy stocks—or all the same kind, no matter what kind that is. The riskiness of the overall portfolio depends on the *covariance* of its holdings—how they are all related to each other—rather than on the average riskiness of the separate investments evaluated separately.[4] You have to own different kinds of securities. But Markowitz's essential insight was to state that you cannot diversify your risk to zero, no matter how many securities you include. Nor would you want to diversify your risk to zero, since the return you get from your portfolio comes from its risk.

For example, imagine that you have a portfolio composed of mostly unexciting U.S. large-cap stocks. It is not considered to be a terribly risky portfolio (although post-2008, we look at all risk differently). Then imagine you want to buy some emerging markets stock, securities issued by companies that are located in India, Argentina, and Poland. That sounds *really* risky. Yet adding them to your portfolio could actually cause overall risk to decrease because their performance in the marketplace will be so different from the performance of your large-cap stocks; in other words, their covariance with your large-cap stocks is low. Adding a risky security could cause overall risk to decrease.

You not only have to have diversified securities, you have to have the right kind of diversification. These are Markowitz's own words from his 1952 article:

> *In trying to make variance small it is not enough to invest in many securities. It is necessary to avoid investing in securities with high covariances among themselves. We should diversify across industries because firms in different industries, especially industries with different economic characteristics, have lower covariances than firms within an industry. . . . It is generally more likely for firms within the same industry to do poorly at the same time than for firms in dissimilar industries.*[5]

Markowitz himself says he does not know when his theories gained the name of modern portfolio theory, but what you might call the old portfolio theory—prior to the introduction of his ideas—focused almost exclusively on return. Analyzing how to select securities for optimal performance within a portfolio was an unknown concept.[6] Even the great John Maynard Keynes, arguably the greatest economist of the twentieth century, thought there was a good argument to be made for concentrated investments under certain circumstances.[7]

One of the hardest parts of accepting modern portfolio theory is accepting up front that when the strategy is working, some *portion* of the portfolio is always decreasing—that is, losing money. The other side of that is hoping that there will always be some asset classes that are going up. What makes the whole portfolio work is having different asset classes reacting differently to the various economic and market forces. If you can get over the mental hurdle of expecting that some part of your portfolio will always be decreasing, you will be able to construct a sustainable portfolio.

Figure 5.1 is a simplistic illustration of how this would work if we had two assets with perfect negative correlations, meaning that they move exactly opposite to each other in response to market conditions. (This perfect negative correlation is expressed as –1.0.) Although both of these ideal asset classes have an overall upward slope over the long run and each asset

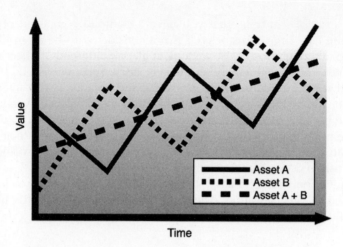

FIGURE 5.1 Combining Noncorrelated Asset Classes Reduces Risk and Increases Return

Source: Forum Financial Management, LLC.

class will provide a reasonable rate of return over the long run, in the short run, one will win and one will lose, resulting in an average upward slope. The ultimate result is lower volatility or risk and a smoother path for your portfolio's increase. You want to select diversified investments to provide this kind of effect.

If there is ever a time in your investment life when you find that all sectors of your portfolio engine are moving together in lockstep, you should see red flags, because it means your portfolio is not truly diversified, although no one ever overanalyzes the situation when markets are going up. Lack of diversification creates an unacceptable level of volatility and will also lead to lower returns over the long run. Not to mention what it does to your gas mileage.

Creating an Optimal Portfolio

Harry Markowitz followed the publication of his thesis with a book called *Portfolio Selection: Efficient Diversification of Investments*. He presented a case using 10 securities, 9 risky securities plus cash. He wanted to use 25 securities but did not have the necessary computing power; the 1950s were several lifetimes ago in technology. Markowitz could not have worked with asset classes then if he had wanted to because there was no way to calculate them. So I am jumping many years ahead when I say that we view these theories now from the perspective of asset classes, not individual securities.

As simple as the idea of not putting all your eggs in one basket appears to be, implementing a true diversification strategy is not simple at all. First, you need a diversification plan, which we call an *asset allocation strategy*. Next, you need some way to invest in asset classes. Finally, you need asset classes that are negatively correlated to each other. Just like the pistons in the engine, you want some to move up while others move down, with the net result of sustainable progress forward. Calculating those correlations requires statistical analysis, and the longer the term of the analysis, the more confidence we will have that it is right.

How can you invest in an asset class? Recall my struggle, in Chapter 2, to use mutual funds to represent asset classes. We would buy a certain mutual fund believing it would provide us with the performance of a certain asset class, only to find that the mutual fund manager had extremely wide discretion to buy anything he could find to improve performance. Style drift also famously occurs when a new manager decides to change the direction of the fund.

Remember that this style drift was a big problem for us in our effort to construct and deliver a diversified asset allocation for our clients. You might not even notice it until some market disaster brought it to your attention. In the late 1990s, when everyone wanted to own technology stocks, investors might have bought five different funds without realizing that those funds were 95 percent invested in the same stocks! (All five funds would have been very likely to own GE, Microsoft, and IBM.) This has been one of the most common and ruinous things to happen when individuals have tried to diversify on their own without reading a pile of prospectuses carefully.

To construct a portfolio containing assets that truly complement each other and thus have different risk factors, we use a correlation table, which is easy to construct with today's computing power and 83 years of detailed observations of securities. A correlation table compares the performance of each asset class to the performance of each other asset class, and analyzes how much the movement in one asset class is like the movement in another asset class.

We construct the table using statistical analysis to evaluate, for example, how similar U.S. small-cap performance is to two-year global bond performance. (The answer: not very much alike, -0.14.) Perfect correlation would be 1.0; extremely high correlation, meaning two different asset classes are very similar to each other in the way they behave in the market, would be 0.8 or 0.9. Perfect negative correlation, like that drawn in Figure 5.1, would be -1.0. If the correlation is zero, the relationship between the two securities is random.

Markowitz and the Efficient Frontier

The efficient frontier represents a set of investments (for us, they will always be combinations of asset classes in a portfolio) that provide the highest expected return for a given level of risk, or the least amount of risk for a given amount of expected return. If our investment or our portfolio is not on the efficient frontier, then we can get more return for the amount of risk we are taking, or we can get the same return for less risk.

Part of Markowitz's insight was that he allowed for the idea that individual investors have different appetites for risk, which is why the efficient frontier demonstrates varying amounts of risk rather than just one efficient portfolio. Each investor has a different idea about the amount of risk appropriate to his circumstances. Imagine the amount of market risk a retiree might find acceptable, compared to the situation of a young person just out of college and starting a career. An investor's sensitivity to risk and return is called the *utility function*. A rational investor will hold only a portfolio that lies on the efficient frontier.

Figure 5.2 shows how we might draw a generic efficient frontier today. It is far more sophisticated than the first efficient frontiers Markowitz was working with, and he would not have been able to calculate it at the beginning of his career, due to lack of computing power. Building a portfolio

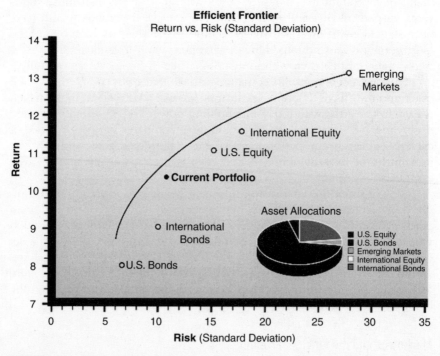

FIGURE 5.2   Sample Efficient Frontier

Source: Forum Financial Management, LLC.

using this kind of efficient frontier requires that we analyze every possible combination of securities or assets in order to find the most efficient way to combine them. We have to estimate the expected return for each asset class in the portfolio, and we have to know the covariances. The frontier is curved rather than straight because the formula for covariances is quadratic—it uses mathematical squares.

The process of calculating this optimal portfolio is called *mean-variance optimization*, which means finding the combination of assets that will allow us to invest on the efficient frontier according to our personal appetite for risk. The term *mean* refers to the long-term *expected returns* from the portfolio, and to the fact that returns always come back (revert) to the mean, the statistical center. *Variance* is the statistical term for riskiness and means the same thing as standard deviation. This is where this model reaches its limitation, as I found out for myself at Terra.

To get the optimized portfolio, we have to know the expected return for each asset, the standard deviation of returns, and the correlations among all the assets. While the standard deviation can be calculated for historical returns, and correlations (or covariances) can be calculated statistically, how do we figure out what the *expected return* should be, since expected return looks forward? This was my big problem when I first started working with optimization, as I related in Chapter 2, and it is still a problem. Should I take the average annualized return for 80 years of history? This is the essence of the dilemma of pure optimization. What should one use for the expected returns of each asset class?

The idea was to optimize using indexes and then pick the best funds to represent each asset class. If you're using active funds to represent asset classes, then you get the problem of style drift, as I also discussed in Chapter 2. Small differences in expected return can make a very large difference in the way the portfolio looks. At Terra, we would use historical return because we could not see any better way of estimating expected return. This would result in a portfolio that was optimized for the market cycle that was just past so the asset classes that had been in favor—and were likely to be out of favor very soon—were overrepresented. This was a big flaw for someone who tried to work strictly within the Markowitz world.

Sharpe and the Capital Asset Pricing Model

William Sharpe first introduced the capital asset pricing model (CAPM) in 1964. He shared the Nobel Prize in economics with Harry Markowitz (and Merton H. Miller) in 1990. At the beginning of this chapter, I mentioned that there is a world of financial theory that most people have never heard of. That is even truer of the CAPM itself. If you have a degree in finance or an

MBA, you will have studied it in depth; otherwise, you have probably never heard of it. Sharpe worked closely with Markowitz, further developed his theories, and to this day continues to say how much of a debt he owes to Markowitz. The capital asset pricing model is also considered to be a part of modern portfolio theory.

Sharpe began by studying certain aspects of portfolio analysis according to the model suggested by Markowitz. He wanted to explain how risky assets would be priced. He used Markowitz's idea that an asset should be evaluated relative to how adding it to the portfolio affects the portfolio's risk. Sharpe thought it would be possible to evaluate the risk of each asset relative to some common factor or portfolio.[8] How the assets behaved in relationship to that portfolio would tell you how much market risk that security represented. This covariance of any asset with existing holdings is what determines its risk premium and allows you to determine its price.

He called his model the *single-index model*, although it is now referred to as the *single-factor model*. Basically, he did not look at individual port-folios of assets. Instead, he thought that a stock's expected return was a function of its volatility relative to the volatility of all risky assets together. And the most efficient portfolio is the entire marketplace of risky assets.

This model says there are two kinds of risk, but each equity is a com-bination of both these kinds of risk:

1. *Market risk* is the risk of investing in the capital markets. You have this risk with any investment in the markets and you cannot overcome this risk by diversifying which securities you buy. This is called *systematic risk*, because it is the risk of the whole system. It is also called *beta*.[9] We have said that diversification means not putting all your eggs in one basket. Market risk refers to the fact that you have eggs, no matter how many baskets you put them in.

2. *Nonmarket risk* is firm-specific, the risk of investing in a particular com-pany or security rather than in a different company or security. This is the risk that your Starbucks stock will decrease in value if consumers drink less coffee, or that Toyota will increase because car buyers are crazy about the new Camry. You diversify that risk by creating a port-folio of securities of companies that have different businesses, so when food-related stocks are not doing well, auto stocks will be. You can see that this is the basic strategy of using a wide variety of baskets to put your eggs in. This kind of risk *can* be overcome through diversifica-tion and is also called *nonsystematic risk*, because it is the risk of one security only and not of the system as a whole. Nonmarket risk is also what you might call *sector* risk, the risk that I have invested in energy companies rather than in airlines.

The CAPM holds that the most efficient portfolio is the entire marketplace of risky assets; thus it provides the intellectual foundation for a mutual fund that invests in the entire market. Beta puts a price on each asset relative to the whole marketplace. For example, an asset might have a beta of 1.3. That means it is 30 percent more risky than the entire market. If the market—whatever you think of as constituting the entire market—goes up by some amount, then you would expect this risky asset to go up 130 percent of that amount. In other words, it bears more risk and will provide a reward that is in excess of what the underlying market provides. Conversely, whatever amount the market goes down, a stock with a beta of 1.3 will go down 130 percent of that amount. The volatility of every asset is related to the volatility of the overall market and that can be expressed as a percentage. High-beta stocks are the riskiest and thus have the highest expected return. You would expect that risky stocks, like some technology stocks during the tech bubble, for example, could easily be seen as having high beta, because they went up in price much more than the market, and they also fell in price proportionately more.

There is a great deal more to this pricing model; MBA students study it in one course after another. Sharpe believed that the market should settle into equilibrium, as the low-beta stocks that he thought most investors would see as most desirable got bid up in price, and high-beta stocks that no one wanted would drop in price.[10] The expected return of each asset would be determined by three factors:

1. The *risk-free rate* available on Treasury bills or government-guaranteed savings.
2. The market rate of return because the asset was invested in the market.
3. The beta of the individual security, meaning its relationship to market risk as a whole.

But he expected the whole market to move to equilibrium. This starts to build the case for the efficient market theory we discuss later. At equilibrium, all stocks are fairly priced and all are equally attractive to the investor, who then would really want to own all stocks or the whole market.

More about the CAPM and Its Issues

Simplifying greatly, Sharpe offers three practical messages.

1. Diversify as much as possible so you hold market proportions of risky securities, which can then be modified to suit your own risk tolerance.
2. Hold a broad portfolio in market-value proportions.
3. Bearing market risk should result in a higher expected return as a reward.

However, the kind of risk you bear must be the risk of the overall market (beta). Investors should not expect markets to reward them for risks that can be diversified away; they should expect compensation only for bearing systematic risks.

If you take your money out of your mattress and invest it in any security in the market, you will take on market risk along with the risk that is specific to the fortunes of the particular companies you have chosen to invest in. If you decide to invest in Microsoft or Apple, you will have market risk—the risk of the market in general—first of all, but you also have the nonsystematic risk of the particular company.

What if you had invested all your money in Enron? Oops, that was a bad idea, and now you have lost everything. But what if you had held a diversified portfolio and less than 1 percent of your overall portfolio was invested in Enron? Even with Enron's value going to zero, your overall port-folio was not affected that much. This is one of the great lessons the public had to relearn in 2008. If you held a portfolio that was truly diversified, you experienced a loss, but it was the loss of the market as a whole, the same rate of return as that experienced by the market as a whole. If you held a portfolio with large positions in Lehman Brothers, Fannie Mae, AIG, or Washington Mutual, or any of the other great failures of that year, you experienced a loss greater than that of the overall market, because you held too much unsystematic risk, the risk of individual securities that could have been diversified away.

When you buy only one or two stocks, both of which have risk, you should not expect the return on those two securities to compensate you for that risk. You might do very well with two securities or you might not, but the result will be due to random chance, not to your skill as an investor. You have to own enough stocks in enough different companies so that if one company goes bad, your portfolio is not devastated; you need to be diversified across enough different sectors so that if one sector goes bad, you do not lose everything.

Let us be clear as to what this means in plain English. Someone won a Nobel Prize for proving that one *cannot* by definition be adequately rewarded for picking individual stocks! In fact, this man said that you should want to own the entire market, and a little later we introduce the idea of the index funds that start to make that possible. This new way of thinking threatened the universe of the financial services that was devoted to the idea of investors paying for the privilege of learning what stocks to pick. He also said that the market tends to equilibrium, which leads to the efficient market theory, also discussed in a moment.

The publication of the CAPM fell on deaf ears. Sharpe wrote the original article in 1961 and gave it the title, "Capital Asset Prices: A Theory of Market Equilibrium under Conditions of Risk." After some wrangling with the editors of the *Journal of Finance*, who expressed skepticism about his ideas, his paper was finally published in September 1964. He was elated to see it in print and expected the phone to start ringing—and was met by total silence.[11]

However, he certainly had the last laugh, because in 1989, Wells Fargo Investment Advisors wanted to celebrate the twenty-fifth anniversary of the article's publication, so they ran "an electronic tabulation of citations of the article but had to stop 'after two thousand citations and references, because [their] budget ran out.'"[12] Wells Fargo "pointed out that Sharpe's model, in addition to serving portfolio managers as a means of predicting both risk and expected returns, had spawned valuable measures of portfolio performance, index funds, applications in corporate finance and corporate investment, and procedures for setting utility rates, as well as major theoretical innovations in the study of market behavior and asset valuation."[13]

While in some ways the CAPM has been superseded, it provided an essential foundation. Its brilliance was recognized by the Nobel Prize. Sharpe's message about diversification is the foundation stone of my investment philosophy.

Fama and the Efficient Market Hypothesis

Eugene F. "Gene" Fama was another of those economists who discovered the power of computing early on. He earned a PhD in economics at the University of Chicago in 1964. He told Peter Bernstein that UC had an IBM 709, "the first serious machine," and, in the whole university, "for a long time, only he and a member of the physics department... knew how to use it. 'We were like kids in a candy store.'"[14] It is not a coincidence that theories about markets and stock prices made significant advances as computing power developed—the power necessary to crunch and mine prices and all kinds of market data.

In the early 1960s, Fama was not the only one who was thinking and writing about the idea of stock prices as a random walk, but the publication of his PhD thesis in 1965 set him on the road to being widely recognized today as the "father of modern finance."[15] The *Journal of Business* published his entire 70-page PhD thesis in its January 1965 issue: "The Behavior of Stock Market Prices." The editor of the *Financial Analysts Journal* considered it to be so important that he published a simplified version, "Random Walks in Stock Market Prices," nine months after the first version had been published. Then the English analysts' journal reprinted it in 1966, and finally *Institutional Investor* reprinted the article in April 1968.[16]

Central to Fama's thought is the principle now called the *efficient market hypothesis*. It states that, at all times, markets incorporate and reflect all information, so stock picking is futile. This is the theoretical explanation for all the empirical evidence that stock picking does not work. In an efficient market, all securities are priced fairly and current market prices are the best approximation we can reach of their intrinsic value. In his thesis, he cited studies that had already been made demonstrating the impossibility of outperforming the market, including a groundbreaking study done by Michael Jensen, one of his graduate students. Remember that this was long before the invention of index funds, before Dalbar's studies, even before modern portfolio theory had become accepted in the marketplace. This groundbreaking study, already cited in Chapter 4, looked at the performance of 115 mutual funds over 10 years, from 1955 to 1964. The results? "On average, investors who held mutual funds for ten years would have been worth 15 percent less than if they had merely bought and held a broadly diversified portfolio of common stocks with the same level of risk."[17] Forty-five years ago, there was already a study showing the futility of active management! We are still using and teaching that same essential thought today.

If you do not agree with the idea that markets are efficient, imagine that they are not efficient. That would mean that individual money managers should be able to predict *consistently* (not just occasionally, which is only getting lucky) which stocks are going to outperform. In an inefficient market, insider information would allow some money managers to outperform others *in some consistent way*. An inefficient market would also say that a few of the legions of market analysts are better than the rest, and are better at identifying the companies that will outperform over the next few years. Do you know how many people in the United States are employed in trying to figure out which companies are the best to invest in? And that does not count the thousands or hundreds of thousands of individual brokers and average investors who spend their time trying to locate the next source of outperformance. If markets were truly inefficient, some—at least a few—of these people should show consistent above-average performance over the years.

Is there such a thing as insider knowledge? The efficient markets hypothesis says there is not; that the marketplace has already priced in all the information that is possible about every security in the marketplace. Peter Bernstein points out that the last person who was able to make insider information work was Nathan Rothschild, who "made millions when his carrier pigeons brought him the first news of Wellington's victory at Waterloo."[18]

That does not mean that market inefficiencies or mispricings never happen. The "madness of crowds" results in the occasional bubble or panic. Of course assets get mispriced occasionally, but such opportunities occur randomly and not in a way that a money manager could take advantage of systematically and over the long run. The efficient market hypothesis further states that stock prices remain in equilibrium and the value of a security is determined when the price at which a number of people wish to sell is the same as that at which a comparable number of people wish to buy.

The implication of this is that, by definition, active management cannot add value by selecting stocks and timing the market, and stock picking cannot work. So when you turn on the TV and the guru of the moment tells you the market is undervalued or overvalued—or overbought or oversold—think about the foolishness of this position. On the day you saw the guru, about 1.5 billion shares traded on an open and free market and determined the market price at the close. So 1.5 billion shares voted and determined a price, and according to the guru, they are wrong and he is right. That might be the definition of *chutzpah*!

Although this devastating research has been around for a long time, it took me 15 years of working at Terra to figure this out for myself through painful trial and error. All the energy that is placed into picking stocks and picking sectors (technology sector is going to outperform; buy energy companies now) is just wasted.

Gene Fama still teaches at the University of Chicago and has been affiliated with Dimensional Fund Advisors for most of its years of existence. He has continued to make landmark contributions to the field of investing; keep reading. Many people predict a Nobel Prize in his future.

I remember meeting an investor who told me he did not believe in efficient markets, even after I showed him all this data. He was a long-time stock-picker. So I asked him a simple question: "If markets are not efficient, why are you not a millionaire from your stock investments? You are smart, well-read, and have an MBA. If stocks are so mispriced, why have you not been able to find this mispricing and become rich?" He could not answer that, of course, and eventually became my client.

If you have trouble believing markets are efficient, where is the evidence that they are inefficient? Hedge funds were supposed to find this mispricing, and although they charge an extraordinary amount of fees for their supposed expertise, more hedge funds have gone out of business during the bear market than mutual funds.

People always want to talk to me about Warren Buffett. The fact that there could be this one phenomenally successful investor over the entire history of the market does not in itself prove anything about efficient or inefficient markets and stock picking. Beyond that, Buffet knows the advantage of not having the market be aware of his moves. In the early years of managing Berkshire Hathaway, he did not disclose his large purchases of public stock because he did not want other investors coat-tailing, as he called it, on his picks. He knew that if others saw him buying Coca Cola—or whatever company—the price would climb. Buffett managed to do this for many years until the SEC forced him to disclose his holdings. As told in his biography, *Snowball*, after that, for a long time he stopped making large investments in public companies.

Even Buffett is subject to efficient markets. As I write this book, he has made many large investments in public companies but he usually got his own special deal. Finally, please note that Buffett is a buy-and-hold investor above all; he buys stock and he buys whole companies and he holds them *for years*. He has been an incredibly successful investor over the years, but he is not anything like a typical active manager.

Creating Index Fund Investing

According to Sharpe, the market portfolio is the most efficient portfolio of all. If all you have to do is buy the market, or an index that replicates it, who needs anybody to carry on the traditional activities of a trust department?[19]

By 1970, many people were raising questions about active management. Some parts of the financial world had read Markowitz on the importance of

What Is an Index and Why Is It Important?

An index is generally used to benchmark or measure the market's movements and its performance. Many investors are familiar with the Dow Jones Industrial Average and the S&P 500 Index. These indexes have been used for a long time as proxies for or indication of market performance. If you invest in the marketplace, you can always find out the price of an individual stock at the stock market's close. But if you want to get a picture of what the market as a whole did, you need something to act as a bellwether or composite picture. The Dow Jones Industrial Average has been providing that information since 1882, and the S&P 500 since 1957, and there was an earlier version of the S&P that was started in 1923. Today's technology is capable of crunching together the prices of all stocks, but we still rely on the indexes that have been giving us market information for a long time.

The widely recognized and quoted Dow Jones Industrial Average was founded in 1882. It tracks only 32 stocks that are chosen by the editors of the *Wall Street Journal*. The Dow uses a price-weighted (not market-weighted) calculation, which means that a large change in one company's stock price (even though it might be the smallest company in the index) can have a dramatic effect on the price movement of the index.* For example, a $1 change for a $10 stock is much more significant (percentage-wise) than a $1 change for a $100 stock. The Dow Jones index simplified the amount of calculation you had to do in those days before computing power: At the end of a day of trading, you had to add up the prices of the individual stocks and then divide by the number of securities in the index, something many people could manage before calculators, and it gave you a great deal more information about the market than nothing. Now the Dow is so well known and has so many years of history that it is still how many people conceptualize market performance. We are still stuck with it for some aspects of securities and market analysis because it has the longest history.

Since the S&P 500 Index includes 500 stocks, not just 32, it is far broader and more representative of the market than is the Dow, but it is still a far cry from representing the whole universe of stocks, since Standard & Poor's as a rating service tracks almost 10,000 stocks for all of North America. The calculations used to compute the index are more complex than those for the Dow but provide a much more accurate picture of market activity. The index is market-weighted (i.e., each stock's weight in the index is proportionate to its market value) and has a heavy weighting of large-cap stocks due to its requirement that a company must have at least $5 billion in market capitalization. Standard & Poor's defines the index by saying it includes "500 leading companies in leading industries of the U.S. economy," so we know that it represents only the U.S. economy in its definition of "leading industries."

Although it is true that the companies in the S&P 500 Index together constitute approximately 75 percent of the U.S. domestic equity marketplace as measured by market capitalization, the index represents only one or two asset classes, depending on how you classify them (either it is only U.S. large-cap, or it can be divided into U.S. large-cap growth and U.S. large-cap value). The most powerful argument against its being able to represent the market is the fact that, as of March 31, 2009, the 10 largest companies in that index comprised 21.61 percent of the index. That is to say, 2 percent of the number of companies constituted more than 21 percent of the market capitalization of the

(continued)

(*Continued*)

index. The S&P 500 represents, essentially, the market performance of 10 gigantic U.S. growth companies that do business around the world.

---

* When a stock market index is *price-weighted*, each stock makes up a fraction of the index that is proportional to its quoted price. For example, a stock trading at $50 will make up 10 times more of the total index when compared to a stock trading at $5, but it will not make a difference to the index if one stock has a market cap that is 10 times greater than that of another stock; it is all about price. This is different from a *market-weighted* index where stocks are included based on the market capitalization of the underlying companies—in other words, the quoted stock price multiplied by the number of shares outstanding. A price-weighted index does not reflect the growth in underlying market values. A small company might have a stock that sells for $50 while a large company stock might sell for $5. Thus a change in the larger price of the smaller company would drive the price-weighted index because the higher price means it makes up a larger part of the index, although the combined market values will not be affected very much; that would require changes in the price of the larger companies in the index. This kind of index calculates the appropriate weight for each stock in the index and requires constant rebalancing to keep the stocks in the index at a weight that is appropriate.

A *market-value-weighted* index—also called a *capitalization-weighted* index—weights its component stocks according to the total value of their market capitalization, meaning the total market value of their outstanding shares. That means that the effect of a stock's price change is proportional to the stock's size in proportion to all the stocks in the index. A change in the stock price of the largest stock in the index will have a much greater effect on the overall index value than will a change in the stock price of the smallest members of the index. A stock's market capitalization is the share price of the stock multiplied by the number of stock shares outstanding.

---

considering risk as well as return and the importance of diversification; had read Fama on the efficient market hypothesis; and had read Sharpe on the importance of diversifying nonsystematic risk but the impossibility of escaping the risk of the market as a whole. There were people like Burton G. Malkiel, who wrote in *A Random Walk down Wall Street*:

> *What we need is a no-load, minimum-management-fee mutual fund that simply buys the hundreds of stocks making up the broad stock-market averages and does no trading . . . in an attempt to catch the winners. Whenever below-average performance on the part of any mutual fund is noticed, fund spokesmen are quick to point out, "You can't buy the averages." It's time the public could.*[20]

So how much diversification do you need and how many securities do you have to own to get a market rate of return? And how do you buy the market anyway, so as to get a market rate of return? Remember that this is not that long after Markowitz had been forced to use only 10 securities in his sample portfolio because he could not muster the technological resources to use 25. Owning hundreds or thousands of securities in one passive mutual fund, as Dimensional Fund Advisors does now, would be impossible without today's technology.

There were three important pioneers in this attempt to let investors own *the market*, although the limitations of systems and operations proved to be huge obstacles. Instead of owning the market, you could own an index fund that could be said to represent the market. An *index fund* is a mutual fund that is designed to replicate as perfectly as possible the performance of an investment index. That is, the fund would hold the same securities and in the same proportions as the index that the fund wants to replicate, with the stated investment goal of achieving financial performance that is equal to that of the index. The costs of managing the fund are minimized because the fund simply buys what is in the index, although every fund will have fees for administration, reporting, and maintenance.

Inventing Index Funds

So where was the index fund invented? For institutional investors, the first index funds were used at Wells Fargo Bank on the West Coast and American National Bank in Chicago. John Bogle, who has become one of the best-known figures in retail investing, was the first to make an index fund available to retail investors.

Wells Fargo was not successful at using active management in its trust business. This motivated them to be a pioneer in using passive investment. But it worked for them. By the end of the 1970s, the only money management strategy they used was passive.[21]

David Booth and Rex Sinquefield both studied under Gene Fama at the University of Chicago while working toward their MBAs. After graduation, Sinquefield accepted a position with American National Bank in Chicago, later becoming head of the trust department. As he evaluated the bank's money managers, he discovered just what Fama had predicted: Actively managed funds that invest in large company stocks collectively do no better than the S&P 500 index and in fact do worse, once you count their fees. He proposed the idea of a fund that simply tracked the index. While it was not easy to convince the bank to implement this idea, in 1975 he and American National launched an index fund intended to track the S&P 500 index.

DFA's First Fund

Rex Sinquefield and David Booth founded Dimensional Fund Advisors in 1981. Their first product was the DFA 9-10 Fund, which invested in the smallest companies in the marketplace (the ninth and bottom deciles, when ranked by stock market value) and eventually became DFA's micro-cap fund. Although S&P 500 index funds were experiencing reasonable acceptance, institutional investors were still not investing in the smallest sectors of the stock market. Booth and Sinquefield thought that a fund that did invest in the smallest sectors would offer diversification.

As true believers in market efficiency, Sinquefield and Booth bought the whole market for their fund—all the relevant firms in that market segment. They did not attempt to pick which ones would be winners and they did not start a research department, thereby keeping costs much lower than those charged by other firms. They just bought any security that fit the parameters of the fund in terms of size. The fund would have the efficiency of an S&P 500 index fund but, due to the small-cap effect, had the potential to provide higher returns in the long run.

There were challenges at first. Although they obtained some institutional clients relatively early, from 1984 to 1990, small stocks went through their worst seven-year period since 1926. As Sinquefield says, "There were some extremely trying times," but "most of the clients hung on."[22] Booth said, "At least it discouraged the competition."[23]

DFA hung on because Sinquefield and Booth had not told clients that small stocks would outperform large stocks in any given period, even seven years. They did say that their fund would beat most small-cap funds, since most of those had high fees. The results were as they predicted: While all small-cap funds underperformed the S&P 500 index, DFA did better than most. Since 1990, the small-cap market has consistently outperformed the S&P 500.

John Bogle and the Vanguard Funds

John McQuown at Wells Fargo and Rex Sinquefield at American National Bank in Chicago both established the first Standard & Poor's Composite Index Funds for institutional clients; individual investors were excluded. John Bogle introduced the index fund for retail investors.

Bogle changed the entire game of retail investing. He has won many honors, including being named one of the "world's 100 most powerful and influential people" by *Time* magazine; winning *Institutional Investor*'s Lifetime Achievement Award; being named one of the investment industry's four "Giants of the 20th Century" by *Fortune* magazine; and winning the Woodrow Wilson Award from Princeton University for "distinguished achievement in the Nation's service." He has been a powerful advocate for retail investors over a lifetime of investing. He has written many books on both index investing and commonsense investing and is still often quoted on money management issues. He has devoted followers who call themselves "bogleheads" and are easily found online.

He was not part of the University of Chicago academic world, but was very current with the new thoughts about indexes and passive investing in the early 1970s. He founded the Vanguard Group in 1974 and in 1975 started the First Index Investment Trust, based on the S&P 500 Index. It is now named the Vanguard 500 Index Fund.[24] John Bogle's analyses of the costs of active management have been groundbreaking; I use them in this book. He has remained one of the most vocal proponents of low-cost index fund investing. Assets in Vanguard indexed funds are more than $100 billion. As Bogle himself says, "We have come a long way since 'Bogle's folly'—a phrase I heard all too often from the late 1970s through the early 1990s."[25]

To us now, using an index as a proxy for investing in the wider market seems so obvious. However, I wonder why we thought it was so important to match the performance of something as arbitrary as the S&P 500, chosen by a committee. Maybe following an index was a necessary discipline at the beginning of the passive strategy, and the S&P 500 was preferable to the Dow Jones 32. At the time, the computing power available to manage this kind of fund might not have been sufficient for larger funds like the Russell 1000.

As a result of Sharpe's research, and recognizing the importance of the efficient market hypothesis, investors began searching for a way to diversify and invest in many of the stocks available on the exchanges or, simply put, the broad market. The concept of investing in an index was developed.

Indexes are massively important to the marketplace. For any investor to evaluate the performance of his investments, there has to be a bench- mark someplace, and indexes provide it. The Standard & Poor's web site (www.standardandpoors.com) says some $4.5 trillion is benchmarked to the S&P indexes, and that is only one index family (although the largest).

According to the Investment Company Institute (ICI), in 2008, the per- centage of equity mutual funds (and only equities) invested in an index fund was 13 percent (and of that 13 percent, 40 percent were invested in S&P 500 Index funds).[26] Some $604 billion is invested in some form of index, whether regular mutual fund or ETF, and including bond, international, and hybrid indexes; and 368 mutual funds and 766 different share classes are devoted to index investing.[27] Amazon tells me there are some 1,600 books devoted to the subject of index investing. Being able to invest in low-cost mutual funds using a buy-and-hold strategy has been an enormous benefit for individual investors. Because Wall Street never misses an opportunity, you can also find a plethora of index-like funds offered by the money management firms but with a twist purporting to improve on index investing, such as the use of puts or hedges that will supposedly protect your investment on the downside. This of course comes with the usual high fees of active management.

While I believe any investor is better off using indexes rather than active managers, there are both some issues with index investing and some opportunities beyond it.

The Problems with Indexing

While this whole group of academic financial pioneers have been talking about investing in "the market," what leap of faith do you have to make to get from the market—a theoretical portfolio comprising every investment and security in the world—to the Dow Jones Industrial Average or the S&P 500?

My goal as an investor is to invest in the market using asset classes, and any given index is not the market and is also not an asset class. Even the Wilshire 5000, which invests in the stocks of the largest 5000 companies, is an *index*, not an asset class. In fact, you can well imagine that buying all companies in that way ensures that you are not making a distinction among asset classes. The S&P 500 and most of the other indexes were created as vehicles for reporting the performance of some companies and were never intended to be investment vehicles.

Over the past 25 years, as asset allocation has become an important part of investing, indexes have been created to try to offer the characteristics of asset classes, but the main point of that has been more to create benchmarks rather than investment vehicles. The S&P 500 Growth Index, for example, was intended to be a proxy and a benchmark—something a large-cap growth manager could be measured against—rather than an investment vehicle.

Another important problem with an index fund, whatever its original definition and purpose, is that it reconstitutes—makes changes in its component securities—only annually. During the year between reconstitution dates, there will be many changes in the markets and in the securities that comprise the index. A small-cap stock may become mid-cap or be sold to a large-cap company, or a growth-type security may change enough to no longer belong in the growth category. An index may itself experience significant style drift over the course of a year. In Chapter 6, I discuss how DFA deals with these issues.

Matching an index is not an investment strategy, and investing in an index is not the same as having a diversified asset allocation approach. Think about the goal of the manager of an index fund: to have zero difference between the results of the index fund and those of the index itself. While this is not the same kind of active management you find elsewhere on Wall Street among the funds that are trying to pick winners for you, someone, somewhere, is buying and selling individual securities so that the fund in which you invest provides exactly the same investment return as the index itself. In fact, the manager of the fund is evaluated according to how close the return of his index fund is to the index itself.

Another part of the story is that indexes are constantly reinventing themselves. What do you think happens on the date a change is made? When an index sponsor announces the securities to be added to or deleted from its composition, managers seeking to closely track the index must buy and sell to adjust their portfolios on the reconstitution date. Remember that the index itself is just an index; it does not actually own any securities. But a manager who wants to replicate the performance of the index actually has to buy those securities. By some estimates, a stock added to the S&P 500 increases up to 5 percent in price on the day that it is added. Prices may be temporarily distorted by the spike in demand from numerous index managers seeking to buy or sell securities on the same day. Other market participants take advantage of this temporary demand. The index manager has no choice but to buy the new security on the precise day that it is added to the index.

This reconstitution costs you money and is not the same as a buy-and-hold strategy. It can result in significant trading costs, aside from the costs of moving the market. Index replication requires executing with prespecified transactions, stocks, amounts, and trade dates. Timing lag between the reconstitution announcement and effective date enables nonindexers to buy additions and sell deletions before tracking-sensitive investors do, when prices are often more attractive.

Market impact is a zero-sum game; to the extent one party is penalized by the reconstitution effect, someone else enjoys a benefit. In any negotiated transaction, the party in a hurry to make the deal is at a disadvantage. Although index managers may successfully track the index, their trading strategy may penalize the return of the index itself. Investors who make low tracking error a priority bear the costs of this activity.

Brinson and the Importance of Asset Allocation

Most of the discussion so far has focused on investment philosophy and investment strategy. Expenses and fees are also essential to the discussion of what kind of investing is best for the long haul. But next I want to introduce yet another landmark study, first published in 1986.

Gary Brinson managed the mergers and acquisitions (M&A) department at the First National Bank of Chicago in the early 1970s. In 1989, Gary Brinson and his unit were allowed to buy themselves out of First Chicago to create Brinson Partners, which went on to incredible success; at one time, Gary Brinson was managing more than a trillion dollars.

But long before all this happened, Brinson, Hood, and Beebower did a study of the factors that had the greatest effect on portfolio performance, and considered asset allocation, market timing, security selection, and more. The result was reported in the *Financial Analysts Journal*: "Investment *policy* (the allocation of assets) dominates investment *strategy* (market timing and security selection), explaining on average 93.6 percent of the variation in total [pension] plan assets."[28]

This is an extremely difficult statement to parse and is surely one of the seminal and most quoted statements in all of modern finance, but it is probably also one of the most misunderstood statements as well. This finding was reaffirmed by the authors in 1991 in a follow-up article which this time said that, for the 10-year period ending in 1987, asset allocation determined 91.5 percent of this variation.[29]

Since these two studies said that all of Wall Street's expensive expertise on picking securities is essentially useless, they rocked Wall Street, although the real meaning of their statements is not as obvious as it is sometimes made out to be. Brinson, Hood, and Beebower (BHB) did *not* say that your asset allocation decision *determines* the returns of your portfolio. They said that asset allocation policy made "an overwhelming contribution... to the return performance of a sample of 91 large pension plans.... Investment policy explained, on average, 91.5 percent of the *variation* in quarterly total plan returns."[30]

Perhaps it is a question of semantics, especially because it has become widely recognized how important the asset allocation policy—that is, the asset allocation strategy—is to the performance of a portfolio. John Bogle simplifies the discussion: "Long-term fund investors might profit by concentrating more on the allocation of investments between stock and bond funds, and less on the question of what particular stock and bond funds to hold... as long as cost is held constant and low."[31] In any event, there is no misunderstanding this sentence from BBH: "Active management not only had no measurable impact on returns, but... it appears to have increased risk by a small margin."[32]

This study influenced me profoundly at Terra. Since I often felt that I was on a lonely mission in trying to figure out how to optimize portfolio performance for my clients, when this study burst upon the scene, first in 1986 and then again in 1991, it made me feel personally vindicated for all the time and trouble I had taken over the years trying to get the asset allocation mixture right.

In fact, this study says that the best way for an adviser to spend his or her time is the way I had spent so much of my time: trying to figure out how best to allocate investment dollars using a sensible mix of asset classes that have a low correlation to each other. You choose the appropriate asset allocation and then stay invested over the long term. The most important decision in allocation is how much should be allocated to bonds versus equities, because this determines how much you will allocate to safe assets (bonds) and how much to risky assets (equities). Once you have made that decision, then you will figure out how to allocate your stock position among the various growth and value, domestic and international, large- and small-cap stocks.

Weaknesses in the Theories

Much of modern finance is founded on the idea that investors are rational, which is probably where you have to start to build any investment theory, and that investors can be counted on to take the actions that maximize their return and minimize their risk. But as we discussed in Chapter 3, in real life, investors are rarely rational, let alone completely rational, and at times are subject to sweeping waves of irrationality. Some examples are very well known: tulips in seventeenth-century Holland or tech stocks in the late 1990s; it is the same kind of behavior.

Beyond that, these theories consider that investors know and understand risk and share similar views about it. If you want to see different perceptions of risk, compare the views of the preboomer generation who lived through the Depression and then talk to a member of Generation X. If you want to compare how differently investors view time frames, ask a day trader to talk to Warren Buffett about the outlook for a stock.

Modern portfolio theory assumes the marketplace has securities and asset classes that are truly independent of one another so that an investor can diversify completely. But just as positive market sentiment can result in a series of years where all asset class performance is positive, there are times like 2008 when there is almost no positive asset class performance anywhere worldwide. In times of such enormous market stress, investments that in theory ought to be independent in fact act like they are tied together—and everything heads down. The downward effects create a vicious circle and the weakness in one part of the economy weighs heavily on the rest.

Both modern portfolio theory and other financial principles such as asset allocation depend on the idea that there are no transaction costs for buying or selling; that any amount of buying and selling can take place without moving the market; and that all securities are perfectly liquid, meaning one can buy or sell any amount of any security at any time. In fact, although the larger the size of the transaction, such as for large pension funds, the greater the economies of scale in terms of transaction costs, the other side of that coin is that those very large transactions are most likely to move the price of a security as they are executed. Liquidity is not always available, especially for smaller stocks. These theories also never take taxes into consideration, whereas individual investors live in a world where every transaction is potentially a taxable event.

Fama and French and the Three-Factor Model

In this chapter so far, I have discussed modern portfolio theory and the need for diversification, and the capital asset pricing model, which says that you can diversify away only the nonsystematic risk of individual stocks but you cannot diversify away the risk of the market itself. But in fact, you do not want to diversify away all risk because it is the risk that provides the return. Both of those theories are primarily concerned with increasing returns by reducing (not eliminating) risk—or, you might say, by *managing* risk. William Sharpe said that it is very hard to beat the market and you are typically not rewarded for trying.

I also introduced the efficient market hypothesis, which says you cannot predict market performance and individual managers cannot outperform the market over time. In fact, if individual active managers want to beat the market, not only do they have to do as well as the market, they have to do better, in order to compensate investors for the fees charged by those managers.

Finally I raised the question, why not just buy the market, especially as represented by one of the indexes such as the S&P 500 Index? I come back to this question at the end of this chapter.

In the context of modern portfolio theory, I said that many investors have trouble accepting the idea that reducing risk means giving up a little of the total potential return they might otherwise have. This does compromise returns somewhat, especially for investors who believe that they might be different from almost any investor who has ever lived and will somehow be able to pick the best-performing sectors much of the time. Is the additional safety worth it? The short answer to that question is yes, but you have to wait until the next chapter where I show you how to build portfolios using asset allocation and then compare risk-adjusted performance.

But there is one more essential element to this story before we get there. I mentioned Gene Fama earlier as the author of the efficient market hypothesis and one of the founding fathers of modern finance. Kenneth French has been part of the Tuck School of Business at Dartmouth College for many years. French and Fama have both been associated with

Dimensional Fund Advisors for many years as well. Together they developed what they call the three-factor model, which further develops the ideas expressed in Sharpe's one-factor model and provides additional information on how securities are priced in the market.

The explanatory power of the capital asset pricing model offered investors a new way to understand risk and market performance, but it was the one-factor model, and it could not explain everything. Fama and French wanted to understand more, and the model they developed says that the price of a security is explained by three factors:

1. A premium for investing in an equity rather than in a fixed-income security; the equity has a higher expected return because equities have more risk than fixed-income securities.
2. A premium for investing in value stocks (based on the ratio of book value to market capitalization), which have a higher expected return than growth stocks (keep reading for more information about the definitions of value and growth stocks).
3. A premium for investing in the stocks of small companies. Measured by market capitalization, smaller companies provide higher expected returns (on average) than larger company stocks; they are also riskier.

Fama and French decided to analyze the components of the S&P 500. They classified all the companies in the index according to whether they sold above or below book value. What does that mean? A simple example is to look at the value of your home. You take the fair market value of your house, which you might have bought a number of years ago, and say it is worth $300,000 today. Then you subtract the amount of your mortgage that you still owe. For the sake of this example, say your mortgage is $200,000. Then the book value, or the equity you have in your home, is $100,000. In this case, your home is worth more than its book value.

Companies also have equity, which is basically what the company is worth minus what they owe to third parties. Companies that are like this example, with a price in the marketplace that is higher than the book value of the firm, Fama and French defined as growth companies. These are the companies the market loves. Investors are optimistic about their earnings potential and their future growth possibilities. Everyone tells you to buy these companies; investors are willing to pay more than the actual current value of the company because they believe its growth prospects are so good.

Now say that you had bought your home just before the housing market dropped and it is now worth $200,000, whereas your mortgage is $300,000. That would make you like what is called a value company, where the actual market value of your home is negative and worth less than the book value, what you owe on your mortgage. Companies like this are out of favor and financial advisers tell you not to buy them.

Fama and French used this factor only—above or below book value—to divide the S&P 500 companies into two categories. (Remember that the companies in the S&P are all large companies.) If a company sold above book value, it was in the large-cap growth category, and if a company sold at significantly below book value, maybe 30 to 40 percent below, it was put into the large-cap value category. There was no attempt to evaluate good or bad company or good or bad management or anything else.

The results of their analysis can be seen in Table 5.1 which is updated to the current year. Look at the returns. The average annual return of the

TABLE 5.1   Size and Value Effects Are Strong around the World

Index	Annualized Compound Returns %	Standard Deviation %
U.S. Large-Capitalization Stocks, 1927–2008		
U.S. Large Value	10.04	27.21
S&P 500 Index	9.60	20.69
U.S. Large Growth	8.64	21.99
U.S. Small-Capitalization Stocks, 1927–2008		
U.S. Small Value	13.03	35.05
CRSP 6–10	11.11	31.08
U.S. Small Growth	8.40	34.30
Non-U.S. Developed Markets Stocks, 1975–2008		
International Value	14.95	24.60
International Small	14.82	28.61
MSCI EAFE	10.29	22.58
Emerging Markets Stocks, 1989–2008		
Emerging Markets Value	14.58	39.24
Emerging Markets "Market"	10.70	35.47
Emerging Markets Growth	8.69	34.96

In U.S. dollars. Indexes are not available for direct investment. Their performance does not reflect the expenses associated with the management of an actual portfolio. Past performance is not a guarantee of future results. U.S. value and growth index data (ex utilities) provided by Fama/French. The S&P data are provided by Standard & Poor's Index Services Group. CRSP data provided by the Center for Research in Security Prices, University of Chicago. International Value data provided by Fama/French from Bloomberg and MSCI securities data. International Small data compiled by Dimensional Fund Advisors from Bloomberg, StyleResearch, London Business School, and Nomura Securities data. MSCI EAFE Index is net of foreign withholding taxes on dividends; copyright MSCI 2009, all rights reserved. Emerging markets index data simulated by Fama/French from countries in the IFC Investable Universe; simulations are free-float-weighted both within each country and across all countries.
Source: Dimensional Fund Advisors.

large-cap growth companies is 8.64 percent and for large-cap value companies it is 10.04 percent. The difference between those two annual rates of return is 140 basis points or about one and a half percentage points.

Fama and French were intrigued by these results, and wondered if this methodology also worked with small companies. So they analyzed small companies the same way. Table 5.1 includes an index you might not be familiar with. The CRSP 6-10 (from the Center for Research in Security Prices) represents the bottom 50 percent of the number of all stocks traded in the United States. Earlier in this chapter, I told you about the Center for Research in Security Prices and how its data series all began in 1926. This is an index based on that research. Small companies are those with a market capitalization representing the bottom 50 percent by number of companies of all U.S. companies, traded on any exchange. Fama and French repeated their research, taking all of the companies trading below book value and putting them into the "small value" category, and those selling above book value went into the category of "small growth." The result this time is an average annualized return of 8.40 percent for small-cap growth and 13.03 percent for small-cap value: a whopping large difference of 463 basis points, or approximately four and a half percentage points. Active managers lie awake at night dreaming of attaining that kind of outperformance! And these were the results of the securities themselves, without any active manager to choose them.

Since these are averages over more than 80 years, that means that in any given year you will not get exactly these results. There have been years in which growth companies did better than the index and value companies did not do well. But it points to an interesting phenomenon we have discussed elsewhere in this book: Few active managers beat an index in any one year or for a couple of years. There is no active manager or series of active managers at a mutual fund company who has been able to sustain outperformance over 80 years.

Now on a roll, Fama and French decided to look at non-U.S. companies in the developed world, and then they looked at emerging market countries, meaning non-U.S. nondeveloped countries. In each case, the same relationships were true. It is interesting that it would be true in countries that are not well developed and which may not have efficient markets, and yet even so see value securities outperforming growth securities or an index.

This seems to contrast starkly with the advice you get from most advisers, who tell you to buy the great companies, not the lousy companies.

I have an analogy that might help explain this. Say that two people came to you to borrow money, and one person had a great credit history and the other person had a very poor credit history. Who would you charge a higher rate of interest to? I hope your answer was the person with the poor credit history. Why? Because there is more risk associated with lending to the person with the poor credit history.

If that makes sense when you loan money, it should also make sense when you invest in stocks. If you think about it, those large blue-chip companies, according to the Fama and French model, are expected to do well and so have less risk; that means that they will also have a lower rate of expected return.

Small companies in general (as defined by the CRSP 6-10) outperformed large companies in general (as represented by the S&P 500) by 151 basis points—more than one and a half percentage points. Of course the higher return comes with higher risk—which is why the return is higher. Small value stocks have the highest risk of all and they outperformed large growth stocks by 439 basis points. That is almost four and a half percentage points per year over 83 years. No active manager can approach this record.

Beyond Index Investing

There is one more strand to this part of the indexing story. David Booth had started working at A.G. Becker in New York City, advising pension funds on investments, when he wanted to start a small-cap index fund but was laughed out of the office. The next day he decided to start his own firm in the spare bedroom of his Brooklyn Heights apartment.

The research of another graduate student of Fama's, Rolf Banz, was the first to demonstrate that small-cap stocks produce higher returns than large-cap stocks over the long term, something that most professional investors accept today without question: Small companies have higher risk and thus higher cost of capital and higher expected return. Sinquefield followed Banz's research while still at American National, and proposed a small-cap index fund in addition to the S&P 500 fund. The bank turned him down. Soon afterward, Booth called to say that he was starting a new firm in order to offer just the kind of fund that American National had turned down. Sinquefield quit his job and joined Booth. Dimensional Fund Advisors was born, but it took me another 15 years to find them.

In the years since it was founded in 1981, DFA has grown to over $127 billion in assets (as of June 30, 2009). It continues to be unique in the marketplace for offering mutual funds that are defined strictly by asset class.

Remember that I raised the question earlier, why not just buy the market, especially as represented by one of the indexes such as the S&P 500 Index? That question is answered by the three-factor model. An index is not an asset class and is not the market; the S&P 500 is certainly not the market. Now, using the DFA funds, it is possible to buy pure asset classes, which you use to tilt toward small and value and improve on pure market or pure index performance.

DFA and I believe that it is possible to use a passive approach that saves significantly on transaction costs and pay for the active manager, and still do even better than an index by tilting your portfolio towards the small and value securities that have outperformed over time. During this recent, most brutal market since the Great Depression, we learned to focus our attention on *safety* above all. But one of the most important reasons for working with this strategy is the *performance* part of the story, that tilting towards the higher-risk/higher-return parts of the marketplace that can get you higher rewards over time.

The negativity in this marketplace caused a temporary correlation of what seemed like all assets—everything going down at once (except some short-term fixed-income asset classes). A bear market, even this kind of bear market, is a natural and normal occurrence in the marketplace, however painful. There were some corrections that were due and some that were overdue. But no matter how grim prospects ever seem, bear markets always end. Or at least they have so far in our history, and I am confident that that will continue to be true in the future. As the market comes off its lows, once again investors will be trying to figure out how to get the best performance.

In the next chapter, I explain how to put together all the pieces of the story I have told so far, to build an investment strategy for the long term.

CHAPTER 6

Implementing the Strategy

L et me recap some of the things we have learned so far in this book. Active management does not work. We know that from the empirical evidence, but now we have also learned from the academic theories why it cannot work. We found that using index funds to build a portfolio is better than trying to use active mutual funds, but index investing also has its drawbacks. Then we found out from the three-factor model that we can actually improve on index investing.

Now that we have that whole background of explanation and information, how do we create an investment strategy that we can implement, and use it to sustain our investing for the long term? That is the question this chapter tries to answer.

Continuing the Search for a Sustainable Investment Strategy

Partly because my mission in this book is to save you from my mistakes, and partly because stories about other people's mistakes are interesting, I am going to finish the narrative I started in Chapters 1 and 2 about my search for a sustainable investment strategy. My colleagues call this the "Norm on a bus" story—and roll their eyes. However, the events related here changed my life—and resulted in a major change in Terra's entire business model. I still tell this story because it was so important to the way I do business now.

In 1994, I departed for a conference for institutional investors in Phoenix offered by Schwab. This time I expected to get access to a whole new level of very smart people; I thought I would be able to transcend the retail business because Schwab was going to give us access to some famous brand names on the institutional level. The conference would also give me an opportunity to meet and talk with other advisers.

When I arrived in Phoenix, I started asking other advisers how they used the optimization programs. I explained how I had to rig the optimization and put constraints on it so I did not wind up with a portfolio that was proportionally overloaded in REITS. I was very surprised to learn how many advisers did not even attempt to use optimization or other analytics and said that they just came up with something for asset allocation—which was exactly the approach that I had tried to avoid when I started with the optimization software.

William Sharpe, Nobel Prize winner in 1990, discussed in Chapter 5 for his groundbreaking work with the capital asset pricing model (CAPM), was one of the speakers. I anticipated hearing important insights from him. He asked how many of us used optimization software. I proudly raised my hand, along with about half the audience. Then he said, "Have you ever noticed that if you change the expected return number by just a little bit, you get radically different results?" A light bulb exploded in my head! This was an epiphany. I realized I could not rely on pure optimization any more. In fact, I was already not relying on pure optimization because I had to constrain the program so as not to wind up with wacky results. This was despite the fact that the software technology had clearly gotten better since the first program I had used. It now could run 5,000 scenarios in three minutes. Yet the powerful software was flawed in this important way.

The exhibitors at this conference included some of the important institutional money managers not available to retail clients. As I talked to the many different exhibitors, each with a little toy or highlighter to give out, I thought I must have finally found the really smart people here.

Over in a lonely corner was a guy with no toys and no marketing material. When I asked him what he did, he answered something like, "I work for a company and we do a kind of complicated academic thing." Instead of marketing materials or toys, all he had was a prospectus.

Finding DFA

When the conference was over and I was on the shuttle bus taking me to the airport, I met a crotchety guy from Kalamazoo, Michigan, Jake Miller, who berated me for collecting toys and talking to the fancy managers. To my utter amazement, when he saw my prospectus from the company no one had ever heard of, Dimensional Fund Advisors (DFA), he explained that he was a fee-based adviser and had a large practice for a small town. I asked him why he used DFA.

He explained. "Look, I used to manage $4 billion in pension assets in the early 1980s. I have heard every one of these institutional guys you're looking at. And it's all the same garbage. You're going to wind up with the same results." During the 45-minute bus ride, he lectured me on his prior experience of trying to pick active managers; his story pretty much tied into mine except he had done it for about 30 years longer than I had.

I wound up attending one of the conferences DFA puts on for the advisers who use its funds. Like every other adviser attending that conference, I came in loaded with questions. The speakers and firm managers were all academics and the only thing that drove their answers and perceptions was data—but not 5 or 10 years of data. They believed you could not know anything about financial matters or the marketplace without at least 50 years of data, preferably more.

Finally I had found a financial firm that confirmed my own observations about the inevitable disappointment of active money managers. The DFA academics helped me understand why it is impossible to predict what the markets are going to do and impossible to figure out who the next Warren Buffett will be. Their belief in efficient markets fit perfectly with my frustration with the Really Smart Guys—who might be smart today but tomorrow would produce mediocre results. I had spent so many years and used so many different techniques to try to find the best managers for my clients, and the results were always the same.

DFA endorses the modern portfolio theory I discussed in Chapter 5, which says that, in the long run, active managers fail. We know that from the evidence. The theory tells us that active managers *have* to fail because markets are inherently efficient; by definition, an individual investor or money manager cannot have secret information or secret insight that will allow him or her to gain an advantage over the market. It means that stocks are always fairly priced. Of course there are exceptions and securities might occasionally be mispriced, but how do you identify those situations *consistently*? You can try to do it, but you will not succeed. It cannot be done consistently over time, so you might as well accept that for all practical purposes the markets really are efficient.

In addition to DFA's academic, theoretical approach to the markets, they also offered pure asset-class mutual funds that were not actively managed but were highly diversified collections of stocks that satisfied certain asset-class criteria. Each of their asset-class funds might own hundreds or thousands of separate stocks; each asset-class fund would hold all of the stocks that satisfied the screening criteria, which usually consisted of size and value/growth characteristics.

I came back to Terra and announced that I thought the people at DFA had revealed to me some important truths about the marketplace. We started using the DFA funds right away and we were certainly believers—but we were not yet 100 percent believers, nor were we sure if our marketplace was ready for 100 percent of the DFA theory. We wanted to build a model with a core of DFA funds but decided to include some of the no-load funds we had access to, with well-recognized managers with track records who could deliver value to our clients.

Living Through the Internet Bubble

We continued to develop this program and offer it to clients through our advisers. We worked on it through 1994, 1995, and 1996, but by then the technology sector of the stock market was starting to really take off. The idea of efficient markets became a tough sell because so many individuals believed that they themselves had discovered investment nirvana through the tech boom. Our program offered an extremely diversified approach using 13 asset classes. According to our investment philosophy, we continued to buy the small cap and value funds that were very much out of favor. Meanwhile the technology sector—one *sector* in one *asset class*—was going up 30 to 40 percent per year. Individuals thought they had outgrown the need for financial advisers and were busy trading their own accounts online.

Our clients told us they could do better than we could. During the years when the Internet bubble went up, our portfolios also went up, of course, but not as much as pure technology portfolios. Clients who were still invested with us (and not directly in the market through online trading) were screaming at us and at our accountant advisers to buy more technology stocks. At that point, the stocks comprising the S&P 500 Index included something like 30 to 40 percent technology, so we said that we were just not going to buy more than that. My worst month was January 2000, when it seemed that every time I looked around, someone was telling me that we were in a new paradigm where stocks did not need to show earnings or profitability—you were supposed to buy companies based on the dream that was inspiring the company's founders. But we stuck to our guns and our 13 asset classes, and I told people that I had believed in asset allocation and diversification for going on 15 years and could not wake up one morning with a different belief system.

Then the crash came and some people lost their life savings. Among my own clients were some I had begged to sell their Lucent and Cisco stock. They just would not do it—and they got devastated. A friend of mine had a 20-year-old son who had bought some technology stock for $2,000. It soared in value until it was worth $750,000. I sat with him to explain why he needed to sell it. I urged him to sell it; I begged him to sell some of it and put some of the proceeds into CDs. Imagine how much education that would have paid for! He did not take my advice, of course, and lost it all—lost it *all*. I could blame this particular example on the inexperience of youth, but Vegas syndrome is not limited to the young. It is not exactly simple greed; it has to do with starting to win and then feeling invincible about winning and determined to let it ride. Behavioral finance understands that most of us are not able to say, "This is enough. Let's take some of the winnings off the table." We get caught up in believing that what goes up will continue inexorably to go up more, and if we sell too early, we might miss that last bit of gain. This is how all those Las Vegas casinos are built.

Our portfolios held up well. Our tax professional advisers had been through hell during this time, dealing with their clients. Due to their accounting background—which was very different from the sales backgrounds that traditional brokers might have—many of them had found it difficult to meet client objections and stand their ground about the importance of asset allocation. Those years of the Internet bubble were a crazy time, but we were eventually redeemed. We learned an important lesson: By sticking to our guns we survived very well.

Giving Up on Active Managers

We learned another intriguing lesson as well. We found out that we were better off using only DFA funds on the equity side. The few active funds we still tried had the same style drift that had been causing us problems for years; nothing had changed. Active managers still invested outside their stated style when they thought it would give them higher performance, and it did not matter if the fund was a load or a no-load fund. We had thought there might be some possibility of finding great managers among the five-star funds, but now we just gave up. Trying to find the best active managers was not even our value proposition any more. There was no such thing as *best money managers*, and if we kept trying to find them, we would inevitably be disappointed. Instead, our value proposition to our clients had become: Let me find you a sustainable investment strategy for the long run.

That does not mean that I will hit a home run for you today. And while I freely admit that I cannot hit that home run, I do not think anyone else can hit it either, because it does not exist. I will help my clients manage their wealth but I cannot make them rich through investments alone. Finishing the race is more important than trying to win it. Trying to win usually leads to taking too many risks, while finishing means you achieved your goals and took less risk. Wealth is created through a long-time program of saving and managing risk.

My job as an adviser is to help my clients manage that wealth. If you are on the low side of wealth, I can help you accumulate and sustain it, but I am not going to make you 20 to 30 percent per year; I am not even going to try to do that. The problem for people who have not been able to save enough is that they are driven to take inordinate risk to make up for it.

So now we have the basics of our belief system. How can we design and implement an investment strategy using these ideas?

Figuring Out the Approach

So now you are intrigued and want to know how to implement this kind of strategy. There are no mutual funds out there called Fama/French. And you know by now that even if you were to find an active manager whose fund had *growth* or *value* in the title, that would not mean that the manager would actually stick to that kind of investing.

I return now to Dimensional Fund Advisors, the institutional investment company that has taken the Fama/French research and developed asset-class-specific mutual funds based on the three-factor model. Their funds are style-consistent and have extremely low internal costs and turnover. They are passively managed, meaning that if a security fits a certain asset class, it is included without regard to the opinion of any manager or the financial condition of the company. (DFA does run certain screens, and does not buy companies that are in bankruptcy or have certain other very negative characteristics.)

It is essential to realize that the asset-class mutual funds DFA constructs are not managed actively. Finally we get a break from active managers who think the mandate of their mutual fund is only a general guideline. Passive managers do not make selections based on an opinion about the worth of a stock; the only criterion is whether the security or stock has the characteristics of that particular asset class. This eliminates both the human factor and luck. Each one of their asset-class mutual funds will hold every security that fits the characteristics the mutual fund is constructed to deliver, which could be dozens or hundreds of securities. In other words, based on a stock's size and book value relative to price, it is placed in a certain asset class irrespective of hypothetical future earnings or anyone's ideas about its growth prospects. Since these managers and I both believe that performance is random, trying to pick which one is going to be this year's winner is impossible and investors should own all of them.

How do you get to these DFA funds? DFA is an institutional fund manager and does not sell directly to individuals because it does not want constant retail flows moving in and out of its mutual funds (and generating taxable events). As of the time I am writing this book, if you want to use these engineered asset-class mutual funds, you will have to work with a fee-based adviser who can help you construct an asset allocation strategy that is appropriate to your own circumstances. You can also probably get something close to a small-cap, value strategy using index funds or ETFs.

So now we have a strategy based on long-term results rather than on the track record of a hot manager. It provides a higher return than that of the overall market. If this is so great, why is it the best strategy you have never heard of? Because it is not in Wall Street's best interest to promote a low-cost strategy that makes their research irrelevant. Wall Street analysts and savants make hundreds of millions of dollars every year performing their research and sharing their opinions with investors, and this strategy says they are irrelevant.

Some investors may conclude that the best results may be achieved merely by buying index funds. Although buying index funds is far better for your wallet and your future than betting on an active manager, my strategy is *not* an indexing strategy. As defined in Chapter 5, indexes are constructed to serve as proxy benchmarks for a certain sector of the marketplace. Beyond that, they are used as benchmarks against which to measure the performance of an active manager; how can you tell how well an active manager has done unless you have a point of comparison? An asset class, by contrast, is a basket of securities that demonstrate and deliver the same risk and return characteristics. The kind of small and value asset class investing I recommend is designed to use pure, engineered asset-class mutual funds to capture the incremental return available through the small and value size and style factor tilt as described in the Fama-French three-factor model.

The Cost of Active Management

Throughout this book, I have been talking about *active management,* meaning a (high-priced) money manager actively buying and selling securities based on judgment, opinion, research, and stock analysis. *Passive management,* by contrast, is a buy-and-hold strategy that seeks to provide broad asset class or market exposure and market-consistent returns. It does not include or exclude a stock based on research, judgment, or opinion.

Now let us try to imagine that our active manager thinks he is such a good manager that he can not only make up the cost to pay him, along with all the hidden costs, but he can do better than that.

Ignorance may be bliss, but turning a blind eye to the expense of actively managed funds can be costly. Mutual funds have two costs that reduce their return. The *expense ratio* is the amount a fund takes out of its assets each year to cover its expenses. *Transaction costs* are not included in the expense ratio and are generated when a fund buys or sells a stock holding. Just like individual investors, active managers have to pay transaction costs to buy or sell a security, but they pay on a different kind of scale than a retail investor. Few active investors are aware that there are transaction costs for all the active trading that a manager does, but they are hidden very well within the investment results and not reported in a fund's prospectus; these hidden costs can create additional drag on performance, further lowering returns.

These costs are not reflected in the reported expense ratios. According to a study[1] by the Zero Alpha Group, which examined more than 5,000 domestic equity funds, these funds had average trading costs 43 percent as large as the disclosed annual expenses. In some instances, unreported trading costs exceeded the funds' annual expense ratios.

These hidden expenses can be difficult to track, as John Bogle suggests in his book *Bogle on Mutual Funds: New Perspectives for the Intelligent Investor* (Irwin Professional, 1994). The costs represent a combination of brokerage commissions and market impact costs. While brokerage commissions are reported to the Securities and Exchange Commission (SEC) and can be quantified, market impact—the effects on prices of buying and selling—is more difficult to measure. Stock purchases tend to push prices up, while sales drive prices down. Imagine the manager of a very large fund decides he wants to sell out all of his IBM stock one day. The first 1,000 or 10,000 shares he sells might be absorbed easily by the market, but what if he wants to sell 100,000 shares? What if the stock is not IBM but a stock that is small and thinly traded? In that case, the market might move after only 1,000 shares have hit the market.

The managers at DFA have a unique approach to trading. They are not trying to match the performance of an index, basis point to basis point. Rather, they are trading within overall guidelines. They trade patiently and wait for the market to come to them. Since they hold basically every viable security in the entire marketplace, if one security is not available at a given time, another one probably is. Furthermore, the more illiquid the market—meaning the markets in the small and value stocks favored by the strategy—the more important it is to trade quietly and not move the market as you execute your strategy. Having to execute all your trades on the same day as everyone else in the marketplace, which is what happens when an index fund has to follow a change in the index, is a good way to ensure you pay top dollar.

Mutual funds report their *turnover ratios*, which means the amount of their holdings that are bought and sold—or turned over—in a given period. The classic kind of very active manager who trades for momentum might have an annual turnover rate of 100 percent or 200 percent or more. That manager's trading expenses will be far higher than those for a more conservative buy-and-hold manager. The active manager has to have better luck with performance in that case because he has higher expenses to overcome.

To account for these factors, Bogle estimates that a trade costs, on average, 0.6 percent of the amount of the transaction. In order to determine the impact of trading on a fund, he suggests doubling the turnover ratio (to account for the purchase and then the sale), then multiplying that figure by 0.6 percent. So if the average actively managed large-cap-blend fund has an 82 percent turnover and the reported fund expense is 135 basis points, you add those together to get the total expense of 231 basis points (or 2.331 percentage points) to subtract from the yield.[2] The Bogle calculation methodology is useful but not precise, and provides only a rough rule of thumb. The more actively a fund trades, of course, the higher the trading

TABLE 6.1   Active Managers Generate Much Higher Transaction Fees, Including the Hidden Expenses

Fund	Turnover Ratio	Expense Ratio	Trading Cost, Bogle Calculation	Total Expense and Trading Cost
DFA U.S. Large Company	6%	0.15%*	0.07%	0.22%
DFA U.S. Large Value	19%	0.28%	0.23%	0.51%
Average passively managed (index) large-cap-blend funds	25%	0.59%	0.30%	0.89%
Average actively managed large-cap-blend funds†	82%	1.35%	0.98%	2.33%

*Pursuant to DFA's Fee Waiver and Expense Assumption Agreement, DFA has agreed to assume the U.S. Large Company Portfolio's direct and indirect expenses to the extent necessary to limit the expenses of the fund to 0.15 percent.
†Actively managed, large-cap-blend funds are defined as the universe of large-cap-blend funds excluding index funds.
Sources: John C. Bogle, *Bogle on Mutual Funds: New Perspectives for Intelligent Investors* (Irwin Professional Publishing, 1994), 204; Bogle methodology; data from Morningstar as of December 31, 2008; Dimensional Fund Advisors; and Genworth Financial Advisers Corp.

expense will be. Thus, actively managed funds generate far more transaction costs than passively managed funds, due to their higher turnover ratios. And all of this still does not account for any movement in the market that a large manager has caused by selling mostly at one time.

A passive or index strategy conducts far fewer trades and generates lower transaction costs, resulting in a lower cost strategy. However, a pure *index* mutual fund will follow set protocols requiring mandatory trades. As an example, an S&P 500 Index fund will need to buy and sell to maintain the identified 500 stocks. As Table 6.1 illustrates, the total average for the passively managed, large-cap-blend funds (0.89 percent) has almost four times the total expense of a similar DFA fund (0.22 percent) but is only about one-third of the cost of an active fund (2.33 percent). These fees can inflict a significant penalty on net investment returns and terminal wealth.

If you think these small amounts of 100 or 200 basis points are not important, think again. Over the longer run, these fees make a huge difference on net investment returns. They have a proportionately greater importance when investment returns are low. For example, if you are expecting a gross investment return of 4 percent and you pay fees of 2 percent, you have lost half of your return to fees. Table 6.2 illustrates the difference these fees would make over a 30-year period. Imagine you start with $1 million

TABLE 6.2   The Importance of Fees: Estimated
6.5 Percent Annualized Return over 30 Years on
$1 Million

1 percentage point fee	$ 4,983,951
2 percentage point fee	$ 3,745,318
3 percentage point fee	$ 2,806,794

Source: Dimensional Fund Advisors.

and achieve a gross investment return of 6.5 percent. These are the end
amounts you would have if fees of one, two, and three percentage points
are subtracted from your investment returns annually. Those small amounts
aggregate to a huge difference over the long term.

For better or worse, a good financial adviser will always remind you
what it costs to invest. High fees, hidden trading costs, and high turnover are
things you should generally avoid, but are oftentimes part of the package
with active management. This can create significant drag on the performance
of your investments. With passive management, based on the philosophy
that markets are efficient, you can avoid these significant cost disadvantages.

Implementing a Sustainable Investment Strategy

Working with DFA over the past dozen years has been a very valuable
experience for me. It continues to be on the forefront of academic research
and, as of this writing, is unique in its approach to engineering asset-class
mutual funds. But this strategy does not depend on DFA's existence alone;
it could be implemented using similar mutual funds or ETFs from someone
else. This is not the *DFA* strategy: It is a passive, massively diversified strategy designed to capture the extra returns from small and value stocks while
managing risk through the use of bonds and an appropriate asset allocation. DFA's uniqueness is its implementation of the Fama/French strategy.
Improving technology has made it increasingly easier for vendors of index
funds to offer more and more finely segregated collections of securities, so
perhaps one day some of the indexes will be more suitable than they are
right now for implementing this kind of strategy.

I believe that an adviser's most important job is to develop a sustainable,
transparent investment strategy that is going to last for the long term. That
also means no surprises, such as, "Oops, I have 10 percent of my portfolio
in AIG," or "I had no idea I was in a hedge fund at all, let alone one that
made a very bad bet and then I found out six months later that I could not
liquidate any of my holdings."

Random Asset Classes

Fama and French took their three-factor model and applied it beyond U.S. borders. Working with DFA, they kept engineering mutual funds to represent asset classes so that the advisers who used their mutual funds could devise whatever asset allocation they wanted. They also identified other asset classes with low correlations to mainstream U.S. equities, such as REITs, resulting in a very wide choice of asset classes.

Figure 6.1 portrays the main asset classes identified by DFA and listed year by year in order of performance for each year, with the highest performance on top and lowest on the bottom. There is a black line in most years that separates positive performance from negative performance. Using this figure and showing it to clients is central to my practice. I invite you to look closely at this figure—which I admit is more impressive to look at in color—and tell me where you see the pattern.

You can't see a pattern? Of course you can't. There is *no* pattern for asset class performance. That is the point of the efficient markets. That is why active management does not work.

As you look at Figure 6.1, reflect on the events of those years. Do you see any pattern for years with wars or floods or riots? Again, there is *no* pattern. A war may start during the year, but that could easily be good for the markets rather than negative. Even during times of great economic turmoil, many asset classes will have positive returns. Even during 2008, arguably the most difficult year economically since the Great Depression and with the second-worst return since 1931, at least three asset classes were positive. (Only two of them show in this chart because it includes only the most significant asset classes.) It is true that, during a crisis, some or many equity asset classes may turn negative, but which ones? For how long? This appears to be random. Asset allocation works.

Advantages of Using a Passive Strategy

A passive strategy has a number of important advantages:

1. Not paying a high-priced manager and other investment staff.
2. Very significantly reduced transactions costs—both for buying and selling and also moving the market.
3. Significantly reduced taxes.
4. No style drift.

I discuss each of these four in turn, both what it means and then how DFA further adds value.

The Randomness of

	1994	1995	1996	1997	1998	1999	2000
Highest Return	16.17	40.09	37.05	36.94	28.58	66.42	31.04
	14.77	37.58	22.96	33.75	23.11	33.01	8.96
	9.20	30.63	22.36	33.36	11.95	30.16	8.28
	3.38	26.66	19.97	25.79	10.24	28.41	7.33
	2.66	13.39	17.43	19.66	9.69	21.51	4.01
	2.48	12.71	10.23	7.27	8.41	21.04	-2.01
	1.32	12.24	7.67	7.12	7.75	6.99	-3.08
	-0.33	10.32	6.04	5.93	5.91	4.37	-6.40
	-0.63	7.92	5.49	0.39	-2.33	4.04	-9.10
	-0.79	3.96	4.54	-11.59	-10.04	3.55	-12.26
	-2.03	0.99	3.49	-14.55	-17.01	1.90	-12.26
Lowest Return	-7.31	-5.19	2.80	-15.12	-25.33	-2.58	-30.60

U.S. Large Cap   U.S. Small Cap   U.S. Real Estate

U.S. Large Cap Value   U.S. Small Cap Value   International Value

FIGURE 6.1   The Performance of Asset Classes Is Random

Source: Dimensional Fund Advisors.

NOT PAYING A MANAGER AND INVESTMENT STAFF   How many times have you read in the financial news about some money manager getting paid millions or (for certain hedge funds) a *billion* dollars for a year's work? Who do you think pays those fees? When you say that the mutual fund family pays those fees, that is in effect stating that the investors who pay the mutual fund fees are paying the salaries of those managers. Furthermore, for every mutual fund manager, there is a staff of well-paid research analysts using expensive, high-powered computers, software, and other research tools, all no doubt working out of attractive offices.

The low costs of passively managed mutual funds offset the cost of an adviser that you hire and pay yourself. When an adviser is employed by a mutual fund family or insurance company or other product provider, the

Returns Annual Return (%)

2001	2002	2003	2004	2005	2006	2007	2008
40.59	7.62	74.48	35.14	34.54	35.97	39.78	8.83
18.04	5.11	69.18	33.16	24.13	32.99	8.16	6.60
12.35	3.82	66.79	32.11	22.63	32.59	8.04	4.75
8.44	3.58	60.25	30.58	15.10	27.54	6.35	-37.00
7.28	3.39	57.81	27.33	13.82	26.32	6.31	-38.64
6.44	-2.85	56.26	25.95	9.70	21.87	6.24	-39.20
-2.37	-8.00	36.43	19.15	5.61	21.70	5.95	-42.54
-2.71	-11.72	36.18	17.74	4.91	17.08	5.49	-44.49
-6.48	-13.84	28.69	10.88	4.45	15.80	-2.61	-45.12
-11.89	-19.87	2.04	2.65	3.08	4.32	-12.24	-47.11
-15.41	-22.10	1.95	1.35	2.36	4.09	-17.55	-53.14
-16.75	-30.28	1.47	0.83	1.34	3.75	-18.38	-53.18

International Small Cap
International Small Cap Value
Emerging Markets
One Year U.S. Fixed
Five Year U.S. Goverment Fixed
Five Year Global Fixed

solution for every financial need will be the product the adviser represents. I believe that, for many investors, the best solution is having an independent adviser who is paid to be objective and sit on your side of the table. This is more valuable for you than buying highly rated mutual funds or stocks—which, as we have seen, is not a strategy for success. An adviser's fees might be around the same cost you would pay for some moderately priced, actively managed mutual funds, but having this adviser who reports only to you and uses a low-cost, passive strategy is the best formula for success. Furthermore, this SEC-regulated adviser is obliged by law to put your interests before his own (it is called *fiduciary responsibility*), while a registered representative is obligated only to follow the duty of suitability, which is a much lower standard of care.

TRANSACTION COSTS VERY SIGNIFICANTLY REDUCED Because DFA does not trade stocks actively, its turnover of stock is extremely low, particularly in comparison to an actively traded fund. It has low turnover even in comparison to an index fund, because index funds have to buy and sell securities when the underlying index makes changes to the securities it contains. This is the index reconstitution required to accurately track the index that the fund represents. This can result in sales and transactions that create unnecessary gains and costs. These are relatively small in some instances but can be larger in some others depending on the index being tracked and the volume of trade in the market.

DFA and other asset class strategies do not have to reconstitute at a particular point in time. This can lower costs enough to result in performance approximately two percentage points better each year. Refer back to Table 6.1 to see the actual results. This advantage comes from not trading actively and not having to track an index. In an active fund, these additional expenses are subtracted from net return and the investor does not get them. This alone accounts for the superior performance of many passive funds over many active funds. Imagine as an active manager you have to beat an index—and you start from a two-percentage-point disadvantage.

REDUCTION IN TAXES   There's more bad news for those investing in actively managed funds: taxes. Actively managed funds cost more in fees and transactions costs, and all those transactions generate taxes the investor has to pay. In general, the higher the turnover, the higher the tax consequences, because when an active fund sells securities that have gains in them, those gains get passed through to the mutual fund investors. When markets are surging, active mutual fund investors may not notice the impact of taxes on their returns. You get a tax statement from your mutual funds every year telling how much you have to report in long-term and short-term capital gains. These taxes can add pain to bad results. For example, in 2007, the markets were mostly up, and many mutual fund investors had to pay significant taxes on their investments—only to see the market tank in the early part of 2008. In April, mutual fund investors were paying capital gains taxes on mutual funds that were already worth far less. It is one thing to pay taxes on portfolios that have seen significant gains; it is another thing to pay taxes on portfolios that in the meantime have seen significant losses. Sometimes the volatility in markets over the course of a year means that, even by year-end, the investor has to pay taxes on accounts that have seen losses. Investors get confused and upset by this.

Taxes are owed only when the money manager has realized gains by selling. The less the manager trades, the lower the taxable events will be, which is another advantage of a buy-and-hold strategy. If an investor's wealth is to grow over time, all the activity generated by the investment manager has to create value above and beyond the transaction costs and the taxes the investor will owe, and the taxes owed on capital gains generated by the sale of a stock can represent a significant drag on a fund's performance and can substantially reduce an investor's potential returns over time. Hence, passively managed funds which by definition trade as little as possible will generally have fewer capital gains to distribute than funds with higher turnover rates.

Recognizing that some clients are tax-sensitive while others may have their investments largely in tax-deferred accounts (such as IRAs), DFA offers several tax-managed strategies that target market segments like value stocks and small-cap stocks. DFA's tax-managed portfolio strategies attempt to offset capital gains and losses. Equity portfolios generate dividends that traditional tax management typically ignores, even though taxes from dividends may be higher than taxes from capital gains. This is especially true among small-cap and value stocks that distribute more income than large-cap growth stocks. The challenge becomes reducing dividends without diluting exposure to the factors that drive returns. DFA's tax-managed strategies simultaneously attempt to minimize taxable gains and dividend yield, without sacrificing precise asset class exposure and solid, broad diversification. In summary, DFA creates asset classes to implement a client's portfolio to capture the benefits of not only the value and small-cap effect, but also to reduce trading and tax costs.

NO STYLE DRIFT   DFA funds have eliminated the style drift that gave me so much trouble over the years. Remember how much trouble I had executing an asset allocation strategy when a small-cap manager would decide he could do better for his investors if he also dabbled in large cap? DFA has rules about which securities belong in which asset classes, and you can be sure that a small-cap value fund is going to give small-cap value results, whether that is up or down.

But *passively managed* does not mean no changes ever. DFA has protocols for ensuring that each asset-class mutual fund remains true to what it is supposed to be, no matter what happens to the individual securities that comprise the asset class. When an individual security grows too large to be a small-cap stock or changes from being a growth stock to being a value stock, DFA will make an adjustment to the mutual fund. Passively managed means that the mutual funds own all the securities in the marketplace that fit the definition of the asset class, and the mutual fund is managed only so that it retains its asset class characteristics.

In contrast, in general, index funds are not necessarily supposed to represent a certain asset class, for one thing. Secondly, indexes usually reconstitute only once a year, which gives a long time for any particular security to change in size or style characteristics. By the time the reconstitution date comes around, an index may have drifted quite a bit from its characteristics at the preceding year's reconstitution date.

Finally I have a way to implement a pure asset allocation strategy with asset classes that retain their asset class characteristics through any market. I do expect that ongoing developments in technology may allow stated index funds and ETFs to be defined more and more tightly, thereby allowing an investor to implement an asset allocation strategy similar to DFA's without the DFA mutual funds.

Understanding Volatility

Before we talk about the essential role of bonds, I need to remind you about volatility one more time.

Investment Risk as Volatility

It is impossible to talk about performance without also considering risk. Traditional investment risk is thought of simply as your investments not doing well, and refers to both your entire portfolio and individual parts of your portfolio. I think that the most important lesson I have learned throughout the years is the same insight Markowitz had theoretically: Managing money and achieving return is all about managing risk.

We know that the academicians have come to define risk in terms of volatility; we do not really have any other way to talk about it. But of course the volatility we hate is the volatility going down. No one ever complains about volatility when the markets are going up.

The markets are volatile; the S&P 500 Index (or any equity index) goes down for as many months as it goes up. If you follow your investment every month, you can easily get discouraged. In fact, as I have pointed out, behavioral science studies have shown that following the volatile *monthly* performance of investments can lead investors either to invest too conservatively or to chase performance and trade too often. The performance of a single month is almost irrelevant; even a single year is less important than the long-term perspective of investing for retirement.

There are two essential truths about volatility:

1. Volatility, or market risk, is the reason that equities have return. The *volatility* of the equity markets represents the *risk* of the equity markets—and that risk is the reason equities have a higher long-term return than fixed-income securities.
2. Managing risk, rather than trying to eliminate it, can result in higher investor returns as well as a better investor experience.

To be able to manage risk, you have to be able to measure it. In Chapter 5, I summarized the history of the academic understanding of risk

TABLE 6.3 . Higher Volatility Increases Risk and Decreases Returns—Hypothetical Example

	Portfolio A		Portfolio B	
Year	Return	Total $	Return	Total $
1	18%	$118,000	8%	$108,000
2	35%	$159,300	8%	$116,640
3	21%	$192,753	8%	$125,971
4	−50%	$ 96,377	8%	$136,049
5	36%	$131,072	8%	$146,933
Average Return	12%*	5.6%†	8%*	8%†

*Straight average
†Average annual compound total return
Source: Forum Financial Management, LLC.

and risk measurement. Any discussion of market risk always starts with volatility—how often the security price goes up and down and how wide the swings are—and is expressed in terms of standard deviation, the statistical term we use to indicate volatility.

To summarize: Standard deviation is a relative measure of how much actual results varied from the average rate of return for a given historical time period. The larger the difference between the actual return of a security and its average return (or expected return), the higher the standard deviation will be. The larger the standard deviation, the greater the volatility, and the greater the risk of the market.

The completely hypothetical Table 6.3 shows how higher volatility can result in lower compound returns. Portfolio A shows highly volatile return percentages that come to a straight average of 12 percent while portfolio B's returns have a lower straight average of 8 percent. Yet the average annual compound total return is higher for portfolio B and the actual dollars in the portfolio are also higher because this portfolio did not experience losses that had to be made up before more profits could be generated.

In general, managing risk means giving up the hope of getting the highest market return and instead trying to get a sustainable return over the long term; this chart shows that lower volatility actually can result in higher returns. Lower volatility is most likely to result in higher returns when it results in less negative performance.

Investors may confuse volatility with loss, but they are not the same thing. If you sell your securities at the bottom of the market, you will certainly experience a loss, but volatility in a portfolio that is meant to be held for the long term is not the same as a loss. We all want to avoid losses but we *manage* volatility. Volatility may affect individual securities in a way that results in permanent loss in value, but widely diversified portfolios are subject only to market risk and not to the unsystematic risk of individual stocks, managers, and stock pickers.

Introducing Bonds

Bonds are an essential part of our portfolios. When used properly within a portfolio, they can reduce volatility and the degree of fluctuation in daily values, and provide downside protection when the stock market is in decline.

Investors often think of bonds as a safe investment without understanding that bonds do carry considerable risk. When not used properly, investors may receive unintended results.

There are two primary forms of risks inherent in bonds:

1. *Credit risk.* The risk that a bond issuer will default can be low but is, nevertheless, present. The level of risk for a particular bond is reflected in its rating (A, AA, etc.), but no rating system can encompass every possible eventuality for a given issuer.
2. *Interest-rate risk.* Interest rates affect bond prices; increases in interest rates cause the market value of existing bonds to decrease. The longer the bond has until maturity, the more a given change in interest rates will affect the current value of a bond. Furthermore, the longer the bond has until maturity, the more time is available for changes in marketplace interest rates to occur, thus also increasing the volatility.

When selecting bond investments, investors often focus more on overall yield rather than on the length of time until maturity. Longer-term bonds are more speculative than shorter-term bonds and often offer higher rates of return, thus leading some investors to purchase these instruments for their increased yield. More often than not, however, the additional return is minimal relative to the increased risk, due to interest-rate fluctuation over time. Investors are generally not fully compensated for the additional risk incurred.

In Table 6.4, the lowest returns are for those fixed-income securities with the shortest maturities—one-month T-bills in this example. Going from the shortest maturities to the longest (20-year government bonds), the rates of return grow quite evenly from just under 6 percent to more than 7.5 percent.

The third column is standard deviation, which by now we understand to be a way to measure risk. You can see that the break in the risk/return ratio comes between the one-year notes and the five-year notes, where the risk goes up dramatically: 5.46 percent is *three times* as much as 1.8 percent, and then 10.22 percent is almost double 5.46 percent. From the one-year

TABLE 6.4   Using Shorter-term Bonds Reduces Volatility and Risk, 1964–2008

Time Period	Annualized Compound Returns %	Annualized Standard Deviation (Risk) %
One-month T-bills	5.69	0.78
Six-month T-bills index	6.46	1.14
One-year notes index	6.66	1.80
Five-year T-notes	7.50	5.46
20-year government bonds	7.87	10.22

This table uses total return data, meaning that dividends and capital gains are reinvested.
Source: Dimensional Fund Advisors and Genworth Financial Advisers Corporation.

notes to the 20-year government bonds, you get an extra 121 basis points of return in exchange for approximately five times as much risk. That is why our portfolios stick with fixed-income securities that are no more than one or two years in term.

Tying up funds in longer-term maturities does not have a significant impact upon increasing returns; it does, however, substantially increase the risks. Yet investors consistently purchase bonds having 10- to 20-year maturities. There appear to be two reasons for this:

1. Investors fight for yield; normally, this means buying longer-maturity and/or lower-quality bonds.
2. Brokers make far more money selling longer-maturity bonds (this is due to the basic mathematics of bonds, which is beyond the scope of this short section).

Many investors would argue that the second reason would not apply to them since there was no commission listed when a given bond was purchased. Again, there are only two likely reasons for this:

1. The broker is willing to work for free (remember what you know about those who work on Wall Street).
2. The commission was hidden.

As there appear to be few individuals willing to work for free—on Wall Street or otherwise—it is safe to assume that the second explanation is more likely. How?

Many times, brokers will sell bonds out of the brokerage house's inventory and mark the bond up (raise the price) so the commission is not obvious. Of course this reduces the yield over the entire term of the investment. The largest markups occur on the longest-maturing bonds, again due to the basic math of bonds. Also, a brokerage house will often buy bonds in large blocks at *discounted* rates, which then add to the profits when the bonds are sold on the market at nondiscounted rates.

Some Concerns about Investing in Bonds

Following is a list of concerns about investing in bonds.

- *Avoiding credit risk*. Bonds come in all flavors and can be quite complex. We believe in avoiding credit risk. Remember, today's AAA credit can be tomorrow's Enron. It is easy to avoid credit risk altogether: Buy U.S. government securities (also called Treasury securities) or insured municipal bonds and notes. Buying relatively short-term, highly rated bonds also helps reduce credit exposure.
- *Keeping your bond strategy safe*. In the opinion of many qualified investment advisers, the bond portion of the portfolio is the safe portion of the portfolio. It should avoid strategies that attempt to predict interest rates or increase yield by extending maturity.
- *Uncertain pricing*. Investors who purchase longer-term bonds from brokers and then later wish the maturities were shorter may find themselves worse off financially than if they had chosen shorter instruments in the first place. Shortening maturities requires selling the bonds prior to maturity. Investors have to rely on their brokerage statement to provide them with an estimate of what the bonds are worth. Unfortunately, with the exception of Treasuries, the prices listed on brokerage statements are only estimates. Furthermore, what you earn on a bond is not the quoted yield; it is a factor of what you paid for a bond. Thus, when an investor does liquidate, he may find the bonds worth 5 percent less than the estimate, or worse. Consider what it would be like to take a loss of $5,000 on a portfolio of $100,000 when you expected full value. It would have been a better investment to have bought a shorter maturity in the first place, at a slightly lower yield, than to end up with a possible overall loss.
- *Foolhardy predictions*. The market in Treasury bills, notes, and bonds is enormous: larger than the daily trading volume of the New York Stock Exchange. The Federal Reserve controls only short-term interest rates. This means that although Fed policies and market actions can have an effect on long bond rates, the market is really what controls interest rates. Attempting to predict the long-term direction of interest rates is as difficult—and as fruitless—as predicting the direction of the stock market.

- *Use of bonds within portfolios.* The role of bonds in a portfolio is to stabilize value; it is the safety portion of the portfolio. The goal is to use bonds to minimize credit risk for the bond portion of the portfolio. In the strategy I use in my practice, for the most part I use select mutual funds for the fixed-income portion of the portfolio, and the diversification provided by the mutual fund helps minimize credit risk. If I use individual bonds, I buy only bills, notes, and bonds issued by the U.S. government or insured municipal bonds (the insurance on the bond eliminates the credit risk). The program minimizes interest-rate risk by buying maturities of five years or less. Finally, I never act in the role of broker when buying municipal bonds.

Building the Portfolio: Overweighting in Value and Small Companies Improves Performance

In Chapter 5, I defined index funds and mentioned that they were an improvement over the old style of active management. But index funds are not the final choice: I explained the Fama/French three-factor model, which says that tilting a portfolio towards small and value companies can provide an extra two to three percentage points of return over time.

There is a caveat to this, which is that markets are unpredictable, volatile, and random. That means that you can never predict in which years you are going to surpass the index returns and in which years your DFA portfolio will underperform. All you know is that this has worked over the long term, which we define as the 83 years of data that the academics use. In years like 2008, where all markets seem to be perfectly correlated in their descent, it may be hard to keep in mind the strong theoretical basis of this strategy. Even so, it has worked over time and I, along with the DFA people and my colleagues at the Forum and a whole lot of other people who also use this strategy, believe that it will work. We have a way of portraying graphically the kind of portfolio I recommend, although some people may find the presentation to be quite technical.

Figure 6.2 divides the entire universe of U.S. domestic stocks into four quadrants based on company size (from smaller cap to larger cap) and style (from value to growth). You can see the location of the S&P 500 Index at the bottom of the figure. It consists of stocks that are mostly growth stocks with the largest capitalization in the marketplace. Since the Wilshire 5000 represents the market as a whole, it sits on the intersection of small and large, value and growth. To achieve a higher rate of return, the portfolio has to contain more value stocks and more small stocks than either the S&P

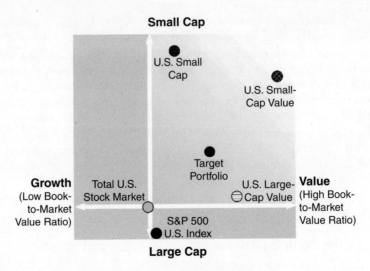

FIGURE 6.2 Comparing Target Portfolios to the Marketplace

Source: Dimensional Fund Advisors and Genworth Financial Advisers Corp.

500 Index or the market as a whole. I believe this provides investors with a risk/reward advantage over the long term.

This requires investing in a way that is the antithesis of what financial publications and other advisers have led you to believe; you need to tilt your portfolio away from blue-chip companies and toward—meaning buy proportionately more—smaller, value-oriented companies. Do you still need large, well-run companies in your portfolio? Absolutely, but not to the exclusion of these other asset classes.

Using the Fama/French strategy and investing disproportionately in small and value stocks can increase the expected return of your portfolio by two to three percentage points over the return of the nominal market (which we call *beta*). For the investor, this will provide a significant increase in the ultimate value of the portfolio—and is something few active managers have ever achieved.

Building Portfolios

Table 6.5 shows two portfolios that use these strategies. Our convention is to list the amount of equity in the portfolio first, so an 80/20 portfolio is 80 percent equity, but spread over 11 different asset classes, with fixed-income represented by two asset classes. The portfolio in the second column is half equity and half bonds.

TABLE 6.5   Some Sample Portfolios

	80/20	50/50
Short-term fixed-income (Barclays Capital Treasury Bond Index 1-5 years)	5.00%	12.50%
Inflation-protected fixed-income (Barclays Capital US TIPS Index)	5.00%	12.50%
Emerging markets (DFA Equally Weighted Emerging Markets Index)	7.20%	4.50%
International value (Dimensional International Adjusted Market Index)	14.40%	9.00%
Dimensional International Small-Cap Value Index	7.20%	4.50%
Marketwide index with small and value tilt (Dimensional U.S. Adjusted Market 2 ex-Micro Index)	18.40%	11.50%
Small-cap blend (Dimensional U.S. Small Cap Index)	3.20%	2.00%
Small-cap value (Dimensional U.S. Targeted Value Index)	7.20%	4.50%
Dow Jones Wilshire REIT Index	8.00%	5.00%
Global bonds (Global Government Bond Composite Index, hedged Citigroup)	5.00%	12.50%
Merrill Lynch One-Year U.S. Treasury Note Index	5.00%	12.50%
International equities (MSCI EAFE Index gross div.)	7.20%	4.50%
Large-cap blend (S&P 500 Index)	7.20%	4.50%
Total	100.00%	100.00%

Source: Dimensional Fund Advisors and Forum Financial Management, LLC.

Now I want to look at the portfolio's performance over the past 38 years. We start in 1970 just as a convenient starting place, and end in October 2008. Sometimes you are restricted in what you can show in the way of historical performance by the inception date of the indexes you are using.

Table 6.6 represents the heart of my investment philosophy. You can see that the return of both the portfolios I built, the global neutral 80/20 and the global neutral 50/50, have a higher return than the S&P 500, which is so often considered to be the nirvana of the marketplace and is certainly 100 percent equities. My portfolios have 20 or 50 percent lower-yielding but less-volatile bonds, and performed better. The growth of a dollar means that if I had started with $1 in my portfolio in 1970, this is how much I would have on October 31, 2008. This is more often seen in terms of hundreds or thousands of dollars. If I had started with $10,000 in 1970, in 39 years I would have $635,200.

The most essential part of this essential table is the annualized standard deviation, which represents risk. I got this higher return with significantly less risk! Compare the standard deviation of the S&P 500 at 15.41 and then

TABLE 6.6   Comparison of Risk and Return in Sample Portfolios

	Annualized Return %	Growth of Dollar ($)	Annualized Standard Deviation (%)
Global Neutral 80/20	11.28	63.52	11.62
S&P 500 Index	9.69	36.24	15.41
Global Neutral 50/50	10.00	40.50	7.48

Source: Dimensional Fund Advisors and Forum Financial Management, LLC.

look at the 11.62 for the 80/20 portfolio and 7.48 for the 50/50 portfolio. For the 80/20 portfolio, my return was approximately 16 percent higher but my risk was 30 percent less. And for the 50/50 portfolio, the return was a little higher but the risk was about half! This is statistically a significant factor.

It is important to remember this is not the track record of a stock picker—it is what a passively managed asset class did historically. This strategy does not depend on a stock picker repeating his historical feats of magic. *This is what makes it significant.* Can and will you lose money at any point in time? Yes, absolutely. But it will not be caused by the failings of a bad manager. It has much more to do with the asset classes you use and how they are allocated. This is a much more manageable process that is based on the performance of 12 to 14 asset classes that are managed passively along with the effect of the tilt towards small cap and value in the portfolio.

Table 6.7 demonstrates once again how important it is to take the long-term view. The one-year numbers can be huge, but they even out over the longer term. The worst thing you can do as an investor is to focus on the short-term volatility, because it will keep you from being able to take the long-term view.

Rebalancing

A diversified investment strategy is further enhanced by implementing a disciplined rebalancing strategy. This risk management technique helps us follow the first rule of investing: Buy low and sell high. Rebalancing will realign a portfolio back to its original allocation when a stronger- or weaker-performing class has exceeded or become underweighted from its original percentage. As an example, let's suggest a 10 percent allocation to small-cap value has grown to 15 percent due to that asset class's positive performance. The rebalancing strategy will sell off the gains to rebalance back to the stated 10 percent and use the sale proceeds to purchase shares in an underper-forming or underweighted asset class. This will bring the portfolio back to

TABLE 6.7 Best and Worst Portfolio Returns, 1970–2008

		1 Year	5 Years	10 Years	20 Years
Global Neutral 80/20	Average annualized return	13.4	13.2	13.7	14.1
	Best return	50.0	30.1	21.6	17.2
	Worst return	−35.6	0.3	6.2	8.6
S&P 500 Index	Average annualized return	12.3	11.8	13.0	13.6
	Best return	61.0	29.7	19.5	18.3
	Worst return	−38.9	−3.8	0.4	8.8
Global Neutral 50/50	Average annualized return	11.2	11.3	11.7	12.0
	Best return	34.9	22.9	17.3	14.1
	Worst return	−22.4	3.0	6.0	7.9

Source: Dimensional Fund Advisors and Forum Financial Management, LLC.

its original asset allocation target, which was determined by the investor's risk tolerance.

Because the asset classes that have done well will be overweighted in the portfolio and the asset classes that have not done well will be underweighted, rebalancing forces us to behave like contrarians in every market, buying what is out of favor. We know that investors in general are very emotional. Investors are always trying to sell their investments at lows and buy more investments at highs. Processes like systematic rebalancing help us overcome our tendency toward emotional decision-making, and can serve the interests of our portfolio for the long run. Protecting our clients from that behavior is part of our value proposition.

Rebalancing means selling your winners to buy the stocks that have decreased in price. Rebalancing can actually also help reduce your portfolio's volatility. Table 6.8 shows the performance of two hypothetical portfolios with an allocation of 50 percent stocks and 50 percent bonds over the past 20 years. Portfolio A has never been rebalanced. Portfolio B shows what would potentially happen if the portfolio were rebalanced annually. The table gives the average annual total return and the maximum 12-month loss for each portfolio.

While the returns for both portfolios over the 20-year period were similar, the volatility was significantly different. The nonrebalanced portfolio experienced a loss of 25.62 percent over one 12-month period—almost

TABLE 6.8   Effects of Rebalancing

	With Rebalancing	Without Rebalancing
Average annual return	8.42	7.96
Maximum 12-month loss	−18.52	−25.62

As of December 31, 2008. For illustrative purposes only. The example is based on a hypothetical portfolio consisting of 50 percent S&P 500 Index and 50 percent Barclays Capital Aggregate Bond Index. The portfolio was rebalanced annually every December 31 during the 20-year period.
Maximum loss is based on any rolling 12-month period during the 20-year period.
Source: Dimensional Fund Advisors and Genworth Financial Advisers Corp.

800 basis points more than the 18.52 percent largest 12-month loss of the portfolio that was rebalanced annually. Rebalancing can potentially help to insulate portfolios from steep declines, making it easier for investors to stick with their investment plan over time.

Rebalancing is important but emotionally it is very hard to do in a bear market. It does reduce the value of a portfolio when you take money out of the bonds, viewed as the safe assets, and put it into stock asset classes that are falling. This is not easy psychologically speaking. But the practice of rebalancing is ultimately based on your belief that markets and asset classes do go up in value (not necessarily individual stocks).

It is true that buying and selling for rebalancing creates taxable events for taxable portfolios, but I believe the beneficial effect of rebalancing on a portfolio far outweighs the taxes that may be incurred. Those taxes affect only taxable portfolios, of course, not portfolios that are tax qualified (such as IRAs).

Table 6.9 is an example of how it would actually work with a portfolio. Let's assume that you have a $1,000,000 portfolio that you have divided

TABLE 6.9   Hypothetical Results of Rebalancing

	Asset Class 1	Asset Class 2	Asset Class 3	Asset Class 4	Total $
Beginning investment	$250,000	$250,000	$250,000	$250,000	$1,000,000
Return (%)	20%	−10%	5%	5%	
Return ($)	$ 50,000	($ 25,000)	$ 12,500	$ 12,500	$ 50,000
New value	$300,000	$225,000	$262,500	$262,500	$1,050,000

Source: Forum Financial Management, LLC.

equally into four asset classes that have low correlations with each other. Our goal in this case is risk reduction. These asset classes have been chosen with the idea that they are noncorrelated and when one goes down, another will go up. For this strategy to work, it is essential that the respective balances of the various classes be maintained at the initially selected ratios (in this example, each class is 25 percent of the total).

Now, of the four asset classes you've selected, let's assume the following: Asset class 1 grows by 20 percent, asset class 2 declines by 10 percent, while asset classes 3 and 4 grow by 5 percent each. (See Table 6.9.)

At the conclusion of the investment period depicted, the allocations have become unbalanced: Asset class 1, by virtue of its return, has become heavier than the others. In this simple illustration, $37,500 of asset class 1 will need to be sold off and invested in asset class 2 in order to balance all the classes at $262,500. For most investors, however, this creates a dilemma; why sell off a winner? There are two reasons:

1. Because of the randomness and unpredictable nature of asset class returns, today's winners are very likely be tomorrow's underperformers, as we saw in Figure 6.1.
2. Avoiding risk is more important to the long-term growth of the portfolio than trying to get the highest possible short-term returns.

Counterintuitive as it may seem, studies indicate that the discipline of selling off winners in order to rebalance your allocations can reduce portfolio volatility significantly. This is reaffirmed by the Table 6.8, which indicates a 30 percent difference between the maximum 12-month losses of this hypothetical example.

The only dilemma in implementing rebalancing is that I have never met a client who will unemotionally do this on her own. Why? We all want to buy more winners and not losers. We cannot help ourselves. We are unable to set our emotions aside and do what we intellectually know is correct when it comes to money.

Use of Risk Tolerance and Its Impact on a Sustainable Strategy

Everyone handles risk and adversity differently. Understanding one's own risk tolerance is critical in developing a sustainable investment strategy. Studies have shown that individuals believe they have a higher risk tolerance than they do, as is evidenced by the number of people who just want out after an extremely bad market. I remember these people from the collapse of the tech bubble, just as I saw them in my office in 2008.

Many investors discovered the hard way in 2008 that their stomach for risk was not what they thought it was, now that worst-case scenarios were not hypothetical any more. The disparity between what people think they can tolerate and what they *can* tolerate can cause significant problems in designing a portfolio. What happens if your need for a certain growth rate is inconsistent with your ability to tolerate risk?

If, for example, you need an 8 percent expected return to meet your goals, but your risk tolerance indicates you should have a portfolio that results in only a 6 percent expected return, you have a problem. The dilemma is that if you implement the more aggressive portfolio, it may not be sustainable; you will be tempted to bail out following a downturn. Conversely, if you implement the more conservative portfolio, it will probably not meet your goals. The resolution of such conflicts requires you to work with an adviser. Most advisers will use a risk-tolerance questionnaire and will incorporate some generally utilized guidelines.

Time horizon is one of the key guidelines in deciding how to allocate your investments. The more time you have before you need access to your funds, the more (in theory) you can allocate to equities versus bonds. In other words, if you won't need the money shortly, you can accept greater risk, as—if it declines—you have more time during which it can recover. The first step in allocating your portfolio, therefore, is determining what percentage to allocate to equities. A simple formula is the following:

$$100 - \text{your age} = \text{percent allocable to equities}$$

Using this formula, if you are age 35, you would allocate 65 percent to equities (100 – 35 = 65 percent). While this is only a very simple formula, it is a very good guideline.

Even people who are close to reaching their financial goals can make emotional mistakes that upend the financial security they thought they had. People in this situation often fall into one of two opposing camps. One group wants to aggressively commit a large allocation to equities simply because—irrespective of having reached their financial goals—they believe the race is never over. Unfortunately, this does not make a lot of sense since they are taking a risk that they do not need. To illustrate this point, many retirees overallocated to equities in the 1990s and lost good portions of their nest eggs.

The other group says they do not have to take any more market risk and instead want everything invested in bonds or CDs. Unfortunately, they do not take into account risks from taxes and inflation. In the past 50 years, CDs and T-bills have rarely provided positive after-tax and after-inflation returns.

A simple example illustrates this point: The 41-year average rate of inflation is 4.6 percent (I am taking this set of calculations from my financial planning software; there is more on this topic in Chapter 7). Assuming short-term bonds or CDs earn 4.5 percent and the tax rate is 33 percent, the after-tax return is 3 percent. After inflation, the rate of return is −1.6 percent (subtract the inflation rate from the after-tax return), a *negative* 1.6 percent. By the time the tax man and inflation have taken their cuts, your return is negative. Few individuals can afford to have a portfolio that is 100 percent bonds or fixed-income because—in real terms—they are losing money every year. In addition to income taxes, inflation is like an annual tax on purchasing power that you have to pay every year.

The issues involved in determining bond-versus-equity ratios for a given portfolio are complicated; they involve not only analytics, but emotions as well. If these are not in balance, it is unlikely your investment strategy will be sustainable. If we define risk as volatility, we need to understand how it affects the ultimate value of your portfolio—and then how that affects your emotions.

Your risk tolerance also depends on other factors in your life. If you are an entrepreneur starting a business, your risk tolerance for your investments will be lower than it might be later in life, when you are well established. There may be a point in your life when you are feeling well established, when you can take on more investment risk. There are a myriad of factors that can affect your tolerance for risk, and it does not remain the same throughout your lifetime. At the end of 2008's difficult markets, many people wanted to lower their risk profile—although, ironically, as a bear market works its way through the economy, great opportunities for growth may be available.

A psychologist administering a test to measure psychometric values would use the term *risk tolerance* differently from the way I use it. From a purely psychological point of view, risk tolerance is one's true ability to handle risk and losses. As a planner, this needs to be countered with the practical implementation required to get a person to meet his financial goals.

Living through Bear Markets

On the one hand, market risk—systematic risk—is inescapable. On the other hand, there would be no markets at all without it. Market risk is what powers market return. The 2007–2009 markets left all investors in pain, so market risk looks like pure bear market to us. When the markets start up again, we forget these times. Then we get another bull market and forget that the markets were ever down.

I love to quote the picturesque terminology of market sage Nick Murray, who says that bear markets are as common as dirt[3] and happen far more often than we think. We just act like human beings and block them out once they are over. We live in the continuing hope that the last bear market will really be just that, the last. As always, in recent years we have forgotten that. We were shocked by the arrival of the vicious bear market at the end of 2007, for many of the reasons we discussed in Chapter 3. As investors, we tend to overextrapolate the recent past. As people, we tend to overweight our most recent experiences, and the past tends to become happier in retrospect.

In 2003–2006, all asset classes turned in positive performance for the year. Even 2007 saw positive performance for most asset classes, so your overall investment return might have seemed reasonable to you, depending on how you were invested. The nasty negative returns following the demise of the tech bubble, in 2000–2002, probably seemed a long time past by then, and the patina of the past was already starting to make them less troublesome in retrospect.

In those same four years, 2003–2007, we also became accustomed to levels of market volatility that were much lower than normal, so we forgot about the other kinds of markets. This recession is the worst since the Great Depression. Most of us were not here during the Depression, so it is the worst we have experienced in our lifetimes. Where can you go and what can you do when every asset class (except very short fixed-income securities, some of them yielding approximately zero) and every sector of the marketplace is down? And down by double digits; down by percentages that seriously erode wealth and are causing large sectors of the population to rethink their retirement strategy.

Every day I faced levels of emotion and stress that I had never seen before. For younger clients, I—along with most market professionals—believe there will be a strong recovery. The problem is the timing. How often do you think there is a bear market in the United States? Would you guess once a decade? Once every 15 years? Once there is a bear market, how long do you think it lasts, on average?

The answers surprise everyone. Since 1900, there has been a bear market, defined as 20 percent loss or more, every three years—every *three* years! There have been 31 such declines since 1900.[4] How long does a bear market last? The average duration of a bear market is 367 days—a whole year. To repeat: *Based on more than one hundred years of data, we might expect to see a significant bear market every three years.* Our last bear market ended in 2003. From the historical perspective of a long-term market average, a bear market in 2008 might be seen as overdue.

The real problem with much of the data on bear markets is the fact that the focus tends to be on the S&P 500 Index, which represents only one asset class out of at least 14. A typical portfolio using the asset allocation I recommend and executed using DFA mutual funds will hold on average

10,000 different stocks in 40 countries. Figure 6.1 shows how random the performance of asset classes is. So when we talk about a recovery, we do not need the S&P 500 to recover; we need any 5, 6, or 7 asset classes out of 14 to recover. Once a crisis stabilizes, the low or negative correlation among the asset classes will be reestablished.

Where Do We Go from Here?

Although the triggering events this time are different from the events and circumstances that have triggered downturns in the past, the economy has absorbed the various blows and restabilized each time. Despite the astonishing events of the past year, we do not believe that the underlying fundamentals of our overall economic system have changed. We expect to continue to see the economy move through cycles, typically triggered by significant economic or financial factors.

When times are bleakest—as they often seemed this past year—it may appear that moving to a 100 percent cash position is the safest course of action. But we believe that, over the long run, cash is not and cannot be the solution. For an investor with a longer time horizon, we believe the best way to meet your goals is to stay invested in the equity markets. Table 6.10 helps illustrate why.

If you divide the market into only the three most basic asset classes—cash, bonds, and stocks—cash has been the best investment in only 6 out of 73 rolling 10-year periods in 82 years, while bonds were the best in 9 of those periods and stocks were the best in 58 out of 73 times. Furthermore, cash was the best only during the period 1970–1982, which was an unusual, unprecedented, and so far unrepeated period of extremely high interest rates.

Table 6.10 shows every decline in the S&P 500 Index greater than 20 percent from 1950 through 2008. History demonstrates that swift market recoveries can make sitting on cash a costly move.

While each individual investor's situation is different, we believe that the best course of action for most investors is to stay invested in a broadly diversified portfolio designed for their specific investment objectives.

Living with the Equity Premium

The premise of this book is that capitalism works, and as long as that is the case, there will be a risk premium for equities. If you want to get a return higher than that of inflation and taxes, then you have to invest in something

TABLE 6.10 Performance Returns for Bull and Bear Markets

Bear and Bull Markets for the S&P 500 Index; Period of Bear Market	Peak to Trough Market Decline %	First Year after Decline %	Second Year after Decline %	Cumulative Effect Two Years after Decline %
July 1957–Oct. 1957	−21	31	10	44
Dec. 1961–June 1962	−28	33	17	56
Feb. 1966–Oct. 1966	−22	33	7	42
Nov. 1968–May 1970	−36	44	11	60
Jan. 1973–Oct. 1974	−48	38	21	67
Nov. 1980–Aug. 1982	−27	58	2	61
Aug. 1987–Dec. 1987	−34	21	21	56
July 1990–Oct. 1990	−20	29	6	37
March 2000–Oct. 2002	−49	34	8	43
Average	−32	36	12	54

Source: Forum Financial Management, LLC.

other than bonds, because, over the long term, the highest return you will get from bonds, in a good year, is approximately the inflation rate.

Go back to the simple example about fixed-income yields, taxes and inflation that I gave several pages ago in the section, "Use of Risk Tolerance." When I invest in CDs or other fixed-income securities, my return after inflation and after taxes is a *negative* 1.6 percent. I lose money every year! How can you create wealth without obtaining a return greater than inflation and taxes? In other words, to create wealth, the portfolio has to have risk in the form of the equity premium.

Ask an academic about the expected return of the market: What is the long-term performance of equities? Calculations for the equity premium say that it is about 6.5 percentage points more than the yield on Treasury notes. If you believe that Treasuries have a long-term yield of about 4 percent, and you add the 6.5 percentage points for the equity premium, then you can expect the long-term performance of the stock market to be about 11 percent (rounding up). My job as a financial adviser and wealth manager has always been to persuade clients to stay invested in equities for the long term. That job was as difficult as it has ever been during the first three months of 2009, when the declines of the bear market meant that the S&P 500 Index showed a negative return for the previous 10 years. At that point, I just wanted to be able to assure my battered clients that the markets would not go down any more (I couldn't, unfortunately).

If you believe markets are efficient, then even 11 percent is not that easy to get. (In fact, 11 percent seems to me now like a remarkably high return.) It might require you to put all of your money into the stock market, and most prudent investors do not want to be 100 percent invested in the stock market. A much more prudent investment might be 50 percent bonds and 50 percent stocks, which gives you an expected return of around 7.5 to 8 percent. This should put into perspective any money manager who claims he can make you 20 to 30 percent per year. It does seem to be possible over a short term. I could tell you stories about the clients who have bragged to me that they have gotten their 20 to 30 percent for a while. But in the longer run, they are always disappointed because getting that kind of outsized return requires taking an outsized risk. If someone is going to give you a 30 percent return, there is also a reasonable chance you could lose 30 percent.

The fact is that markets work. They are like sausage—we like the result, we just don't like to watch how it is made. Living with risk is difficult; living without it is impossible. We need to manage risk and our expectations. Markets do not fail us; it is our expectations that cause us to fail. We see the neat linear graph that tells us we will have a certain amount of money in so many years, but that prediction inevitably fails to occur and then we conclude that the markets have failed.

While this book has been full of statistics about specific securities and asset classes, figuring out how to deploy those statistics is more of an art than a science. You have to take a step back and take a very broad look at your own life in the context of the whole marketplace—and look forward, not backward. It is not easy to present the story of how equities outperform the other asset classes over time, after inflation and after taxes, but that is the single most essential part of the entire story. In the long run, only equities protect you against inflation even after taxes. It is one thing to take a simple rule of thumb and subtract 33 percent as a tax rate; it is another thing to tackle that project knowing that twentieth-century tax rates in the United States ranged from 1 percent in 1913 to a marginal rate above 90 percent in 1944–1945 and 1951–1953.

The award-winning Jeremy Siegel, professor of finance at the Wharton School of the University of Pennsylvania, has been writing and lecturing about the economy and financial markets for almost 40 years. In his book, *Stocks for the Long Run*, he reports on his in-depth research on tax rates and the financial markets. He says that an investor in the top tax bracket who started with $1,000 in Treasury bills at the beginning of 1946 would by now have *lost* 86 percent of his purchasing power, ending up with $138 after taxes and after inflation. However,

> ... *a highest-bracket investor would have turned $1,000 into over $5,719 by buying stocks, a 470 percent increase in purchase power.... For someone in the highest tax bracket, short-term Treasury bills have yielded a negative after-tax real return since 1871, even lower if state and local taxes are taken into account. In contrast, top-bracket taxable investors would have increased their purchasing power in stocks 269-fold over the same period.*[5]

Finally, the smart guys at DFA have produced a chart for me that shows how equities, as represented by the S&P 500, have outperformed U.S. long-term government bonds and one-month Treasury bills over the past 83 years after taxes and after inflation. I have to provide the qualification that producing a chart like Figure 6.3 requires certain simplifying assumptions because tax rates have changed so much over time. Furthermore, equities are typically held for the longer term and therefore might not be sold and taxed, and different classes of securities are taxed at different rates (dividends are taxed differently than long-term capital gains, for example). However, even after trying to be conservative about making these assumptions, the result is clear: Over the long term, it is equities that provide growth even after taxes and inflation are taken into account.

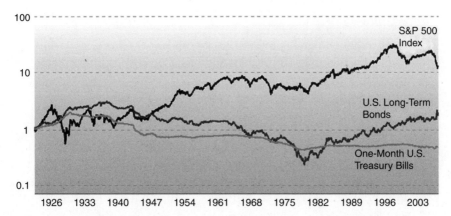

FIGURE 6.3 Performance of the S&P 500 Compared to That of Fixed-Income Securities, Taking into Account Taxes and Inflation, 1926–2008

Source: Dimensional Fund Advisors.

Letter to My Clients

I originally wrote this after the third quarter of 2008. The emotion of recent market events made me want to write bluntly, but regulatory oversight requires me to communicate with my clients in a way that is fair and balanced. For example, as an adviser, I am not allowed to point to the bad results of other investments because that is considered "cherry-picking," picking out the worst examples in the marketplace to make me look better. There would have to be lots of disclosure and evidence to balance assertions and statements. I was able to incorporate some of the spirit of this into the third-quarter newsletter that I sent out, but you had to read between the lines to understand exactly what I meant.

After the markets got the news about Bernie Madoff and his $50 billion fraud, I wanted to add another paragraph and reissue the whole letter—which I still could not do in exactly the language I wanted to use. The Bernie Madoff fraud raised a dozen issues about many aspects of regulation and compliance, but the worst was the harm Bernie Madoff did to the clients whose life savings he lost. In my mind, however, there is one particular issue that stands out above all: the number of investors who came to the Madoff funds through feeder advisers and funds and never had any idea that their money ultimately ended

(continued)

(Continued)

up with Madoff. So imagine how shocked they would be if they said to themselves, well, at least our funds are with X, and not with the Madoff funds—only to discover that their money *was* in the Madoff funds and was now missing. So I added one more item to my list.

What I Didn't Do for You

I knew that would get your attention. Many times advisers tell you all the things they have done on your behalf to protect and manage your wealth. When markets are as turbulent as they have been recently, I would like to offer up some things that I did *not* do for you.

Now before I get to my lapses, please keep in mind I am not now nor have I ever claimed to be as smart as the gurus of Wall Street. Thus these lapses were partly the result of my inability to understand the unique investment opportunities the smart guys were offering.

I did not recommend the purchase of individual stocks because I believe markets are efficient. Because of this, I have diversified my clients away from the specific risk of specific, individual stocks. Accordingly, I never recommended that any client buy positions in any of the following stocks: Fannie Mae, Freddie Mac, AIG, Lehman Brothers, Bear Stearns, Wachovia, or Washington Mutual. Instead, I invested your money in a portfolio of 10,000 stocks in 40 countries.

I did not recommend auction-rate municipal bonds or auction-rate preferred securities as alternatives to money market accounts. This market froze up and some investors found their safe money was "not immediately accessible"—for months. It has taken law suits—or the threat of law suits—to get some of those clients' funds made available to those clients again. Meanwhile, when the funds were not available, brokerage firms were offering to let you borrow against those "not immediately accessible" funds—in essence, letting you borrow your own money—at a price that was not zero.

I did not recommend hedge funds because these products are illiquid, lack transparency, and, quite frankly, I could not figure out how clients were supposed to make money after paying a management fee of 2 percent annually and 20 to 30 percent of the profits.

I did not recommend so-called "structured products" or alternative investments, not only because I thought they were too complicated and in many cases used derivatives, but also because they relied ultimately on the guarantee of a counterparty such as Lehman Brothers. When that guarantee became worthless because the guarantor (i.e., Lehman) went bankrupt, those notes became worthless as well. A 13 percent interest rate on an underlying value of zero is not an attractive investment.

I did not recommend commodity funds, oil, or gold because I believe TIPs (Treasury inflation-protected securities) funds offer a safer alternative as a hedge against inflation and have lower volatility. Besides, I consider that a commodity that just sits there and does not have an expected return is nothing but a casino bet.

I did not take your money and charge you a steep advisory fee, and then invest your money in some place you had no knowledge of or information about, such as, for example, any of the Bernie Madoff funds, which, by the way, charged more fees on top of the ones I charged you. I invested your money in third-party mutual funds that we gave you a great deal of information about. Your trades are executed by a third-party advisory firm which is also the custodian of your funds and sends you probably more statements than you want to see. All parties involved—the registered investment adviser with whom I am affiliated, the mutual fund company, and the third-party custodian—are audited by well-known auditing firms, not by an obscure, three-person outfit that no one has ever heard of.

I passed up all the latest and greatest ideas generated by Wall Street (and elsewhere in the financial community) and stuck to my simple beliefs: Investments should be widely diversified, transparent, and understandable; customized to your risk tolerance and long-term goals; and held for the long term by a third-party custodian. All the tricks and arbitrages and leverage and structured deals that the wise guys thought up have vanished. The people who are still here and who are still invested are the ones who resisted their siren call. Markets have corrections; we know this and have built our portfolios to withstand those storms. But a market correction is a far cry from the total loss brought about by so many of Wall Street's new ideas.

PART III

Managing Your Retirement

CHAPTER 7

Planning for Your Retirement and Creating Income for Life

I said in the Preface that there are four main parts to wealth management, organized around four main types of risk. Up until now, I have focused on the investment side of wealth management: wealth accumulation. Most people think of investing almost solely in terms of rate of return—how fast your money grows. I see it differently, and I have told the story of my long odyssey at Terra to help my readers understand how I came to this perspective.

My mission as a financial adviser and wealth manager is to help my clients understand the importance of risk: Investing your money is as much about managing risk as it is about getting returns. And in fact you cannot optimize your returns over the long term unless you understand—and manage—risk. I have presented my views on this aspect of wealth management, and now it is time to take a look at the other three kinds of risk: retirement and retirement income; wealth and lifestyle protection; and transferring your wealth. Chapters 7, 8, and 9 are about figuring out how much money you will need to get the lifestyle you want at retirement, and then how to manage your funds in retirement. Chapters 10 and 11 are about protecting your wealth and lifestyle, mostly through the use of various kinds of insurance. Chapters 12 and 13 are about transferring your wealth through estate planning. Finally, in the Epilogue, I sum up the most important things I hope you will have learned through reading this book.

Now we turn to this chapter as an introduction to the subject of retirement planning and creating income to last for the rest of your life. It is relevant no matter how old you are now. In fact, if you are many years away from retirement and you take these lessons to heart, you will be well on your way to creating a prosperous retirement for yourself.

Understanding Uncertainty: Portfolio Withdrawal Calculations Using Monte Carlo

At some point, your nest egg will have to create income for retirement. So instead of focusing on the uncertainty of today's markets, let us take a closer look at how to create retirement income, whether starting today or starting in 20 years.

While the first thought of some investors is to flee to the supposed safety of fixed-income investments, that safety is illusory. I introduced this kind of simple, rule-of-thumb calculation at the end of Chapter 6. The essential part of any investment is how much of the return you get to keep after taxes and inflation, not the nominal yield on the security. In general, fixed-income securities, including CDs and Treasury bills and other kinds of bonds, pay out their return as dividends that get taxed every year as short-term income. If you look at a CD or taxable bond with a 4.5 percent return and your tax rate is 33 percent, the yield after tax will be on the order of 3.0 percent per year. A 4.5 percent return would look pretty good right now and resembles current interest rates better than the rates cited in Table 7.1.

Then you have to account for inflation. We take an inflation rate of 4.6 percent from Table 7.1. Your after-tax, after-inflation return is −1.6 percent, negative 1.6 percent (3.0 minus 4.6 percent), meaning you are losing money over time.

Performing the same crude calculation on the S&P 500 Index, the after-tax and after-inflation return is 3.02 percent. (Nominal return is 10.8 percent; after taxes is 7.0 percent and then subtract 4.6 percent inflation to end up with 2.4 percent.) I admit this is a crude calculation that does not take into account the fact that stocks are often taxed at long-term rates and may not be taxed at all for years, depending on how long a person holds a stock, so the after-tax return could easily be higher than 2.4 percent; the after-tax return on stocks would also depend on how much each one paid out in dividends.

The next problem is that, although stocks have historically outperformed bonds, stocks have risk and volatility, meaning the return over time is not a straight line in one direction. When I was at Terra and first started preparing retirement projections for clients some 25 years ago, we used a cutting-edge Lotus spreadsheet to input a client's assets, assumed a rate of return such as 9 percent and an inflation rate of 4 percent or 5 percent, and also input the dollars a client said he would need to live on after retirement. Then we would run the projection and find out that poof! Everyone would die rich.

Unfortunately, the markets and life are not linear. The S&P 500 Index may have earned an average of 9.6 percent from January 1, 1927, through

December 31, 2008, but not once did it earn that exact rate in a calendar year. In fact, if you have the right statistical chart in front of you, you can easily see that for the 83 years from 1926 to 2008, the S&P did worse than –20 percent six times and better than 20 percent 31 times. In only five of those years did it provide a return between 8 percent and 12 percent. It could be up 30 percent one year and down 15 percent the next year with a crude average of 9.6 percent, but losing that 10 percent would feel much worse for the person who had retired at the beginning of that year. Even given the long-term increase in the market over the years, the *point-in-time risk* is that it could go down for the first three years of *your* retirement, putting a big crimp in your plans for the future. The randomness and volatility of market returns have to be incorporated into investors' plans to convert their assets into an income stream.

To accomplish this, many advisers have abandoned their linear spreadsheet approach (which shows us all dying rich) to take randomness into account. This approach is called Monte Carlo simulation and was originally used during the Cold War to calculate how many people would survive a nuclear attack. Now all that brilliant thinking is put to a better use: to calculate the probabilities of you not outliving your income stream. In essence, the program takes the historical data of the various assets and portfolios and calculates 10,000 different scenarios using a wide variety of possible economic factors. The output is a *probable* result.

In the world of financial advisers, here is the question that is central to long-term retirement planning: "What percentage can I withdraw from my inflation-adjusted portfolio so I have a 90 percent-plus probability of not running out of money until age 100?"

Calculating Withdrawals

Before we try to answer that question, you may wonder why we use age 100. If we used the median life expectancy of age 84 in our models, we would be wrong 50 percent of the time. Advisers should take these calculations to age 90 or 100 to be conservative and on the safe side. Of course, if you happen to know when you are going to die and are willing to share that information with me, I can provide you some very accurate calculations!

Using Monte Carlo simulations, there actually is a widely used answer to the question of how much you can withdraw from a portfolio and still have a high probability of not running our of money. The widely accepted answer is that there appears to be a 90 percent probability of not running out of money before age 100 if withdrawals are between 4 and 4.5 percent.[1]

That answer has an important caveat: It does *not* assume the preservation of principal. That means that we can estimate only that investors do not outlive their money but we do not take into account inheritances that individuals might want to leave to their children. In my practice, I suggest using life insurance as one way to deal with the inheritance issue.

There is also a second important caveat: In most scenarios, we believe one needs an allocation to equities of approximately 50 to 60 percent. When we reach retirement, we are at a point in our lives when we want to reduce the volatility of returns because we are no longer in the accumulation mode, but we have to accept the risk of the stock market and equity returns to provide us with a higher probability of not outliving our money.

I will provide a simple example to illustrate this point. Assume a couple, both age 65, has $1 million to invest. They are risk-averse but want to withdraw $45,000 per year, adjusted for inflation. I ran two scenarios. The first scenario assumes all the money is invested in cash equivalents. The second scenario assumes a diversified portfolio invested 55 percent in equities. Table 7.1 shows the results, based on a Monte Carlo simulation, comparing the probability of success for the two scenarios. Please note that this 5.95 percent total return for short-term bonds and cash is much higher than anything available now; that rate was 1.7 percent for 2008 alone. But I use the historical numbers because I have to rely on our data; those are also the numbers the program uses.

This calculation illustrates that your *probability* of success in meeting your retirement goals is much greater when you have an allocation to equities. The amount of the allocation depends on a client's circumstances. Most of us need to accept some market risk to achieve our retirement goals, whether saving for retirement or in retirement. If you need a withdrawal rate of more than 4.5 percent, other solutions, such as an immediate annuity, may allow you to increase your withdrawal rate to 5.5 percent without lowering your probability of running out of money. (I say more on annuities in a moment as well as in Chapter 8.)

TABLE 7.1   The Risk of Running Out of Money for Two Portfolios

Asset Allocation	100% Short-Term Bonds/Cash	55% Diversified Equities/ 45% Bonds
Probability of success	68%	100%
Total return	5.95%	9.59%
Actual inflation 1970–2007*	4.62%	4.62%

*Inflation rate as used in MoneyGuidePro financial planning software program, which is intended for use only by professional financial advisers.
Source: MoneyGuidePro calculations.

Now we add one more factor. You should look at the asset allocation of your overall portfolio as integrated with Social Security payments and any pension you might receive. These monthly income streams can be viewed as the equivalent of a fixed-income or bond allocation in your portfolio. Imagine that you had a second portfolio comprising only fixed-income investments, and it gave off an income stream equal to your Social Security payment.

Look at the preceding example again and assume the same couple receives Social Security payments of $2,000 per month, for a total of $24,000 per year, in addition to the annual $45,000 the couple say they need from their $1 million portfolio. If you had an investment portfolio that paid you $24,000 annually and you knew that was 4.5 percent of the portfolio, how large would that portfolio be? The answer is almost $550,000. (The calculation is $24,000 divided by 0.045.) To restate: Receiving a certain monthly income from Social Security or other pension is the same as having a portfolio that provided that much income every month.

In fact, we could stipulate that this portfolio investment is very much like having a fixed-income portfolio that can be modestly adjusted for inflation (Social Security payments increase at approximately half the inflation rate). So now we can look at the couple's overall portfolio and asset allocation from this perspective, to see that they have a total portfolio of $1,550,000 with $500,000 invested in equities, which means about 35 percent of the overall portfolio is invested in equities and 65 percent is invested in bonds.

Recap of Risk/Remedy Discussion

Let us recap this discussion:

Risk	Remedy
Inflation	Diversified, rebalanced, asset-allocated portfolio of stocks and bonds.
Health and nursing home/ assisted living expenses	Appropriate insurance products.
Longevity	Determining a sustainable withdrawal rate; consider an annuity.
Volatility	Diversified, rebalanced, asset-allocated portfolio of stocks and bonds.
Point-in-time	Determining a sustainable withdrawal rate; consider a hedging tool.

The reason to consider your investments in this perspective is to help ease the angst of thinking you have too much invested in the stock market. In fact, advisers who use this approach would argue that this couple needs to invest *more* in the market. I am not suggesting that, but it is one way of looking at your asset allocation as a whole.

The bottom line of this analysis is that, for most people, achieving their retirement goals means accepting the risk and volatility of the stock market. As we said earlier, the *safety* of fixed-income investments is illusory and in fact represents a kind of investment trap. Accepting volatility and using an investment strategy that manages that risk is actually the only way that many investors will be able to achieve their retirement objectives.

This raises the dilemma of how to create sustainable or guaranteed income in a way that will last for your lifetime.

Seeing It Clearly

We can see this model clearly: Withdraw 4 percent or less from your portfolio annually, buy proper insurance to protect in the event of a long-term care event, diversify, rebalance, and do not have any unforeseen large expenses, and you have a great chance of maintaining your planned lifestyle during retirement. Here is the catch. When the rubber meets the road, many people will not be able to withdraw only 4 percent from their portfolios and have the lifestyle that they desire during retirement. In fact, when the actual budget is done, most people have to readjust one of the following: expectations, retirement date, or need to supplement income by working in retirement.

It is here that we need to consider another tool that may allow you to create a sustainable income stream that you cannot outlive: an annuity.

CHAPTER 8

Using Annuities as an Income Tool

A nnuities have advantages and disadvantages, just like any other financial planning tool. In this chapter, I explain how annuities have come to earn their negative reputation, then talk about the market abuses that still exist today and provide some guidance as to when annuities are appropriate in a retirement portfolio. I also define the basic annuity terms and products, provide some guidelines for using these products, and then introduce the new generation of variable annuity products that can help you, when appropriate, achieve some peace of mind by guaranteeing that you cannot outlive part of your income stream. I also give you an alternative method for thinking about how to divide your investments into different allocations.

Introducing Annuities

Annuities have traditionally been misunderstood and misused. Although there were times when annuities were appropriate for certain individuals, insurance salespeople have used this investment tool as the Swiss army knife for investing. Annuities have too often been high-commission products that were poor substitutes for investing in low-cost mutual funds.

It is essential to remember above all that annuities are insurance products. They were originally designed to provide a guarantee that a person could not outlive a stream of income. Over the years, insurance companies have used the laws that helped to create annuities to bring to market many different variations, some good, some not so good, in order to capture investment dollars and meet the needs of investors. Sadly, insurance agents have often misused, misrepresented, or only partially disclosed all the terms and conditions that apply to annuities.

There are two phases of an annuity product, *accumulation* and *payout*. In the case of the first kind of annuity I discuss, there is no accumulation phase; a single premium income annuity is pure payout.

Payout Annuity

Originally, when you bought an annuity, you gave an insurance company a lump sum of money and the company guaranteed a payment to an annuitant (the person receiving the annuity) over a period of years, over the lifetime of the annuitant, or a combination of these time spans. The money would be deposited in the general account of the insurance company. The insurance company would determine a growth rate appropriate for that deposit and would then pay out the stream of income that was return of both principal and interest.

A lifetime *single premium income annuity* (SPIA) is the purest form of annuity. But a SPIA is *not* an investment! A SPIA is insurance—insurance against living too long. Many people have tried to compute a rate of return by using the initial investment as the denominator of a fraction, and then trying to calculate the numerator as the sum of the total payments that the annuitant might be paid for the rest of his life. This is an absurd calculation! Remember that the median age for death is about 84, meaning about 50 percent of individuals die before age 84 and 50 percent after. For those who live a long life, a SPIA might be their best investment ever. But it is not an investment, it is insurance! It hedges against the risk of living a long life and then running out of money.

Here is how a SPIA works. An individual gives a deposit to the insurance company. In exchange, the insurance company promises to pay the annuitant a fixed dollar amount for the rest of his or her life. The payment is determined by the current interest rate and the age and sex of the annuitant. The older you are when you buy the contract, the larger the payment will be, because your life expectancy is shorter and therefore the amount of time over which you can potentially be paid is accordingly less.

In the following example, please keep in mind that interest rates change every day. As I am writing this book, interest rates are at historic lows, so this example is not an accurate depiction of today's interest rates. Bill, age 65, deposits $100,000 into a SPIA contract. The insurance company pays him $7,942 each year (I use annual payments to make the math easier; payments are typically made monthly) for the rest of his life. If Bill lives to age 100, then he will have received $277,970. If Bill were to die after only one year, then he will have received only $7,942. If Bill bought the annuity using nonqualified money—meaning it did not come from a tax-qualified retirement plan such as an IRA or 401(k)—then part of each payment will be taxed as ordinary income and part will be tax-free and considered return of original principal. If the original purchase came from tax-qualified money, all payments are taxed as ordinary income.

Most people found this approach unacceptable; people hate to turn over their money to an insurance company with no guarantee of getting it back, regardless of the amazing guarantee the insurance company makes in promising to pay you for as long as you live. To make the proposition more appealing, insurance companies started to offer an annuity with provisions added to guarantee that payments would be made for at least a specific time even if you did not live that long (the remaining payments would go to your heirs). The contract would state that Bill would deposit the same $100,000 in an annuity and the insurance company would guarantee payments for the longer of 20 years (or other specific number of years) or life, whichever is greater. For a 65-year-old with guaranteed payments for the longer of 20 years or life, the new payment would be $6,876. There are different options for different lengths of time.

SPIAs are particularly useful when income needs to be assured for the rest of a life or for a specific period of years to individual or joint lives (in the case of a married couple). They are especially useful to fulfill the obligations of lawsuits, for people who have no need to leave a legacy, or for those who are older who need the highest amount of guaranteed income to meet their needs. As I mentioned, the older you are when you start getting payouts, the higher the amount. The biggest negative is that once you have paid the principal to the insurance company, you need to assume that there is no way to retrieve it in the event it is needed. Since insurance companies want to try to meet every need, there exist some insurance contracts that will provide a present value of the income if it is needed at some time in the future; there are also special purpose companies called *life settlement* companies that will buy the annuity from an annuitant. However, as you might surmise, the economics of these transactions are not favorable to the annuitant.

Remember, a SPIA is not an investment, it is insurance to protect against longevity risk.

Accumulation Annuity

An *accumulation annuity* is initially completely different from an income annuity. You deposit or invest with the insurance company either a lump sum (a single premium annuity) or an ongoing stream of payments (flexible premium annuity), although, for discussion purposes and to make this less confusing, I do not focus on the flexible premium aspect of this product. This deposit can be one of two different kinds of contracts. It can be deposited into a fixed-rate contract called a *single premium deferred annuity* (SPDA), which is invested in the general account of the insurance company. It could also be invested in a *variable annuity* (VA), in which case the investment is deposited into a separate managed account that is like a mutual fund and is completely segregated from the insurance company's general account.

In both the SPDA and the VA, no income tax is paid on the growth of that investment as long as the money stays in the annuity. There are two ways to take money out of the annuity while you are alive. When you take a simple withdrawal from the annuity, all of the taxable gain comes out first and is taxed at ordinary income rates.

The other way is to take a stream of income over an annuitant's lifetime, a specified period of years, or a combination of the two; in other words, you may *annuitize* the value of the contract as if you were buying a SPIA. When you annuitize an annuity, you hand over a sum of money to the insurance company and, in return, the insurance company promises to pay you a stream of income for the rest of your life. (The terminology might seem strange to you at first: *annuitize an annuity*. But it is the way the insurance industry talks.) When you elect this option you *give up* the principal of your investment in exchange for this guaranteed income stream. As the money is paid to you, part of each payment is considered a taxable gain and part of each payment is considered a return of principal and is not taxed. This percentage is determined on a pro rata basis based on the gain in the contract at the time the contract is annuitized, or paid out over a time period. You need to be very clear that you give up your lump sum in exchange for a stream of income for the rest of your life.

In essence, the insurance company is making a deal with you, and it is about risk. Here's the crux of the issue: No matter how useful and secure this kind of investment sounds, as I said earlier, people just hate handing over a lump sum of money to an insurance company. People who have a strong wish to leave money to their children hate it even more. No matter how firmly you believe you are going to live to be 100—and therefore fully recoup all that you invested with the insurance company—as soon as people start thinking about annuities, they imagine they will die tomorrow and lose both the money they invested *and* the income stream.

Advantages of SPDAs and VAs

Accumulation annuities have some unique advantages. When you buy an annuity, you do not pay front-end charges (loads); your entire investment amount goes into the policy and begins earning interest right away. All earnings are tax-deferred as long as they stay inside the annuity (not paid to you). Annuities have certain real and valuable guarantees that are backed by the insurance company (more about this later). For those in retirement, there is the additional benefit that the growth in the annuity is excluded from calculating the taxes on Social Security. (When you are receiving Social Security, there is a certain amount you can earn before triggering a tax on your Social Security income.) In applicable tax and estate situations, this can provide individuals with more spendable income during a given year.

Disadvantages of SPDAs and VAs

Accumulation annuities as a group also have some disadvantages. Only licensed insurance agents can sell annuities, and insurance companies provide an incentive to their agents to sell annuities by paying commissions, which are typically 1 to 7 percent of the dollar amount of the annuity (products with very low commissions typically pay a higher ongoing commission, known as a trail commission). Please note that commissions on some contracts can be as high as 20 percent! High-commission products typically benefit only two parties: the salesperson and the insurance company.

Typically 100 percent of the money deposited into an accumulation annuity is invested. However, insurance companies have to pay commissions and expenses to issue and distribute annuities, so they apply a back-end surrender charge to withdrawals that are taken out before there is enough time to recoup these expenses. A fair contract would have a back-end charge that is a percentage that declines over the first seven years of the contract. For contracts with high commissions paid up front, insurance companies need to hold the money over longer periods of time. In these cases, back-end surrender charges might be very high, sometimes as high as 100 percent, and last for as long as 20 years, or have special provisions that the only way to get the money out is to die or to annuitize the contract. These high-commission/high-surrender charge contracts are totally inappropriate for consumers.

There are also IRS rules that apply to accumulation annuities. If withdrawals are taken before the contract owner is age $59^1/_2$, there is an additional 10 percent penalty for those withdrawals. The first withdrawals are considered to be withdrawals of the growth in the contract and they are taxed as ordinary income. After all of the growth has been taken out, then withdrawals are considered to be withdrawal of the principal and are not taxed. There is no capital gains treatment for any withdrawal even though the investment account inside a VA is really a mutual fund investment but is invested inside the contract. But the worst aspect of these contracts comes into play when you die.

Unlike other investments, annuities do not receive a step-up in tax basis at the death of the owner. *Step-up* refers to the fact that the person who inherits your stocks, for example, is considered to own them at the value they have at your death, not at the price you paid for them. For example, say you bought a stock for $10 and it has appreciated extremely well during your life, so now it is worth $500. Imagine how much you would have to pay in taxes if you sold that stock now. Instead, you bequeath that stock to your son. When he gains ownership of it at your death, his tax basis in that stock is its value at your death, $500, rather than the price you paid for it. If he sold it the day after gaining ownership, he would not have to pay capital gains tax on it. (Estate taxes are an entirely separate issue; see Chapter 12.) Stocks, mutual funds, and most other investment assets all are currently stepped up at death and there are no capital gains or income tax due on the investment. But annuity gains are fully taxed at the death of the owner, thereby diminishing any tax deferral that happened over the owner's lifetime. Annuities are bad investments to die with; this is often not discussed by insurance agents.

Variable annuities have another aspect that has made them less than appealing. Considered simplistically, a VA consists of one or more mutual funds held in an insurance contract. The insurance company is allowed to charge expenses over and above the charges that the investment managers (the mutual fund management company) charge for managing the portfolios. These *extra* charges can be as high as an additional 200 basis points (two percentage points) on top of the investment management charges. Later in this chapter, we talk more about how VAs have been abused by insurance and investment companies.

Why Purchase an SPDA?

SPDAs are typically used as an alternative to bank CDs. They declare an interest rate that is guaranteed for a specific time period, usually one to five years. They typically offer a higher interest rate than a CD and are guaranteed by an insurance company. Upon renewal, they will pay an interest rate that is declared by the insurance company. Unlike a CD, they will also have a minimum guaranteed renewal rate. I occasionally see contracts we sold 15 to 20 years ago that have a minimum guaranteed interest rate of 4 to 5 percent. In this current environment, with CD rates below 3 percent, these are very good investments to continue to own.

SPDAs are not subject to income taxes as long as the investment is held in the annuity. The overall result often means more money available to spend when needed than money that was invested in a CD and taxed annually. They can be an excellent tool for people approaching or in retirement; during the right time periods they provide high fixed, guaranteed returns for money. However, SPDAs have surrender charges, and you should not consider purchasing one if you have a short time horizon for your investment.

Market Abuses of SPDAs

Although SPDAs look simple, marketing incentives created by insurance companies have instituted abuses. Consider that SPDA money is invested in the general account of an insurance company. The vast majority of insurance company money is invested in fixed-income instruments. Because most insurance companies invest these funds in a similar way, the yields from one company to another should also be similar, although large companies typically have more ability to derive higher yields on their investments than do small insurance companies; larger companies buy on a larger scale and probably have deeper research and trading resources.

Although CDs and SPDAs invest in different things and are completely different securities, their yields are not that far apart; both are plain-vanilla, fixed-income securities. Yet sometimes you see unbelievable rates advertised for SPDAs. For example, in our current interest-rate environment, CDs are yielding less than 3 percent, and yet I just saw an advertisement for an SPDA with a first-year interest rate of 8 percent. Too good to be true? Of course! Insurance companies often will declare a "bonus" interest rate for the first year of deposit, but this bonus rate has many strings, the most common of which is long back-end surrender charges that force you to hold the annuity for a long period of time. During this long period, the insurance company has plenty of opportunity to renew your contract—after the first-year bonus is history—at lower than current market rates. And they do it—they are in business to make money.

Many of these high-bonus contracts are offered by smaller insurance companies. They are attractive to shady insurance people because they have a nice market appeal. Additionally, these bonus contracts offer high commission incentives and extravagant vacation-reward incentives to the salespeople to attract their business. Unfortunately, insurance agents do take advantage of these bonuses to attract business. At the end of the contract, at best you will be even with what you would have had with a fairer contract without a bonus; at worst you will have been locked into a contract that declared less-than-market-rates for a very long surrender period.

Why Purchase a VA?

Historically, the pitch was that VAs are tax-deferred. Why pay taxes on money you are accumulating for retirement? Salespeople can easily demonstrate how much faster money compounds tax-deferred for those in a high tax bracket, thus yielding a bigger pool of money at retirement.

Variable annuities often have guarantees that the death benefit will be no less than the original deposit. Sometimes the death benefit will increase by a specified interest rate every year, or it might be reset every year at the anniversary value. These provisions can be valuable when the VA owner dies at a point in time after investment values have tumbled, although this death benefit, unlike that of life insurance, is fully taxable at ordinary income tax rates.

Market Abuses of VAs

In the past several years, there have been some significant innovations to the VA product that have recently made them a very compelling product to include in a portfolio; I talk more about these innovations in a moment. For now, I want to talk about the sad state of the sales practices that have given VAs such a bad reputation.

First, you should understand why salespeople like to sell VAs. Let us contrast mutual fund investing to VA investing. Mutual fund investors receive greater and greater discounts as they invest more money into a mutual fund family. Although sales charges in mutual funds may be as high as 5 percent, as the invested dollars approach $1 million, the sales charge reduces to zero. The commissions that salespeople receive are a percentage of this sales load. (Of course, you may purchase no-load mutual funds directly from some mutual fund families, but you do that on your own, without investment advice.) By contrast, almost all VAs sold today have no discount attached to the amount of dollars invested. The investor pays a level commission no matter if the investment is $10,000 or $1 million. There has been no surge in momentum to change this practice in the industry. These commissions vary by the carrier or the product sold, not by the amount invested.

In order to pay the commission and the marketing and distribution incentives, insurance carriers add a charge to the contract, commonly called *mortality and expense* charges. These charges add an additional one to two percentage points (100 to 200 basis points) to the cost structure. Additionally, the back-end surrender charge ensures that the insurance company will be able to recoup the commissions and expenses paid in the event of early withdrawals.

It is time for some common sense. Let us pretend you are an average investor who earns an above-average wage, owns a home, maybe has a family. In deciding how to invest your money, you might use the following logical hierarchy:

1. Put two to four months of income in a liquid investment as an emergency fund (financial foundation for everyone).
2. Maximize your retirement plan contributions—IRA, 403(b) and especially 401(k) with a matching fund (tax deferred, tax deductible—take advantage of compound interest).
3. Invest in after-tax investments such as mutual funds, stock, bonds; you probably also want to save for the good things in life such as a new kitchen, a second home, maybe a business or some real estate. You would not want to lock up this kind of savings until age $59^1/_2$—you might want to enjoy it before then!

After you have filled all of the first three buckets, then you might consider a tax-deferred investment that locks up your money until retirement.

But the reality is that most people never get to level four. If they do, then a VA might be an appropriate investment. However, salespeople have used VAs in both levels two and three.

The worst abuse of VAs has occurred historically when they were used in qualified plans, especially IRAs. An IRA is already a tax-deferred vehicle, so why put this type of investment in an IRA and pay an extra 1 to 2 percentage point fee every year? To justify the sale, typically salespeople would extol two features of the product in particular:

1. *A variable annuity often includes investments from several different investment companies.* The pitch went like this: You can change your investment accounts between different managers without incurring another sales load. This is true. However, very few people ever took advantage of this feature; they invested once and never changed their allocation. Most major fund families allow you to get a reasonably diversified (although not optimal) portfolio with lower ongoing fees.
2. *Variable annuities have a death benefit.* You have to pay for the death benefit, which could prove to be valuable in certain situations.

The advanced discussion typically included the death benefit pitch along with the diversification pitch, plus one more: You can change funds without causing a taxable event that would cause you to have to pay capital gains taxes like you would on mutual funds that you sold. So I repeat that mutual fund families do a pretty good job of providing investment choices.

Another aspect that salespeople gloss over rather casually is that all distributions from a VA are treated as ordinary income and are not eligible for the lower capital gains tax rate. This result is not insignificant when compared to mutual funds. There is no way to average your cost basis—as you do with stocks or mutual funds—to reduce the tax effect. The first dollars that come out are immediately treated as income; tax basis dollars are the last ones to come out.

One of the disadvantages of holding a VA is that, at death, the effects of tax deferral are minimized because all of the gain is taxable at ordinary income rates. There is no step-up in basis, as there is with mutual funds, so the heirs have to pay taxes on any gain.

Index Annuities—Buyer Beware

The insurance industry's most recent attack on consumers is the *index* or *equity index annuity*. Created originally as a single premium deferred annuity, insurance companies were soon using this structure as the investment account for universal life insurance as well. In both instances, these products are both confusing and deceptive for consumers. They provide insurance agents with the opportunity to generate very high commissions and allow insurance companies and unscrupulous agents to circumvent the protections that the Financial Industry Regulatory Authority's (FINRA's) oversight provides to protect consumers from market conduct abuses.

During the recent bull market, insurance companies created a product that claims you can get the returns of the stock market without any downside risk. Sound too good to be true? This product appeals to insurance salespeople who are not registered representatives of securities broker-dealers and who therefore avoid the regulation, supervision, oversight, and enforcement process of the securities industry, which is designed to protect consumers against market abuse. Instead, such insurance salespeople are regulated through the network of state insurance regulators who have in the past been ineffective in protecting consumers against market abuses. Although registered representatives still commit abuses, this system of oversight is significantly better than that which exists through the insurance regulators.

The SEC has recently determined that these specialized annuities should be treated as investment products and that broker-dealers should have the same level of oversight on them as they have on securities sales. I hope the outcome will be that anyone who wants to sell index annuity products will need to be registered with a broker-dealer so that the outlandish misrepresentations will disappear. Once it is revealed that the emperor has no clothes, the products will disappear from the landscape.

At the highest level, an index annuity is an accumulation annuity where an investor gives money to the insurance company, and that money is deposited in the insurance company's general account and then invested, typically in a portfolio of bonds. Additionally, as the pitch goes, the insurance company uses a portion of that deposit to purchase a combination of options and derivatives that will be used to capture the returns generated by an uptick in any one of a number of selected stock indexes. On the downside there are stated minimum guarantees associated with the contract values that will guarantee that the principal of the investment will show modest growth.

The deposit is divided into two pools. One pool is invested in the general investment portfolio of the insurance company which can generate a fixed return. The other pool purchases derivative products. That means that initially, less than 100 percent of the money will earn a fixed rate of return; the other pool is supposed to be able to enhance the return if the market goes up over a period of time starting when the money is deposited and ending at some point in the future. If the market always goes up, you will potentially receive a return greater than a fixed annuity.

The reality is that the market goes up and down. The vast majority of the returns of the market happen in short periods of time. If those options and derivatives expire when the market is flat or down, they cannot add value to the investor's portfolio. The net result is that sometimes index annuities can outperform SPDAs. But their very structure dictates that, over long periods of time, they cannot outperform properly diversified, allocated, and rebalanced portfolios that participate 100 percent in the market.

The following list highlights some of the characteristics of index annuities that salespeople often minimize or ignore in these contracts. You can see that the potential for outperformance is dramatically overstated.

- When the deposit is made, often the fixed, guaranteed account does not start at 100 percent of the deposit; it might start to accrue at 90 percent of the initial deposit.
- These contracts pay very high commissions, typically 10 to 20 percent of the initial deposit.
- Very long surrender charges are attached to the contract so the insurance company can recover the cost of issuing the policy. A surrender period of 10 to 20 years is most common. Sometimes the contract cannot be surrendered but rather must be annuitized to realize the growth account.
- The contracts for these annuities often state that investors should have time horizons longer than the surrender periods (20 years!). The insurance companies are completely serious about this and, when there is a dispute, they stand behind their disclosure, even though agents minimize this aspect in the sales process. Now ask yourself how prudent it would have been to lock up for 20 years almost any investment you have made, other than perhaps real estate.
- Participation in the index chosen to supply the growth, whether it is the S&P 500 Index, the Dow Jones Industrials, or whatever, excludes dividends from the calculation, and yet dividends are around 30 percent of the return of those indexes. For example, if the S&P 500 returned 10 percent over the measured period, the potential upside for the annuity would be only 7 percent because it would exclude the approximately 300 basis points of dividend returns.
- There is typically a maximum cap on growth in any measured time period, either stated as a specific growth rate (if the index grew at 15 percent, the growth might be capped at 7 percent) or as a percentage of the growth rate (if the S&P grew at 10 percent and the dividends were subtracted, resulting in 7 percent, then multiply that by the cap rate, maybe 80 percent, to give a return of 5.6 percent). The maximum return in the latter scenario is 5.6 percent instead of 10 percent!

TABLE 8.1   Growth in the Value of an Index Annuity Compared
to the Return on the S&P 500

Year	Actual S&P Growth	Capped S&P Growth	Cumulative Net Result
1	15%	8%	8%
2	−15%	−15%	−7%
3	10%	5.6%	−1.4%

Source: Forum Financial Management, LLC, as compiled from
index-annuity prospectuses.

Additionally, everything is not always up. Let us look at an example of three time periods and assume that the measurement period is over 12 months, although many contracts go month to month. Table 8.1 shows actual growth of the S&P 500 Index, the actual credited interest rate capped at 80 percent (as suggested in the preceding bulleted point), and then the net credited results. As you can see, although over three years the actual S&P has grown by 10 percent, the investment account is actually *down* 1.4 percent.

The index annuity will always have a minimum guarantee account. The guarantee is often stated so that at surrender the annuity will be worth a minimum guarantee of 3 percent (sometimes this is compound interest; sometimes this is simple interest) per year accrued to the initial credited deposit. The cumulative guarantee might work like this over three years; this example presumes that the contract is surrendered at the end of that time. The investor deposits $100,000; the initial credited deposit is 90 percent of that (so much for no front-end fees), so the beginning balance for crediting the guarantee account is $90,000. After three years compounded at 3 percent, the guarantee account would be $98,345. This might be the surrender value. Sometimes there will be a surrender charge assessed to this value. Or the surrender values might be the greater of the investment account (−1.4 percent in this example) reduced by the surrender charge, perhaps 20 percent of the guaranteed account. Sometimes even the guaranteed account will be subject to the surrender charge, reducing the $98,345 further!

I continue with the list of features that salespeople are likely to gloss over:

- The cap rates and participation percentages are reset every year at the total discretion of the insurance company.
- There are often special incentives in the first year of the contract that make this again appear like a deal too good to be true. Remember, any incentive that is paid in the first year must be extracted from the

consumer over the period of the contract, otherwise the insurance company cannot make a profit. It is important to note that, at surrender, these bonuses do not contribute to the basis of the contract. That means that even if the surrender value is less than the initial deposit, as given in the preceding example, any bonus that was given in the first year at surrender would be taxed at ordinary, not capital gains, rates.

- During the sales process, insurance companies typically choose one year to illustrate the results of the accounts. I recently saw an illustration that used 2006 as the illustrated year because that particular year would have produced a positive result in the contract. If the product were fully regulated by FINRA instead of insurance regulators, an illustration like this would not have been allowed. They would have needed to show many more years, including the effects of 2008–2009! FINRA requires the presentation to be balanced, not skewed to only the good times.

The bottom line is that in markets that go straight up—which are extremely rare over long periods of time—index annuities might capture a return that is greater than that which you might get in a regular SPDA. However, more often than not, the overall return will be similar to that of an SPDA, or less (take the rate on the fixed return pool of the general account of the insurance companies, and then subtract the cost of the derivatives or options that were bought that expired without any value). These products are not substitutes for SPDAs, or for balanced, low-cost, managed portfolios, or for the new generation of variable annuities that have income guarantees.

Variable Income Annuities Using Income Riders—the Next Generation

Variable annuities have both positive and negative characteristics as vehicles for accumulating money for retirement. Furthermore, historically speaking, the only way to create a guaranteed income stream was to annuitize the contract over the annuitant's lifetime. There are two drawbacks: Once you have annuitized, you no longer have any access to the principal, and there is no opportunity for any market appreciation.

To overcome these obstacles, insurance companies created a new generation of products. If used correctly, there new products will allow investors to use their values to lock in gains, provide an income stream guaranteed never to run out, and participate in market appreciation if the growth is large enough.

This probably sounds too good to be true. Here is the reality. You must understand that insurance provides these guarantees. Insurance companies charge for these additional features in the contracts; they are not inexpensive and they add an additional 50 to 150 basis points charge to the contracts (between 0.5 and 1.5 percentage points). But this is insurance and of course you have to pay for it. The purpose of this insurance is to hedge against two of the most difficult risks to protect against: (1) longevity, the risk of outliving your portfolio, and (2) point-in-time risk, choosing to retire at an inopportune time in the market. Unlike index annuities, these are regulated securities products, which means that costs must be fully disclosed; you are provided with a prospectus and illustrations that disclose the nature of the contracts; and, finally, marketing materials must be balanced and not deceptive.

There are many variations on how these contracts work, and exactly how your contract will work will depend on the *rider* you choose. An insurance rider is an additional feature that you choose and for which you pay an additional fee. For example, with a variable annuity, your choice of riders would determine initial costs and payout rates and whether or not the annuity would require annuitization.

Given the extreme volatility we have seen in the equity markets in our lifetimes, these annuities can offer you some peace of mind by providing what you might call an investment floor, which is guaranteed by the insurance company no matter what the market does. If you buy this product before you retire, you will significantly reduce your point-in-time risk. Typically the income stream is guaranteed even if the underlying portfolio goes to zero. The money is invested in various subaccounts, which invest in the stock market and offer a selection of strategy and asset class, like mutual funds. If the actual investment grows at a high enough return to pay the various fees and charges levied by the insurance carrier, your income stream may grow. Depending on the contract, you may also have access to the principal.

The minimum income stream guaranteed by the insurance company is based on a formula and uses an assumed interest determined by the insurance company and as described in the policy. If the investment account exceeds a certain threshold, meaning the underlying subaccounts investing in stock and bonds grow sufficiently to pay the fees (2.5 to 3.5 percent/per annum) and also exceed the amount of interest used in the formula to calculate the guaranteed income stream amount (5 to 7 percent per annum), then not only may your monthly income increase, you may also retain access to some portion of your investment. In other words, unless the investment account grows (and this varies from contract to contract) by at least 10 percent per year, you probably will not have access to capital but you will receive your guaranteed income stream. Bottom line: When reviewing any proposal for an income annuity product, pay close attention to the page in the illustration showing 0 percent per annum growth because this will describe the worst-case scenario, which is the minimum, guaranteed annual income. This is the amount you should rely on for planning purposes.

The insurance companies are trying to provide everything you might want: You do not have to give up your capital completely, but you might also be able to have an income stream and might even be able to participate in the growth of the stock market as well. The real problem is that these products are very complicated. I do not believe that the average investor understands them. In fact, I do not believe the average insurance agent understands the product they are selling, and the fees can add up to an extra 100 to 150 basis points per year. Although it does seem to be a way to resolve the dilemma of creating an income stream without giving up control of capital, there is now one more important issue: Post-2008, how many people trust that the insurance company they are considering doing business with will be around in 40 years to continue to make good on that guarantee?

In the final analysis, however, it makes sense to consider such products when an investor simply does not have sufficient assets to create the income stream required to sustain his or her lifestyle in retirement. This new generation of annuities is a game changer. The additional cost really pays for insurance that is a valuable tool for retirement. With appropriate consideration, these products can be used for both retirement accounts and after-tax accounts. They are good tools for people who have reached age $70^1/_2$ and who need to take the required minimum distributions from their retirement accounts.

The Newest Risk: Insurance Company Risk

We learned many things during 2008. We no longer take for granted that some stodgy old companies are very conservative and very safe. Investors and advisers have to deal with the additional risk of the long-term viability of the insurance company issuing the annuity. In light of the recent financial meltdown, any person giving money to an insurance company has to consider the risk of the carrier being able to meet its obligations for payment at some point in the future.

Take American International Group Inc. (AIG insurance), described on its own web site as "a world leader in insurance and financial services . . . [and] the leading international insurance organization with operations in more than 130 countries and jurisdictions." This great institution, founded 90 years ago, is at the time I write this (early 2009) trading at a stock price of less than a dollar—like a penny stock! In early 2007, it had assets of $1 trillion,

$110 billion in revenues, and 74 million customers and 116,000 employees in 130 countries and jurisdictions. Yet just 18 months later, AIG found itself on the brink of bankruptcy and in need of emergency government assistance. What happened? One part of the company had engaged in some highly speculative activity and generated gigantic losses for the rest of the company.

Most life insurance as well as fixed-rate annuities have a claim on the general account of the insurance company, meaning your insurance depends on the health of the company in general, while variable annuities have the owner's investments in separate accounts. You can easily check an insurance company's ratings from the major rating agencies, but the credibility of those ratings in assessing the creditworthiness of an insurance company is dubious in light of the market meltdowns we experienced in 2008. The good news is that insurance companies are regulated at the state level and state regulation keeps insurance companies sound. Insurance companies are required to have enough capital in reserve to guarantee a good portion of their obligations. Furthermore, each state has a fund to guarantee a part of your death benefit.

A *Wall Street Journal* writer points out that lower-rated companies sometimes offer better rates than more financially sound companies, which could lead to problems in the future. Another study suggested that insurers might not be charging enough for all the new guarantees they offer, which could result in increased fees at some point down the road.[1] These are all things to consider when buying any insurance product. It is essential that your insurance company be able to pay out your benefit when you need it.

So far, this story has a good ending. Although AIG accepted a large amount of bailout money from the government, it seems as though its dozens of separate insurance companies are still in business and insured persons have not suffered. The point of this story is not to pick on AIG but to point out that you cannot take for granted the soundness and long-term health of any financial partner you deal with. If you believe you do not have the information or qualifications to keep track of which firms are healthy, it is essential for you to have an adviser who does.

On the Horizon: The Deferred Income or Longevity Annuity

Some insurance companies are beginning to develop a new contract for advisers to use, the deferred income annuity. Currently they are very expensive and, because of that, they are limited in their applications. However, there may be a time in the near future when they are more competitive and will complement an investment portfolio.

Annuity Summary

Annuity is an umbrella term that encompasses many different products. In general, you cannot say that an annuity is either good or bad. Annuities are products to consider within the context of a full discussion of your goals and objectives with a competent financial adviser, and they may be valuable tools in some situations. The VA landscape has changed in recent years. If you own an old VA, it is in your best interest to sit down with a financial adviser today to review it in light of your current goals and situation, and to consider whether it should be changed to a product that has an appropriate income rider.

Additionally, the commission structure of annuity products is still not as consumer-friendly as we would like. Our role is to help determine the best products for you from among the choices available, but the environment is always changing. Finally, all investments carry some risk, and the risk of the insurance company's survival and ability to pay the income stream is just another risk that has to be weighed against longevity and point-in-time risks.

So many people are living so much longer, we have to plan portfolio withdrawals as though all clients were going to live until age 95 to 100. If we knew we had to get only to age 85, we could increase the withdrawal rate a little and not worry about outliving our capital. In other words, the planning would be a little easier if a client age 65 knew he had to make the money last to age 85 and no longer. The reality is that for 50 percent of the people this would be a good assumption. The other 50 percent would be in trouble. Can you tell me for certain which group you are in?

One innovation to hedge this risk is the previously mentioned VAs with income riders. Another would be the new generation of deferred income annuities. Purchasing one is the opposite of purchasing a life insurance contract: Life insurance pays when a person dies; the deferred income annuity pays an income at a point in time after the person lives beyond an expected age, such as age 85. So, for example, if a 65-year-old client wanted to spend and enjoy his money without worrying about it lasting to age 100, he could purchase an annuity contract that pays over a lifetime, starting at age 85 and paying until he dies.

This raises some interesting possibilities. For example, this 65-year-old client has $1 million and writes a check for $200,000 to an insurance company. The client now has $800,000 to live on for 20 years. I can tell you it is a lot easier to plan for 20 years than for the 35 years until he turns 100.

Under this scenario, if the client reaches age 85, the insurance company pays an agreed income stream for the rest of his life. That's the good news. Here's the bad news: If the client dies before age 85, the money is lost. Now we are back to giving large amounts of money to insurance companies. However, in theory this should all work to create more income (because the client can plan carefully for the 20 years before the annuity starts). As I am writing this book, the real problem—as mentioned earlier—is that these products appear to be too expensive. Only a handful of companies offer them now, and it will take more market competition to make this a genuinely viable alternative.

The EAGR System: A Model for Retirement Planning

As you can see, there are a myriad of complex issues to consider when creating a retirement plan that will last for your lifetime. The dilemmas of point-in-time risk and mortality pose significant challenges in planning. Convincing yourself that you have solved this is falling into the trap of the RSGs (remember them, the Really Smart Guys?). So what kind of alternatives will really help mitigate some of these risks?

Part of the challenge of planning is that we don't know a client's mortality. As I said before, tell me when you are going to die, and I will create the perfect plan for you. Without that information, we are groping in the dark.

Another method of creating income to deal with point-in-time risk is to create several buckets of investments. The idea here is that time solves most problems when it comes to market returns. This method is used intuitively by many advisers and clients in the amount they allocate in their portfolio to bonds when they are doing the mental accounting to reach peace of mind.

The EAGR system places money into four categories or *buckets*: emergency, annual income, growth, and risk protection. Here's how it works:

> *Goal*: To improve the management of portfolio risk for retirees and those near retirement.
> *Risk*: Retirees withdrawing money from their portfolio during a significant market downturn.

1. *Emergency*. Emergency money is separated from the rest of the funds in an amount equal to 6 to 18 months of living costs plus sufficient funds for any near-term emergency needs or significant

expenditures such as a new car or vacation. While generally money market funds and CDs with staggered maturities may be used, for clients wishing a managed money solution, we offer a capital preservation portfolio that comprises all relatively short fixed-income securities. This bucket should be refilled from the second bucket at the end of every year.

2. *Annual income.* These funds are meant to be used in 2 or 3 to 10 years from now, for living expenses and in purchasing long-term-care insurance. These funds will be invested in an income portfolio (80 percent bonds). For purposes of asset allocation and financial planning, assume the funds in this bucket will have a modest growth rate equal to the bond yield.

3. *Growth.* This bucket of funds is for the long term, to be used in 10 years; based on the client's risk tolerance, a more equity-exposed portfolio such as a growth portfolio might be appropriate. This might comprise approximately 50 to 60 percent equities. On a yearly basis, any excess above the initial balance plus an agreed growth factor (such as, for example, the inflation rate) will be moved from this portfolio to the second or first bucket.

4. *Risk protection.* These funds include three major types of financial protection:
    a. Longevity and point-in-time risks: a guaranteed income annuity as the bucket of last resort. This protects against the risk of outliving your money.
    b. Long-term care: using long-term-care insurance to fund the risk of nursing home or home health care costs.
    c. Family protection: replacing the lost wages of a family provider, replacing potential portfolio losses, transferring wealth at death, or funding estate taxes.

Allocating for Longevity and Point-in-Time Risks

I use an easy-to-understand three-step formula to help clients analyze their retirement cash flow and determine how much should be allocated to protect against longevity and point-in-time risks.

1. List expenses. Determine two categories of expenses: essential living expenses and discretionary living expenses. Although it is an individual decision how to categorize them, the following will give you an idea.

    a. Essential living expenses:
- Rent or mortgage, utilities.
- Food.
- Health care, including vision, dental, medicine.
- Clothing; other personal maintenance.
- Insurance.
- Transportation.
- Others.

    b. Discretionary expenses:
- Entertainment.
- Gifting.
- Travel.
- Cost of second home.

2. List the guaranteed sources of income that you receive.
- Social Security.
- Pensions/IRAs.
- Income annuities.
- Income from a trust fund.
- Income from first bucket.

3. Subtract essential expenses from guaranteed sources of income. If there is a shortfall, you should consider providing a guaranteed income stream that will last the rest of your lifetime

Once essential expenses are covered, creating a predictable income stream from buckets 1, 2, and 3, invested to hedge against inflation and market volatility, will be the foundation for predicting your retirement lifestyle.

Although some advisers have done this kind of allocating, the financial meltdown of 2008 emphasizes the point-in-time risk and may make this a more palatable solution with greater peace of mind. Unfortunately it is not a panacea and still depends on equity markets providing enough return to beat inflation over the long run. As I mentioned, the beautiful idea of a longevity annuity has to be balanced with its current cost issues and the fact that such products, so far, have not been designed with inflation protection.

In summary, if your anticipated withdrawal rate from your portfolio exceeds 4 percent from buckets 1, 2, and 3, to meet your total lifestyle needs you must consider hedging against longevity and point-in-time risk. Using the steps I've outlined will help you determine the type of income annuity you should consider and the amount you need to allocate to an annuity.

CHAPTER 9

Using IRAs and Company Retirement Plans

The purpose of this chapter is to provide an overview of how IRAs, company 401(k) plans, and other self-directed qualified plans work and how you can use them to your best advantage. You should understand these principles, but if you are doing anything except the most plain-vanilla use of your IRA account, please consult a professional. The problem with discussing IRAs in a book is that the regulations change every year.

Introducing the IRA

The Employee Retirement Income Security Act (ERISA), signed into law in 1974, had a profound effect on many aspects of retirement regulation; one of the most important was the introduction of the Individual Retirement Account (IRA). It is estimated that more than $3 trillion is invested in IRAs, and one of every four retirement dollars in the U.S. is in an IRA.

In its simplest terms, the IRA permits investors to deposit funds into an account that allows them to grow tax-deferred, meaning that taxes are paid only when the funds are withdrawn. Investors invest directly in these accounts. IRAs are also used to maintain the tax-advantaged status of funds rolled over from any qualified plan such as company-sponsored retirement plans like 401(k)s or 403(b)s.

When first established, IRAs were intended to be simple and universal, which they more or less were in the early to mid-1980s. According to the Investment Company Institute (ICI), contributions from 1982 to 1986 were an average of $34.4 billion annually. When the first set of restrictions was enacted with the Tax Reform Act of 1986, contributions fell in 1987 to $14.1 billion. And then the regulation and re-regulation of the IRA continued.

My goal is to offer an overview of the best way to make use of your IRA, not to provide a history of the account and its regulations, which can be summarized in two main points:

1. The introduction of the IRA has been a tremendous boon and benefit to individuals saving for retirement.
2. The rules governing IRAs, both for you and, more importantly, for your heirs, have grown to be complex beyond imagining, to the point where individuals themselves, without professional assistance, can hardly expect to gain maximum benefit from their accounts.

In my opinion, the incredible complexity came into play partly because of the IRA's initial success. The government wants you to use the tax-deferred feature but it does not want to wait forever for its money or allow you to lock up very large amounts in accounts that will never be subject to taxation. Hence the requirement to start taking distributions at age $70^1/_2$ and the endless rules about who can and cannot contribute, at what age, and in what amounts.

The majority of Americans today have IRAs or their company retirement plan brethren, 401(k)s, rather than the defined benefit plan that might have applied years ago. For many people contemplating retirement, these assets constitute a significant portion of their overall wealth. Many financial advisers believe that the way you handle your tax-deferred money is the single most important piece of your overall financial plan.

Major concerns regarding the disposition of your IRA include:

- How and when should you take your distributions from your IRA and/or company retirement plan(s)?
- How much should you (or must you) take out at one time, or each year?
- Who should you name as beneficiary?
- When you take money out, or inherit an IRA, what are the tax consequences?

If you have significant assets in these tax-deferred IRA and retirement plan accounts, these are among some of the most important and complex financial decisions you will ever make. The answers to these questions will depend on a number of unique personal factors.

When you leave your employer, you will receive a *retirement plan distribution package*. It will contain important disclosures and forms relating to your distribution options. It is extremely important that you make the right decisions and complete these forms properly. Most people approaching retirement do not fully understand the hidden negative consequences of making the wrong choices. You and your heirs could end up paying enormous—and unnecessary—taxes and penalties. Whether you will be receiving tax-deferred money, are the legal representative for, or are the beneficiary of these kinds of accounts, it is extremely important that you seek the services of competent, informed professionals such as a tax adviser, financial adviser, or attorney.

This chapter discusses the basics of IRAs and company retirement plans, important tax considerations, beneficiary issues, and common mistakes people make with IRAs.

Understanding the Basics

First I am going to talk about the two basic types of *company* retirement plans: *defined benefit plans* and *defined contribution plans*. Both types of plans are referred to as *qualified plans*, because they meet certain requirements of the Internal Revenue Code and, as a result, are eligible—qualified—to receive certain tax benefits. These plans must be for the exclusive benefit of employees or their beneficiaries. Whenever you hear someone talk about a qualified plan or qualified money, you know the funds in question are tax-advantaged. Either type of retirement plans allows the company to make tax-deductible contributions, and employees may also be able to make their own contributions.

Defined benefit plans are the old-style pension plans, where the company promises to pay out a certain amount to you every year (hence the named *defined* benefit, because you know what the benefit will be). In a defined benefit plan, the company you worked for retains the risk of the plan; if the investments for the plan fall short, the company is on the line to make up for them somewhere else in its operations. In this brave new world of *defined contribution plans, you* bear the risk: You contribute a certain amount (your contribution is defined) toward your retirement, and if you do not invest wisely, you will feel the effects of the shortfall in not having enough money—or as much money as you expected to have—at retirement. Defined benefit plans are disappearing fast, leaving you with primary responsibility for funding your own retirement.

Do not make the mistake of confusing *tax-advantaged* or *tax-deferred* with *tax-free*. With very few exceptions, tax-free instruments hardly exist: The IRS always gets paid. However, the enormous benefit of tax-deferred accounts is that the funds are allowed to grow without paying annual taxes on the dividends or growth in the account, thereby allowing the account to grow much faster. Taxes are paid on the amounts as they are withdrawn from the accounts. Funds can be withdrawn from qualified accounts in a number of ways, including withdrawals of large amounts or a stream of income over time. In order to use these accounts to your maximum benefit, you must understand how those withdrawals are taxed so you can organize your investments to owe the minimum amount of taxes.

Individual Retirement Plans: IRAs and Roth IRAs

An Individual Retirement Account, as I have defined it, allows you to deposit an amount of money into it every year, to grow tax-deferred until you are ready to withdraw some of it. When first introduced, it was tax deductible to everyone. The rules started changing in 1986, so that it is tax deductible only if you do not have access to a company-sponsored retirement plan or if you have income below a certain level.

But let me be clear: Everyone with earned income can deposit money into an IRA every year, even if you have a high income and a pension plan at work. This is known as a nondeductible IRA. However, in those cases the money going into the account is after-tax money. You do not get a deduction from your taxes for contributing to this account. However, it is a good way to accumulate investment dollars on a tax-deferred basis.

An IRA is also the vehicle into which you can roll funds from an employer-sponsored plan such as a 401(k) (for most people) or a 403(b) (specific to teachers). If you leave a job for any reason, the money that has accumulated in your 401(k) with a company can be rolled into your personal IRA account. There are rules about doing this. For example, if you have your former company make the check out to you and then you fail to deposit it in your IRA within 60 days, not only will you have to pay income tax on the entire amount, if you are younger than $59^1/_2$ you will have to pay a 10 percent penalty tax as well. It would be best to figure out where you want to open your rollover IRA and have someone at that firm help you get your 401(k) funds transferred so there is no possibility of incurring the penalty tax. A custodian-to-custodian transfer, or a check made out to the new custodian, is generally the best way to go.

The Roth IRA was introduced in the Taxpayer Relief Act of 1997. Named for its chief legislative sponsor, Senator William Roth of Delaware, a Roth IRA differs in several significant ways from other IRAs. The IRS requires the usual, specific eligibility and filing status requirements, but the main advantage of the Roth IRA is its tax structure, which allows it to be managed in creative ways.

Contributions to a Roth IRA are not tax deductible for anyone, regardless of whether you have a company retirement plan. Withdrawals from regular IRAs are generally tax-free but have restrictions. One of the main problems for people starting to withdraw funds from regular IRAs will be figuring out what portion of the funds withdrawn has already been taxed, since nondeductible IRAs are funded from a person's after-tax dollars. The Roth gets around that problem.

There is a long list of the advantages of a Roth IRA over a regular IRA, including easier access to your money if you need it before retirement. However, if you have income above certain levels, you are not eligible to contribute to a Roth and must use a regular IRA if you want one. (For 2009, eligibility for contributing any amount to a Roth ends at $120,000 for an individual and $176,000 for a married couple.) This income limit is adjusted annually. For that reason, I am not going to devote more than just a mention to Roth IRAs; I think they are out of reach for many of the relatively affluent individuals who will be reading this book.

The year 2010 offers a special possibility for those who might normally not be eligible to contribute to a Roth. Anyone owning a traditional IRA is allowed to convert it to a Roth and pay the taxes on it without reference to the income test, thus being able to take advantage of the Roth's beneficial attributes. However, you may not use any of the money in the traditional IRA to pay the tax because that would be considered a distribution.

There are two schools of thought on this:

1. The characteristics of the Roth are so advantageous compared to those of a traditional IRA that you should make the conversion, even if you have very large IRAs and even if you are in your 50s, especially since tax rates are likely to be higher in the future; thus, paying the taxes now provides a clear benefit.
2. If you are nearing retirement, deciding whether to use this much of your capital to make the conversion is a very difficult choice to make. If you are approaching retirement, you are likely to have large IRAs from years of investing, and using your capital, which is probably greatly lessened post-2008, to make the conversion is not necessarily the right choice for everyone. The choice is probably easier for someone in their 20s or 30s.

An IRA is an account type, not an investment type or a security. When you open this kind of account, it works like any other account you have. You can have an IRA account with a bank and invest in CDs or even money market funds (although by now you know that I do not recommend that kind of investment for long-term money). You can open an IRA with a mutual fund company and invest in that company's mutual funds; you can open an IRA with a discount brokerage firm or a regular brokerage firm and invest in stocks, bonds, or mutual funds. What makes this account different is the way dividends, interest, and returns are taxed: They aren't, until you get ready to draw on this account at retirement.

For many years, the maximum annual contribution was $2,000, but that has been increased. For 2008–2009, the maximum contribution for a person under 50 is $5,000, and for 50 and over, $6,000; this amount can be divided between Roth and regular IRAs. From now on, contribution amounts will be increased by $500 increments according to inflation.

Your IRA is different from most other assets in a number of ways. Here are some important rules.

- Gifting: The rules on charitable gifting of an IRA have changed a number of times over the years. At one point you could not do it at all, and later the rules allowed you to make a charitable gift of your IRA. You just have to check the rules at the time you want to do this.
- Required minimum distributions: According to law, IRAs are subject to demands for "minimum distributions"; that is, at certain milestones, a portion of the accumulated monies must be paid out, and taxes paid on these. IRAs are subject to minimum distributions in the following circumstances:
  - When you turn $70\frac{1}{2}$ (or, at the latest, no later than April 1 of the year following the year that you turn $70\frac{1}{2}$). Special relief to this requirement was granted in 2009, so check current law or talk to your tax professional.
  - When you inherit an IRA and properly retitle that IRA by September 30 (October 31 for trusts) of the year following the year that the owner died. (The original owner's required minimum distribution, or RMD, must still be taken by December 31 of the year the original account holder died, if that person was older than $70\frac{1}{2}$.)

Taxes: Don't Take Out Too Little, Too Much, Too Early, or Too Late!

What follows are the essence of the rules regarding distributions from IRAs. The IRS requires you to begin taking distributions by age $70\frac{1}{2}$ and penalizes you if you take money out prior to age $59\frac{1}{2}$, with certain exceptions. Your IRA may be subject to one or more of the following taxes: income tax, estate tax, state taxes, generation-skipping tax, and various penalty taxes. The simple rules you should remember are the following:

- *Too little*: Your distributions should take into account the other taxes you are paying, and you should try to pay the least amount of tax possible overall. This is especially true in the 5 to 10 years leading up to age 70^1/$_2$.

For example, if you have a large IRA and are living on current assets and income that do not take you deep into the tax table, then you should consider taking some money out of your IRA now. You will pay a lower tax on those distributions now, instead of the otherwise higher tax you might pay once you reach 70^1/$_2$ and are forced to take your minimum distributions.

Also, keep in mind that there is a 50 percent penalty for not taking out your full, required, minimum distribution.

■ *Too much*: Don't be forced to pay unnecessary taxes, which can include federal income taxes, state income taxes, estate taxes, and generation-skipping taxes, either while you are alive, or by your heirs after you die, because you did not name a proper designated beneficiary, or because your heirs do not understand the inherited IRA rules! Distributions should take into account other already-taxed assets you may have that you may wish to use first to reduce your overall tax.

Special Comment for Very Large IRAs

If you leave a very large IRA when you die, you may find that the balance left to your heirs is nearly destroyed by estate taxes, income taxes, and/or generation-skipping taxes. In a worst-case scenario, your beneficiaries could lose up to 70 percent of the account balance to these taxes! That happens because an IRA might be subject to gift taxes, inheritance taxes, and income taxes; it is a mind-blowing possibility that has really happened to too many unsuspecting heirs.

One simple way to reduce this overall tax is to prepay the estate tax at a discount by taking partial distributions before you die, paying taxes on those distributions, and purchasing a second-to-die life insurance policy which will cover this triple tax when the surviving spouse dies. I say more on this topic in Chapter 10.

There is no income tax or estate tax when the first spouse dies, assuming that the beneficiary is the surviving spouse and the surviving spouse transfers the IRA over to his or her own IRA. All of these taxes will come due at the death of the second spouse. If this applies to you, isn't it smarter to share a small portion of your IRA with an insurance company now, in order to avoid sharing up to 70 percent with some 300 million strangers (the IRS) later?

- *Too early*: If you take distributions before age $59^1/_2$ (unless you take your distributions under special rules referred to as "Section 72(t)") you will generally pay a 10 percent penalty *in addition to ordinary income taxes*. The special rules and formulas under which early distribution *can* be made without penalty are complex and absolutely require professional advice. If you deviate from the formula you originally choose, you can be required to pay the 10 percent penalty on all of the distributions you have taken up to that point.
- *Too late*: As mentioned earlier, there is a 50 percent penalty for not taking out your full, required minimum distribution. Additionally, if a beneficiary does not properly retitle an inherited IRA by September 30 of the year following the death of the owner and take the required minimum distribution by December 31, the entire balance will have to come out within five years and be subject to tax.

Working with Beneficiaries

Universities could open up whole new fields of research into the science of IRA beneficiaries. It is truly one of the most complex, detail-oriented subject matters you will encounter in the entire U.S. tax code. Furthermore, the rules change all the time.

For you, with your own IRA, the question of beneficiaries is minor, but your heirs will care mightily that you name beneficiaries correctly. What happens to your IRA when you die will depend on who you named as the beneficiary, and then the one or more *designated beneficiaries* or their legal representatives must choose how to manage the inheritance.

It is vital that you attend to your IRA beneficiary forms because they take legal precedence over every other kind of document, including divorce decrees, wills, and signed documents of every kind. I provide here only the briefest of overviews because the technicalities of the rules are so complex that they require a whole law course; I simply cannot give you enough information here to do what you need to do.

Beneficiary designations have two rules that are important above all else:

1. Your beneficiary forms must accurately name the current designated beneficiary.
2. Never name your estate (or any other estate) as the beneficiary of an IRA.

Surviving Spouse

The rules are simplest for the surviving spouse of the original account holder, who can choose to roll over part or all of the balance into his or her IRA; take a lump sum distribution; establish an inherited IRA and take minimum distributions each year; or use a combination of these options after splitting the account into separate pieces. This is not even an exhaustive list of what the surviving spouse may do, but some of this depends on whether the original account holder had reached age $70^1/_2$ and whether the spouse is the sole beneficiary. This is the easiest way to inherit an IRA—from a spouse—but you can see the complexity of the rules already.

Nonspouse Beneficiary

The choices available to a nonspouse beneficiary depend on a variety of factors, including whether the original account holder reached age $70^1/_2$ and whether there are multiple beneficiaries. If there are multiple beneficiaries, it is usually best to split the IRA into separate pieces and establish a separate *inherited IRA* for each beneficiary. If the inherited IRA is not set up this way, then the oldest beneficiary's life expectancy (greater age translates to quicker, larger distributions) must be used to determine annual distributions.

Stretch IRAs are a relatively new entity in the IRA world and have become important. A stretch IRA is a tool for transferring wealth to a younger beneficiary, usually one's children or grandchildren. Stretch IRAs were introduced by IRS regulations in 2002. A beneficiary is now allowed to stretch out the length of time withdrawals can be taken from the IRA. That length of time will usually be based on the life expectancy of the younger beneficiary and will obviously stretch out the period of tax-deferred earnings beyond the age of the individual who originally established the IRA, maybe even for the entire lifetime of the beneficiary. Of course there are rules, rules, and more rules. It is important for you to know that this kind of IRA possibility exists; that titling or retitling the IRA correctly is very important; and that you should run, not walk, to your adviser's office if you should inherit an IRA or intend to set up a stretch IRA. This book does not have room for more information on this very complex subject.

Beyond a stretch IRA, the older rules stated that if a nonspouse is the beneficiary and the decedent was younger than $70^1/_2$, the beneficiary may take a lump-sum distribution; must take out the entire balance by December 31 of the fifth year following the original account holder's death; and, if eligible, may elect to establish an inherited IRA, which will allow the nonspouse beneficiary(ies) to take out distributions from the inherited IRA by December 31 of the year after the original account holder's death.

Distributions are based on the beneficiary's life expectancy reduced by one each year.

It is extremely important to note that a nonspouse beneficiary *cannot* roll over the amount into his own IRA! This is even more important if using a stretch IRA, which must be rolled over and retitled according to very specific rules. Additional rules and exclusions apply; these should be discussed with your professional adviser.

When establishing an inherited IRA, it is important to understand that the IRA account must be retitled by September 30 of the year following the year in which the IRA owner died. It must be retitled as follows: "John Doe, deceased (or decedent), IRA for the benefit of (or FBO) Steve Jones." It is important that the decedent's name *and* the name of the beneficiary *both* appear in the title of the inherited IRA. Beneficiaries pay income taxes as they receive distributions, but they are required to take out only a certain *minimum* amount of money each year and are, therefore, still able to defer the remaining funds in much the same way as the original account holder. By utilizing an inherited IRA in this fashion—withdrawing only the minimum amount each year and leaving the rest to grow—the additional money available to a beneficiary over time is remarkable.

Trust as Beneficiary

A trust may be a beneficiary and there are certain legal requirements that must be met.

Estate as Beneficiary

This is the most onerous of all forms of beneficiary and gives the beneficiaries of the decedent's estate certain options, depending on whether the account holder was older or younger than $70^1/_2$ at death. Consult your estate-planning attorney, your tax adviser, and your wealth manager.

The foregoing only scratches the surface of the rules for IRAs. If you are like most people, your eyes glaze over when reading this kind of thing, and even if you understand it in principle, it would be impossible for you to implement. This is yet another reason why the advice of a professional adviser isn't a luxury—it's a necessity.

The Challenges of Inherited IRAs

An inherited IRA may provide the benefit of spreading tax liability out over a person's lifetime, but IRAs and pension plans are both subject to estate tax and ultimately some form of income tax. It is also possible to make a charity the beneficiary, resulting in no federal or estate taxes. While IRAs have provided an important vehicle for many individuals to accumulate money for their retirement on a tax-deferred basis, the complexities of the rules governing their use can present significant challenges when trying to do estate planning.

IRAs are included in your gross estate for estate-tax purposes, and the beneficiaries of your IRA will ultimately have to pay income taxes on funds distributed from them. Be very clear on this: For a traditional IRA, income taxes always have to be paid eventually, whoever ultimately takes the distributions. (Roth IRAs are different.) An inherited IRA might or might not have estate taxes due on the funds as well. This potential double taxation is the source of the kind of horror story I mentioned earlier, where someone inherits a very large IRA but winds up with a paltry sum after cashing it out and paying all the taxes.

So the first thing I ask when there is a large IRA at stake is whether the person who owns it or has inherited it is charitably disposed and is planning to make a bequest to charity, because using an IRA for that bequest is the easiest thing to do with it. There will be no estate taxes on it because it has been donated to charity, and the charity does not have to pay income taxes on the funds as it withdraws them.

If donation is not in the picture, imagine that I have an estate of $7 million in 2009 (emphasizing that this pertains to that particular year because of the $3.5million federal estate exemption available in that year only). My wife and I together have an estate of $7 million and want to create two living trusts, one for each of us. But this time our total estate consists of $3.5 million in other assets and a $3.5 million IRA in my name. The $3.5 million in other assets goes into my wife's living trust. The IRA belongs to me, so I have to keep it and I put it into my living trust. I name my wife as the beneficiary of the IRA so that she can roll it into her own IRA and not have to start taking distributions right away. There is much more information about family trusts in Chapter 12. You might want to come back to this section after reading Chapter 12.

IRAs also have rules concerning required minimum distributions (RMD) that start at age $70\frac{1}{2}$. In general, an affluent person will want to delay taking distributions as long as possible, to maximize the benefit of the tax shelter that an IRA essentially is. When one spouse inherits an IRA from the other spouse, she can roll it into her own IRA and keep on the same schedule for RMDs that she had before. A 60-year-old person inheriting an IRA from her spouse can go for another $10\frac{1}{2}$ years before having to take any distributions.

But back to my example. Say I die first and my wife inherits my IRA, which she rolls into her own and does not have to take distributions from. But in that case, I have not funded the family trust and taken advantage of my own $3.5 million estate-tax exemption. If I have children, then I have neglected to form the family trust for their benefit.

I could make the family trust the beneficiary of my IRA, but in that case distributions will have to be made based on the life of the primary beneficiary. Since the trust is the official beneficiary and not my spouse, then the spousal rollover exemption would not apply and distributions might have to start right away. Even if the wife is the primary beneficiary of the trust, the distributions would still have to start right away. This may not be as desirable an alternative as having the wife named as primary beneficiary so she can roll it all into her IRA. When the trust inherits my IRA, it has the same name it would have if a person inherited it: "Norm Mindel, deceased, for the benefit of the Norm Mindel trust." But the trust can set up separate shares if it is a qualified trust.

The one way to get around this is to make my wife the primary beneficiary of the IRA and the trust the contingent beneficiary. After my death, my wife can consider all the circumstances and decide whether she wants to roll over the IRA completely into her own or put it into the family trust, where she might have to start taking distributions immediately. If she does take the rollover into her own IRA, she will have lost the opportunity to take advantage of my federal estate-tax exemption and could potentially have to pay more federal estate taxes on her own estate than if the IRA had gone into the family trust. If she decides that she wants the IRA to go into the family trust, she is allowed to disclaim her inheritance of the IRA. Disclaiming is acting as though she, too, were dead, and the money will go to the family trust. Sometimes it is just not possible to figure all this out ahead of time, and the estate plan can leave it up to the surviving spouse to decide after the death of the first spouse.

If my only asset when I die is a very large IRA which owes estate taxes, my heirs have only two choices. First, they can take money out of the IRA to pay the taxes. If the IRA owes $1 million in taxes, the heirs will have to take out some 40 percent more than that to result in having enough cash to pay the tax. Second, if the heirs wish to stretch the payments from the IRA in a way that will benefit them for years to come, they can pay the estate taxes themselves, out of their own funds, with the thought that the IRA will generate more return in the long run through its tax-deferred structure. Just to add to the pain, some states now also tax IRAs.

This whole example is predicated on this being a first marriage for both parties. If it is a second marriage, then the qualified terminal interest property (QTIP) trust would be used instead, and the surviving spouse would not have the same freedom of action. If you are naming your trust as the beneficiary of an IRA, the trust has to meet certain qualifications under the Internal Revenue Code. Again, there is more on this subject in Chapter 12.

Common Mistakes with IRAs, Self-Directed Plans, and Qualified Plans

Now that we have covered the basic rules, here are some of the most common mistakes, divided into five areas. These apply to either or both individual plans (IRAs) and company plans (401(k)s and 403(b)s).

While You Are Accumulating

Mistakes 1 through 4 occur while you are accumulating.

1. *Not participating in your company retirement plans to the maximum extent allowed, or not participating at all.* Your company retirement plan is one of the best places for you to accumulate wealth over the long term, especially when you take into consideration that none of your contributions are taxed for perhaps 20, 30, or 40 years; most employers offer a matching provision for a portion of your contributions; and maximum allowable contributions generally increase every year. It is simply unwise not to take advantage of this company benefit, but you should contribute more than the level of the company match. All of your employee contributions come right off the top of your income and are not reported as earned income. Uncle Sam has given us an incentive to put away as much as possible.

2. *Putting too much of your money in your company's stock (too risky).* A widely accepted general rule of thumb is never to have more than 15 to 20 percent of your wealth invested in any one individual stock—although, personally, I still think that is high. As I have said before, concentrated positions represent concentrated risk, regardless of whether it is the company you know. The risk that you incur is higher than that of a well-diversified portfolio and is beyond the acceptable risk tolerance of most individuals (whether they really understand that or not!). When you see your account balance rising over 15 percent in one stock, it is a good idea to rebalance your portfolio to a more suitable, diversified investment mix tied to your goals, time horizon, and overall risk tolerance. Highly paid executives have other special political considerations that need to be taken into account when implementing this rule, but the rule is still a sound and prudent one.

3. *Putting too much of your money into a money-market account or guaranteed account (too conservative).* Retirement plan participants generally have too much of their money invested in the most conservative investment options. I understand how people feel, after 2008, and I address the seduction of going to cash in Chapters 6 and 7. Being too

conservative means you give up the opportunity to grow your funds with the market. A better approach would be to assess your risk tolerance, develop your allocation from among different asset classes, then periodically rebalance. Keep in mind that the long-term (50-year) return of equities is approximately 10 percent, even post the apocalyptic 2008, and the long-term return of bonds has been approximately 5 percent. The closer you are to retirement, the more conservative you ought to be, but *conservative* is a relative term to be defined by you in collaboration with your adviser.

4. *Trading your account excessively*. It is seductive to believe that you can "beat the market." You can't. (If you still think you can, review Chapter 4, "The Futility of Active Management," or the Dalbar study shown in Chapter 3.) No matter how low transaction fees in your account might be, they add up and subtract from the finite amount of money that you are allowed to invest tax-deferred. Review your allocations periodically and rebalance just a few times a year.

Note: Some companies will allow you to receive a lump-sum distribution or will allow you to directly roll over some or all of your account balance after age $59\frac{1}{2}$ (or even lower, for some plans), even if you are still employed. This is typically called an *in-service distribution*. Is this right for you? That is a subjective question with many other factors to consider, including your age, certain guarantees that may be offered by your current plan, and your desire to exercise more control over your investment choices. Talk to your tax adviser.

When You Retire

Mistakes 5 through 7 occur when you retire.

5. *Not planning ahead*. Waiting until just prior to your retirement date to understand your distribution options can be devastating. When you retire, you will generally have the following four options for your company-sponsored plan, whatever kind it is:
   a. Roll the money over into an IRA.
   b. Leave your money in the plan.
   c. Take a lump-sum distribution.
   d. Transfer the money into your new employer's plan.

   Generally speaking, if you have an opportunity to roll over your retirement plan balance into an IRA, the advantages outweigh the disadvantages. However, you will need to understand both sides of this question to make the decision that's right for you. There will always be some individuals for whom an IRA rollover is not appropriate (if, for example, you are between 55 and $59^1/_2$ and will need some of your tax-deferred funds to live on). Some people feel you should take any distribution you can because company retirement plans are always going to give you less choice than you would have if you controlled your own money, even if it is in an IRA. Unless you plan on spending your entire balance right away, it is generally not a good idea to take a lump sum and pay all of the taxes all at once. For most people, this is often the worst alternative.

If you plan on working after retirement and becoming employed by a firm with a defined contribution retirement plan, you are allowed to transfer your current plan balance into your new employer's plan. Even though current rules allow you to roll over your balance into a new employer's retirement plan, you are generally better off rolling that money into an IRA for the same reasons already mentioned.

As you approach retirement, your concern will naturally shift to *income planning*, and your main concern will be to ensure that your money lasts longer than you do. Many people become more conservative than they were when in an accumulation mode. You should clearly understand your distribution options at least a few months before you need to send in your paperwork to request your retirement distribution. This will give you some time to think through the most appropriate choices for you. Making last-minute decisions about something this important can be dangerous! Once you send the paperwork in, your choices are usually final and cannot be changed.

Some things you will want to consider: Your company retirement plan may offer you limited investment choices, whereas if you roll those funds into what is called a *self-directed IRA*, you control the assets and the investments. With proper guidance, you can make wise investment choices that provide more diversification and that may be more suitable for your risk tolerance and income needs.

6. *Investing too much in your company's stock.* I know I am repeating myself, but this point is extremely important. Owning too much of any one stock is a mistake at any stage of your investment life. It does not matter if you inherited if from your beloved parents or if it is the stock of the company you work for. I actually recommend holding *zero* shares of the stock of the company you work for. But if—for whatever reason—you really want to own shares of the company you work for, do not go above owning approximately 15 to 20 percent of your net worth in any one stock, including your company stock. What if you had worked for Lehman Brothers or Bear Stearns? Both companies were excellent and had good prospects—until the end, which came

very fast. Employees who had invested their life savings with those companies were left with nothing, or almost nothing. The same thing had happened a few years ago with Enron. No matter how great your company is and how much you believe in it, the only prudent action is to diversify. Since your job is with that company, you are already heavily invested in it and its future.

However, sometimes it is not that easy to diversify, especially if you have worked for a company for a long time and bought some of that stock a long time ago. Stock in a company retirement plan requires special consideration. First, if you have low basis in your stock, you may want to take a distribution of that stock and then sell it. You will pay ordinary income tax on the basis, but only pay capital gains tax on the net unrealized appreciation (special rules apply). If you roll the stock over into an IRA, there will be no income tax when you sell it in the IRA, but you will pay ordinary income tax on any distributions that you take out later.

If you receive stock certificates as part of a lump-sum distribution, you will need to be especially careful. If you decide to roll over your stock, make sure beforehand that your IRA custodian will accept the stock. Some IRA custodians will not accept stock certificates. For example, many banks and credit unions only allow investing in CDs or a money-market fund and do not offer the option of a true, self-directed IRA. Also, many investment companies offer you a choice of investments, but only in their own mutual funds. You should look for an IRA that allows proper diversification.

7. *Having too many IRA custodians.* It is crucial to understand the difference between what your IRA custodian allows and what the IRS allows. You must comply with whichever set of rules is more restrictive!

As tax laws have changed over the years, some custodians (this applies to all types of custodians including banks, brokerage firms, credit unions, insurance companies, etc.) have not kept up with these revisions and have not changed their documents to allow what the IRS allows—for example, allowing the establishment of an inherited IRA.

You may, therefore, find yourself in a situation where the IRS will allow one thing, but your custodian requires you or your heirs to do something different—oftentimes more restrictive. The same comment applies to company retirement plans (for example, nonspouse beneficiaries are often required to take all of the money out within one year and pay tax on the entire balance).

Note: You need to know the difference between rolling over pretax and after-tax portions. Under the new tax laws that became effective January 1, 2002, after-tax contributions to a 401(k) are now also eligible to be rolled over. If you roll over or transfer any part of these after-tax contributions, then there will not be a penalty for rolling over too much! But keep in mind that you will need to keep track of the already-taxed amount that you rolled over each year on your tax return. You will be required to submit forms.

When You Reach Age 70¹/₂

Mistake eight occurs when you reach the age of 70¹/₂.

8. *Not understanding the required minimum distribution rules and how they apply to you.* If you don't take out the proper RMD amount, you will end up paying up to 50 percent of the amount you didn't take out as a tax penalty.

Note: You may take distributions for all or any combination of your IRAs in order to meet your RMD. A good idea is just to have one IRA that will allow you to diversify your holdings in one account so you can keep your calculations simple and avoid mistakes.

Before You Die

Mistake 9 and 10 occur before you die.

9. *Naming your estate the beneficiary of your IRA.* As I said earlier, never name your estate the beneficiary of your IRA. This will impose the most restrictive rules on those who will inherit your IRA. If you name a trust, it is a good idea to consider language that will easily allow the different beneficiaries to split their interests in the trust into separate inherited IRAs, so as not to be forced to take money out based on the oldest, or most restrictive, beneficiary.
10. *Not considering the combination of all possible taxes that may be imposed on your IRA.* These include federal and state income taxes, along with estate taxes and possibly generation-skipping tax as discussed earlier.

When You Inherit an IRA

Mistakes 11 through 16 occur when you inherit an IRA.

11. *Rolling an IRA into your own IRA without being the decedent's spouse!* If you do this, you may be subject to a 50 percent overfunding tax penalty!

12. *Not taking distributions over your lifetime versus the five-year option.* The worst option is taking the money out all at once and paying 35 percent or more in federal income taxes!

13. *Not using the correct language when establishing an inherited IRA.* The IRA must be properly retitled by September 30 of the year following the year the IRA owner died, as follows: "John Doe, deceased (or decedent), IRA FBO Steve Jones." It is important that both the decedent's name *and* the name of the beneficiary appear in the title of the inherited IRA. Beneficiaries pay income taxes as they receive distributions, but they are only required to take out a certain *minimum* amount of money and are, therefore, still able to defer the remaining funds in the same way as the original account holder did.

14. *Naming a trust as beneficiary without checking with an attorney.* You must comply with the rules in order for the trust to be considered a designated beneficiary.

15. *Not properly calculating your inherited IRA RMD.* If you take out too little, you will be subject to penalties and more taxes.

16. *Not getting professional advice.* The rules affecting IRAs are constantly changing. Misinterpretation of newly changed rules or continued application of obsolete rules can have a large and potentially devastating impact upon your personal finances and those of your descendants. Appropriate, regular, ongoing professional advice is essential to achieving your goals.

Frequently Asked Questions about Managing Your 401(k)

In Chapter 3, we mentioned in passing some of the mistakes that investors make when choosing the investments for their 401(k) money. When the number of investments options available is relatively small, people tend to allocate their funds evenly across all choices, regardless of what those choices are. Even the famous Harry Markowitz, father of modern portfolio theory, admitted to doing this. When the number of choices is very large, many individuals feel overwhelmed and cannot figure out what to do and so make no choices, thus leaving their money in the money market fund or whatever the default investment is. Another set of investors thinks of this money as very serious money that must be invested very safely—and they choose the kind of investment that cannot lose money, a money market fund or its bond equivalent. Unfortunately, as we have discussed many times in this book, that is probably the most unwise decision they could make, because that money cannot grow and thus cannot keep up with inflation or the need for retirement dollars. Studies regularly indicate that a large proportion of 401(k) dollars is sitting in money market funds.

If you are lucky enough to have been at the same job for many years and you have contributed systematically to your 401(k) plan, you might have built up $100,000 or more in your plan. Highly compensated individuals or those working for a company that makes profit-sharing contributions into their account could have seven figures or more. You must take this money into consideration when looking at your overall financial situation—and yet you cannot direct its investment beyond the choices available to you.

Whether or not you work with a professional financial adviser, your 401(k) account is beyond the reach of your adviser and completely separate from any other investments you have. The available investments depend completely on the plan your company has adopted. You might well have to learn your way around some mutual funds or mutual fund families that you are not familiar with.

The large variety of features and investment options available through 401(k) plans means puzzled clients often go to their financial adviser for guidance. Clients often want to know how to invest and manage their 401(k) so that it works in concert with their other investments. If you have a large amount in your account and you are getting up in years, you also have to be sure to name beneficiaries. Have you gotten divorced since the time you set up your account? Maybe the wrong name is on the beneficiary line for the account. As I mentioned earlier, you need to start planning in advance for this part of your retirement plan.

Addressing wider concerns is beyond my scope here. I just want to offer a few tips concerning the most common questions my clients ask me about investing in their 401(k) plan at work.

- *Should I participate in a 401(k)?* In general, you should invest as much as you can. Not only is it an easy way to save on taxes today, but, as you increase your savings, you could increase the periodic paychecks you receive in the future. Many companies also provide a matching contribution, which is akin to receiving free money on top of the current tax savings and increased resources available at retirement. Furthermore, if you are 50 or older, you may be able to take advantage of additional tax-deductible contributions.
- *How should I allocate my 401(k) investments?* The easiest way to allocate your 401(k) assets is to try to use an asset allocation model similar to the one you use for your other investments, because it corresponds to your risk tolerance and time horizon. But there may be some drawbacks to this approach; see the next question.
- *My 401(k) offers only a few index funds and many active funds; how do I pick active funds to satisfy my asset allocation requirements?* This is far less desirable than using your own overall asset allocation program

customized to your personal time horizon and risk tolerance, but you can keep a few things in mind:

- Many 401(k) plans will not have all of the asset classes that correspond to the asset classes used in our models. You may be able to come close and still have adequate diversification under your asset allocation.
- Many actively managed mutual funds or separate accounts available under other 401(k) plans or to the general public may be characterized as having style drift, as I have discussed elsewhere in the book. A fund may be described as a "U.S. large-cap" fund, but the prospectus may state that the manager reserves the right to invest 15 to 20 percent in international funds, real estate, or short-term bonds. As a result, I do not believe track record is the most important factor in selecting an active fund. Instead, make sure the fund meets the investment criteria for the desired allocation and really invests according to its investment philosophy. You do not get the diversification you expected if, for example, the small-cap fund manager has added large-cap positions.
- When picking fixed-income funds, do not focus on yield, since higher-yielding funds can hold long duration bonds, which in turn increase the volatility of your portfolio, or lower-quality bonds, which increase risk in the part of the portfolio that is supposed to hedge risk. Instead, focus on the duration of the bond funds: Less than seven years is most desirable. Additionally, consider investing the fixed-income portion of your account in a stable-value fund if your plan offers one, since such funds tend to have less volatility.
- A simpler approach is to look for funds that already use asset allocation. Such funds may be called balanced, fund-of-funds, or lifestyle funds. Some plans may have a choice of funds based on your personal risk tolerance or target retirement age.

- *How often should I review the investments my 401(k) funds are going into?* You should review your account once a year, keeping in mind some of these questions:
  - Has over- or underperformance in some sectors resulted in the need to rebalance the portfolio back to the original asset allocation?
  - Is the allocation still appropriate to your time horizon?
  - Are funds meeting their investment goals and representing their asset classes?
  - Once again, ask if your company stock represents more than 10 to 20 percent of your total portfolio. The fact that you are employed by your company means you already have a very large stake in the success of the company; adding a large stock position significantly increases your risk profile.

Final Words of Wisdom

Do I have any other words of wisdom? Just this: *Do not chase returns!*
I keep repeating this because it is so important. You need to stick with
your allocation model and not change it because some funds were
losers and others were winners: This is normal and means you were
diversified. Buying last year's winners and selling last year's losers is
very likely to result in poor performance in the long run.

Wealth Protection:
Facing a World of Risk

Wealth Protection:
Facing a World of Risk

CHAPTER 10

Best Uses for Life Insurance

Howard S. Kite, CFP, CLU, ChFC

In my early years at Terra, I focused a great deal of my time on estate planning, which means that I also did a great deal of work with insurance. Insurance in general is one of the most important tools any estate planner has to work with. It can protect young families financially from the untimely death of a parent, provide for medical care during the last years of one's life (I discuss long-term-care insurance separately in Chapter 11), and transfer wealth from one generation to another. I have always believed strongly in the value of life insurance. No matter what opinions you have about the insurance industry and the way it conducts business, insurance itself is an essential tool in the financial lives of many people. However, as you will read shortly, it can be difficult to separate the importance of insurance as a concept from the sometimes less-than-admirable way the industry—or individual insurance agents—conducts business.

Throughout this book, I have discussed the ethical failures of Wall Street and the abuses of stockbrokers. Based on my experience, I have to add that the life insurance industry and its sales practices are also abusive. But even so, many clients have a real need for insurance products, and I have planned many estates where insurance has preserved a family business or provided a spouse with critical cash at a moment of extreme vulnerability.

In my practice, sometimes I need to call on the expertise of a specialist to help with certain situations. Insurance in particular is one of those areas. Rather than write this chapter myself as a generalist, I have invited Howard Kite, CFP, CLU, ChFC, one of my partners at Terra and now my partner at Forum, to share his insurance expertise with us. Howard is a second-generation insurance professional who has helped hundreds of tax professionals navigate through this complicated and confusing area of financial planning. The remainder of this chapter is written by him.

Confessions of an Insurance Agent

My name is Howard and I am an insurance agent.

Woody Allen said, "There are worse things in life than death. Have you ever spent an evening with an insurance salesman?"

Why do we chuckle when we hear this? In my opinion, it is because the insurance industry's reputation is well earned and well deserved!

In the course of my career, I have learned about the uses, abuses, sales practices, motivation, and greed within the industry, and my partners and I have tried to educate clients and accountants on the good, the bad, and the ugly of the insurance industry. I have three objectives for this chapter:

1. To help you understand that life insurance, like other insurance products, is an important tool to help you hedge against the catastrophic event of untimely death.
2. To help you understand how the industry went haywire and what the consequences were.
3. To provide a template for selecting the appropriate product and amount of insurance.

As Norm said, I am a second-generation insurance agent. My father spent much of his life post–World War II reaching for the American dream by selling small policies to people who needed them to provide for their families. At that time, insurance agents could sell only small cash-value policies that paid high commissions to the agent. In 1955, when gas was $0.23 a gallon and the average price of a home was $22,000, a $10,000 life insurance contract was a significant hedge against loss of a wage earner. Dad used to leave the house on Monday morning and travel to some rural area; he would work day and night all week until he came home on Friday night. The insurance industry had to provide extraordinary incentives to persuade agents to sacrifice their family lives through this much work. The commission structure developed from a business model of selling a large quantity of small policies. Unfortunately for the consumer, this same high-commission structure has prevailed for many years past the time when it made sense, into the 1970s and beyond. Like the market's recent experience with the mortgage industry, this inspired greed and abuse.

When I entered the insurance industry in 1981, fresh from a teaching career, the industry was dominated by people who were more interested in earning commissions than in helping their clients. I was fortunate that the person who hired me was not like that, and I received a broader-based training that included elements of financial planning. I eventually worked with business owners and people who needed insurance as a protection from estate taxes. But at the start, I worked full-time as an insurance agent for an insurance company and my ability was evaluated by the single criterion of production. Like my father before me, I was a product of the environment. I had a new baby; I was paid on commission, and I needed to pay the bills. So I sold.

Low-cost term insurance had been in existence for some time when I began in 1981. The commission on annually renewable term insurance products was 30 percent in the first year and 2 percent on renewal premiums. In contrast, cash-value insurance (which you probably think of as whole life insurance; whole life is one kind of cash-value insurance) was compensated with a 55 percent first-year commission along with incentives that might go as high as 85 percent, with renewals at 10 percent of subsequent premiums. Additionally, cash-value premiums, paid in the first year for the same amount of coverage, could be 10 to 15 times greater than the premiums for term insurance. This was the beginning of the snowball the insurance companies started to roll downhill during the post-WWII recovery, but the result was an avalanche that benefited agents and insurance companies more than the insured.

Agents and insurance companies will probably bristle at that last statement and note how many billions in claims they have paid out over the years to help families and companies survive economic disaster. But here is how agents were originally trained: Ask how much the client wants to set aside on a weekly or monthly basis, and then purchase as much cash-value insurance as possible. The question *should* have been: How much insurance does the client need? And the appropriate action would then be to choose the type of insurance to get the person the appropriate coverage. The cost of $10,000 of cash-value insurance and $100,000 of term insurance was very similar in the first year, yet the commission paid to the salesperson was significantly different.

I know everything the insurance companies would tell you about how cash values create savings whereas term premiums increase over time, and I also know every platitude there is to justify the sale of a cash-value policy rather than a term policy. However, when the rubber hit the road, in 1985, I would rather have delivered a $100,000 check to a young widow to help to insure that the family would be able to retain its lifestyle and support the children through college than give her the same-priced $10,000 insurance check provided by a cash-value insurance policy.

When I was first working with clients almost 30 years ago, the majority of life insurance was issued by *mutual insurance companies* rather than *stock insurance companies*. Mutual insurance companies are literally owned by the policyholders. That means that excess earnings generated by a mutual insurance company are returned to the policyholders in the form of a policy dividend. There are significant tax advantages to this structure and it produced significant benefits for policyholders. The policies issued by mutual insurance companies were called *participating whole life.*

Because the company was owned by its policyholders, all the earnings of the company went into the company's general account to pay all the expenses of running the business plus reserves needed to be set aside for claims to be paid in the future. The interesting aspect of mutual companies is that, when they are profitable, those profits beyond what is needed to operate the company are returned to the owners/policyholders in the form of insurance dividends. Dividend scales are projected at the issuance of the policy, but there is no guarantee the projected dividend scale will be met. People living longer than expected and interest rates going up provided additional earnings in portfolios, and such companies were very profitable in the 1970s and 1980s; dividend projections were very high. Unfortunately for mutual insurance companies, they could grow only as fast as they could sell more policies. If they wanted to grow faster and needed capital to grow, many were forced to turn themselves into normal, publicly held corporations. In making that change, they issued shares in the public company to the old policyholders, and sold shares in the new company on the stock markets. Now those *demutualized* companies' earnings needed to be shared with shareholders as well as with policyholders. Today, there are only a few significant mutual insurance companies left.

By the late 1980s, the industry was starting to come around to the changing economic realities created by inflation in the earlier part of that decade. There was a real need for large amounts of low-cost term insurance. The commission structure began to change so that agents could get compensated based on the amount of the premium rather than on the type of insurance. But the industry mentality was already deeply committed to selling high-cost, high-commission, cash-value policies. Furthermore, now computers could be used to model insurance proposals that put projections in writing. These projections were the beginning of the next great sleight-of-hand to be perpetrated on the consumer. With the high commission structure and minimal regulatory oversight, creative insurance agents and companies used computer projections to extol the virtues of tax-deferred/tax-free build-up of cash values to provide an incentive to purchase large policies as investments. Without regard to conscience, agents and companies devised schemes to sell insurance and annuities that were abusive to the clients—and in some instances destructive to the insurance companies themselves.

This chapter is important because life insurance is the only product that can create liquidity for a family or business at the precise time when it is needed—in the event of a death. It is essential to most financial plans at almost any stage of life. The problem is that the products are confusing and are distributed by insurance agents who have historically put their own income needs before client needs. Even worse are the creative individuals who have taken advantage of a loosely regulated environment to market schemes that are counter to the clients' best interests. Our objective is to help you differentiate between appropriate and inappropriate insurance products through some easy-to-understand illustrations and guidelines.

Insurance is a very complicated financial instrument. Until recently, it was in the insurance company's best interest to spend time training and rewarding people to *sell* rather than to disclose and explain the intricacies of how the product really works. Interest rate and equity market volatility in the late 1980s and early 1990s had a dramatic effect on these creative policies and schemes that were devised by agents and companies—schemes designed to fulfill one primary objective: to sell more high-premium, cash-value products.

Why Do So Many People Dislike Insurance?

Why do people dislike insurance so much? Usually when you spend hundreds or thousands of dollars on something, you expect to receive something tangible in return. But insurance—and especially life insurance—is a very *intangible* product. You pay lots of money, and the insured typically does not receive a tangible reward for paying the premium. The *beneficiaries* receive the tangible rewards, not the insured. Most importantly, partly because of the complex nature of the product, the industry has done a poor job explaining the purpose of cash-value insurance in the big picture. Most people with whom I have come into contact over the years firmly believe that cash-value life insurance is a waste of money.

Auto insurance provides a good contrast to life insurance. Almost everyone has made a claim on their auto policy although, over your lifetime, you will almost certainly pay far more in premiums than you will ever receive in claims paid. Yet strangely enough, people feel better about paying their auto premiums than their life premiums. Why? I believe much of the reason is the appearance of a tangible reward, claims paid, while we are alive. Even though we are quite certain that, over their economic lives, almost everyone will get less back in claims paid from auto insurance than what they paid in premiums, we

(continued)

(Continued)

have gotten paid something. With life insurance, you do not get back anything tangible until you die, and people look at cash values as a wasted asset. Many only consider whether they have the right amount of life insurance when they are ill and mortality is knocking on the door.

So before you decide to skip this chapter, believing that this is just another insurance agent who is going to justify selling cash-value insurance, please don't—because it isn't. After finishing this chapter you will have a clearer understanding of life insurance and be able to at least have an informed discussion of the appropriate type of product for your needs.

Types of Insurance

At the highest level, there are two basic types of life insurance: *term insurance* and *cash-value life insurance*, also called *permanent life insurance*.

1. *Term insurance.* This kind of insurance provides a person with a death benefit for a certain length of time, usually a year. In its simplest form, it can be compared to car insurance. Everyone knows that car insurance is good for a certain period of time. You pay your premium every year for that year's coverage. If you have an accident after your car insurance has lapsed, you have no coverage. Term insurance has no residual cash value and reflects only the cost to keep a policy in force as the insured gets older. It can become extremely expensive, as we will see, to keep a term policy in force as people get older.

2. *Permanent insurance.* As the name indicates, permanent insurance is intended to remain in place for more than just one year. In fact, the usual intention is to have the policy remain in force until the insured dies, no matter when that is. There are two major types of permanent polices, *whole life* and *universal life*, and many variations of each of them. I will concentrate only on the most-used types.

At the heart of every single insurance policy ever issued is a *mortality charge*, the price the insured pays the insurance company for the basic risk that the insured will die that year. This price is assessed by the insurance company. Term insurance includes only the mortality charge whereas cash-value insurance includes an amount that will be invested within the policy—and this is done by various calculations and in various ways—so that the insurance will remain in force throughout the life of the insured.

Term Insurance

Term insurance is a policy that has no cash value and reflects the cost of mortality, or the chance of a person dying at a particular age, each year the policy is in force. It is absolutely essential in most insurance plans because, for a very low outlay of premium, a person can provide large levels of coverage at a point in time for the period of time that coverage is needed. A perfect example is someone with family obligations. A person has a child age two. It is foreseeable that the obligation to support this child depends on someone earning income until a point in time, like the child finishing college or 20 years. In this situation, it would be appropriate to purchase a 20- or 30-year level term policy to cover this obligation in the event that the parent dies during this time period, including the years after college when parents may have depleted their savings to help pay for college or even graduate school.

There are two main types of term insurance, *annually renewable* (premiums go up every year) and *level term* (premiums that are guaranteed to remain the same for a contracted period of years). After that period, the policies either do not renew or become annually renewable at the then-current premium rates. Level term time periods may be 5, 10, 15, 20, and even 30 years. Choosing the appropriate type of term insurance should balance the duration of the need with the amount of money a person is willing to allocate to the need.

I cannot express myself more plainly than the following: The cost for term insurance with long premium guarantees has become so very inexpensive that there is absolutely no reason for people, especially those with young children, not to consider owning large amounts of personal (not group through an employer) term life insurance.

For illustration purposes only, I am including a table to compare the premiums at specific years for different types of term policies. Table 10.1 shows four different types of policies: annually renewable (premiums go up each and every year), 10-, 20-, and 30-year level term policies (premium is level for a specified period of years). Some carriers allow the level term policy to be renewed after the level premium period; others do not. If the policy can be renewed, the premium would typically be similar to the annual renewable premium shown in Table 10.1. The premiums shown here are from a financially strong, major insurance company. Special note should be taken that all insurance is underwritten, meaning that to qualify for a specific premium, the insurance company needs to assess your current

TABLE 10.1   Term Insurance Costs for a 35-year-old Male
Nonsmoker in Relatively Good Health

Policy Year	Annually Renewable $	10-year Level $*	20-year Level $*	30-year Level $*
1	610	450	710	1,020
2	630	450	710	1,020
3	660	450	710	1,020
4	700	450	710	1,020
5	730	450	710	1,020
10	5,550	450	710	1,020
20	12,860		710	1,020
30	36,900			1,020

*Policy is no longer in force after the level premium period.
Source: Forum Financial Management, LLC, as compiled from
mainstream insurance companies.

health situation and family history of diseases. Table 10.1 shows the annual premium payment required for each of the four different types of insurance policies. These rates represent $1 million face amount on a male, age 35, nonsmoker, who is in the second-best risk category.

Permanent Insurance

Permanent insurance policies include a cash-value account that is supposed to grow over the years. This means that the annual premium that you pay goes partly to pay the cost of providing insurance and partly to build up as cash earning a certain return inside the policy.

Risk assessments—the *mortality charges*—are made to policies at regular intervals based on the amount at risk (total death benefit minus cash value) times a mortality (risk of death) charge based on the attained age of the insured. In other words, the insurance company has less risk when there is cash value in the account to pay some of the death benefit in the event of the insured's death, but the mortality charge of course increases as the insured ages.

As I related at the beginning of this chapter, low-cost term insurance has been in existence for 40 years, but insurance companies have created significant economic incentives to sell *cash-value products*. Traditionally, *whole life* is one cash-value product, but the newer variations on whole life, such as *universal life* and *variable universal life*, are also cash-value products. I say much more on this topic later in this chapter.

As an example, consider two large groups of people: (1) everyone in the United States who is age 35; (2) everyone in the United States who is age 85. It is easy to understand that the chance of any one person dying in group 2 this year is significantly greater than that of any one person dying in group 1, right? Thus an insurance company would need to charge more to cover the risk of dying for people in group 2 than for those in group 1.

Now consider the premiums charged for annually renewable term. This is the purest form of life insurance because each year the premium increases, reflecting the increasing mortality charge; the insured has to pay the higher premium every year to keep that policy in force. (The cost to purchase a new policy each year would be a completely different table with variables that I do not discuss here.)

Table 10.1 shows us that, as we age, the cost of keeping the term insurance in force goes up each year. It is important to note that the renewal premiums are not the cost of purchasing a new policy every year at that age. Median life expectancy today is about age 84. That means that 50 percent of the people will die at age 84 or earlier and 50 percent age 85 or later. About 4 percent of the population will die at age 84. In our simple model, it is obvious that obtaining a life insurance policy beyond age 84 is a very expensive proposition with very little economic reward. If you need insurance at age 85 or later, you will need to have done something while you were younger to hedge these high charges later in life. Not only do mortality charges increase significantly as you get older, but you may not be able to get insurance at all, due to health problems you may have developed. This illustration is part of the fundamental logic of why cash values are so important. Cash values, in insurance policies, are the hedge against these extremely high expenses in the future. Let's take a look at how that works.

There are two primary types of permanent insurance: *whole life* and *universal life*.

Whole Life

Whole life is a form of permanent insurance and is the primary kind of cash-value insurance that I would have sold through the 1990s. A simple example would be a policy that has a $5,000 annual premium for a $500,000 death benefit. The $5,000 you pay is more than the annual mortality cost and therefore causes the cash value in the policy to build over time. The rest of the premium (over and above the pure mortality cost) pays into the cash value reserves, which have two components, *guaranteed* and *nonguaranteed* values. The guaranteed values are very conservative contractual guarantees that are designed to increase over time so that at a point in the future the guaranteed cash value equals the guaranteed death benefit.

In the case of a mutual insurance company, excess earnings—the profits from the mutual insurance company's overall operations, including investment return on the company's investment portfolio in excess of the guaranteed return—would be built into the structure of the policy and are returned to the policyholder in the form of a nonguaranteed dividend. This could add up to a significant amount over time, due to interest compounding. These policies could well build up enough cash value earning dividends to eventually pay for future premiums, thus allowing the policy to become self-funding. Whole life is very appropriate to use when an insured can afford the higher premiums and there is a need for the unique guarantees provided by whole life; the cash values become part of the overall solution. Such uses principally include estate planning or specialized business scenarios.

Universal Life

Universal life (UL) is another type of permanent insurance issued by both mutual and stock insurance companies, and in a way was the successor structure to participating whole life. It has a flexible (hence universal) premium structure that allows the insured to raise or lower the premium payments easily. There are two types, *interest-sensitive* (a declared set interest rate guaranteed for a specific interval of time, as declared by the insurance company) and *variable* (invested in the same types of subaccounts that are used in variable annuities; these subaccounts operate like mutual funds and are separate from the insurance company's general account; contract owners select which ones they want to use). Universal life is easier to understand than participating whole life because in its basic structure the charges are just more transparent than those of whole life.

Generally, the risks of interest-sensitive policies are more controllable than those of variable policies and should be used either to accumulate cash values to reduce future mortality charges as the insured person ages or for some other specific, unique, business purpose. *Variable insurance policies should be used only to optimize the internal build-up of cash values.* Premium requirements in these scenarios are very large, and anyone buying such a policy needs to have a thorough understanding of the investment risks associated with the contracts.

Universal life is simpler to understand than *whole life,* more transparent in its fees, and more flexible in its premiums. However, most people do not understand that in building this structure, insurance companies have insidiously shifted to the insured many of the guarantees that are available in whole life. In UL policies, the insurance company has a great deal of freedom to change the interest rate credited to your policy every year and to change other nonguaranteed terms of your policy, including the mortality charge. Its actions could seem quite arbitrary and you as a policyholder would have no recourse. With whole life, you are a shareholder of the company, and you and the insurance company have the same set of best interests at heart.

From the early 1980s, when universal life was initially introduced, on into the 1990s, insurance salespeople and consumers really did not understand the long-term effects of shifting risk to policyholders. Recently, however, in response to the marketplace, insurance companies have designed policies that reflect a need to guarantee that contracts do not lapse during the time when coverage is expected.

Cash Values and Policy Lapse

The objective of this subsection is to provide a brief, simplified discussion of how cash values build in a universal life insurance policy, and to look at what happens when there are insufficient values in the policy. The final subsection under "Universal Life" introduces the newest generation of permanent universal life policies. This is not designed to be a full explanation of how the policies work and the implications of various premium payment strategies or variations in charges that are assessed to the contract—that is beyond the scope of the book. This is a guideline discussion to prepare you for a conversation with an insurance professional.

Simply stated, UL policies work as follows. Premiums are paid to the insurance company. A cash-value account is credited with this amount and any earnings. As mentioned earlier, the earnings depend on whether the contract is *interest-sensitive* or *variable*. At regular intervals, typically monthly, the cost of mortality (the difference between the death benefit and the cash value is the amount of mortality or risk of dying that the insurance company has) and any additional expenses allocated by the insurance company (stated in the contract itself) are deducted from the cash-value account. As the cash value grows, a policy's amount of risk is reduced. (A $1 million policy with $200,000 of cash value really has only $800,000 of insurance risk for the insurance company, because the policy already has $200,000 of value.)

Figure 10.1 illustrates what happens inside a policy when a set premium of $5,411 is paid over the life of the policy for a 35-year-old, relatively healthy, nonsmoking male for $1 million of insurance from a major insurance company. The premium stream is designed with a projected interest rate of 5.95 percent; the current projected mortality charges are then assessed so that the projected cash value and the death benefit, at age 100,

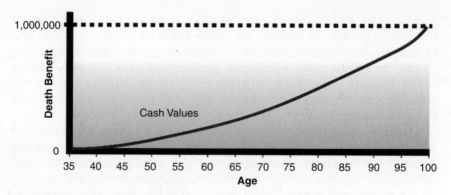

FIGURE 10.1   Cash Value in a Whole Life Policy with Interest at 5.95 Percent

Source: Forum Financial Management, LLC, as compiled from mainstream insurance companies.

are both $1 million. This is a good result. This means that the death benefit will be available when the insured dies.

Figure 10.2 illustrates the same policy with only one change: I reduced the credited interest rate to 4.95 percent. In this graph, the cash value goes to zero at age 91. This means that at age 92, unless the policy owner pays the current mortality charges (think term insurance cost at age 92 for $1 million of coverage), there is no death benefit available to be paid. This is not a good result.

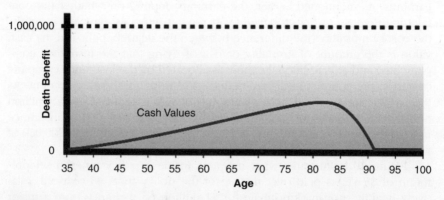

FIGURE 10.2   Cash Value in a Whole Life Policy with Interest at 4.95 Percent

Source: Forum Financial Management, LLC, as compiled from mainstream insurance companies.

The credited interest rate is only one aspect of what can change inside a policy. A few others are:

- *Premium frequency.* A lump sum of $5,411 paid at the beginning of the year does not produce the same earnings as when paid over 12 months.
- *Projected versus guaranteed mortality charges.* Insurance contracts are required to state both a minimum interest rate and a maximum mortality cost that can be charged. All illustrations must show both projected and guaranteed rates and costs. Insurance companies have the option of changing the rate they charge to groups of policyholders, not individuals, anytime during the life of the policy. What do you think the chances are that an insurance carrier will voluntarily lower its charges on existing contracts in the future?
- *Changing the premium amounts and payment frequency during the life of a contract* will have effects on the contract in later years that may jeopardize the availability of the death benefit.
- *Variable insurance contracts*, because of their investment in the stock market, are also affected by point-in-time risk, discussed in Chapter 7.

A New Approach to UL

By now, because of the barely disclosed changes, you might wonder about the morality of the insurance industry itself. However, it works this way because, as I stated earlier, life insurance is complicated. The insurance company is trying to balance the promise to pay a death benefit, sometimes 50, 60, or 70 or more years from now, with having a viable business model and making a profit. But the bottom line is that most people just want an answer to the following question: How much do I need to pay to *guarantee* that I will have insurance when I die, while paying the minimum possible while I am alive!?

The product to answer this need would be like level term insurance *for life*, not just for a 20- or 30-year period. To review, level term means that the term policy is issued to you with a guarantee that it will remain in force for the chosen period of time and the premiums will remain the same for that whole time. But these contracts always have an end.

The newest generation of universal life is essentially that level term insurance guaranteed for life. The contract requires you to pay a stated premium amount that will, on a guaranteed basis, keep the contract in force until you die. This is much easier to understand than the traditional UL and it is a good solution in many planning situations. These contracts do have cash values, but they are intended only for the purpose of keeping the policy in force and are not intended to provide any kind of accumulation. An illustration for this type of insurance contract does show cash values, but they are lower than in traditional UL policies that have the same premium because you are paying for the guarantee that the policy will not lapse.

Abusive Sales Practices

If you have ever talked to an insurance agent and asked for an insurance proposal, you know that reading the proposal is like trying to read a foreign language. These proposals show the policy values growing at a nice steady rate. However, if you flip to the page showing *minimum guarantees,* you see a different picture: The cash value does not grow as fast and there may be very little cash value at all. Most insurance agents do not show clients this page—let alone explain it so a client can understand it.

When an insurance company sells a policy, it shows a projection of earnings for the funds invested in the policy. When interest rates were very high in the 1980s, the companies would extrapolate them into the future. Sometimes agents made sale presentations—and continue to do so even now—as if these earnings are stable and will be paid far into the future. Agents might imply that you as a policyholder will get these miraculous returns, be able to stop paying premiums, and never have a premium increase; all this depended on the sustainability of the dividends, interest rates, or investment earnings. These projections, however, are a kind of estimate and are certainly not guaranteed.

Product innovation and transferring risk from the insurance company to the insured did not end there. The stock market offered a similar opportunity with the bull run in the late 1980s and through the tech bubble. Insurance companies then switched to marketing variable universal life (VUL). You could choose to put your premiums into various equity subaccounts (what the *variable* part of the name implied) invested in a wide array of equities. Now the stock market was supposed to provide outsized future returns for the cash value of your policy, although high fees could put a big crimp in your returns—the fees associated with the investment accounts are typically higher than those of the average mutual fund. The fees could sometimes be as high as 350 basis points (three and a half percentage points). If you had an equity account that earned 20 percent, you might not mind 350 basis points of fees (actual return would be 16.5 percent), but if your account earned 6 percent, you would sure care that fees took more than half of that. Although this UL structure actually provided greater transparency than a traditional whole life policy, the very high costs would make the policyholder much more inclined to choose an aggressive portfolio allocation. Not only that, but when the markets hit the skids, depending on the amount and frequency of premium payments, you might not have enough cash value in the future to keep the policy in force (see Figure 10.2).

As this book has discussed, in a capitalistic marketplace, there is no increased reward without an associated increase in risk. During the bull markets of the 1980s and 1990s, salespeople sold variable UL policies by taking advantage of consumer expectations that the stock market would continue to perform in excess of 12 percent annually. Typically this was done by going to the historical performance page that reflected the scenario of what would have happened to the money if it had been invested in stocks over the past 10 or 15 years, and implying that you would be getting these results. Remember that in this policy, the investment account is a separate fund managed in a way similar to the way a mutual fund is managed, and the premiums are flexible. Proposals were being shown with the lowest possible premium streams to keep the policies in force at projected linear growth rates of 10 to 12 percent. Note that all such accounts bear all of the same investment risks and expectations that you would have for any investment in the markets—but these are compounded in variable UL because the amount of mortality risk charged depends on market results. If the investment return is high, there is more cash value and less mortality risk charge that needs to be assessed. The opposite is true when investment returns are low. Underperformance in VUL has the double effect of a lower cash account and increased charges. The downward spiral is analogous to retiring from the work force at the wrong point in time, as discussed in Chapter 7.

The ugliest part of the story with life insurance is just beginning to play out today. Most of the insurance agents who sold the pie-in-the-sky performance of the 1980s and 1990s are no longer in the business. In fact, I have seen numbers that say as many as 95 percent of agents who started in the insurance business were no longer in the business after three years. That means that many of the policies in force today were sold on unrealistic projections and have remained in the top drawer of the file cabinet without being monitored. Even agents who are still in the business have moved on to other areas and are paying less attention to existing policies.

The result may be premiums that are too low to support the cost of mortality in the contracts. This is especially true with UL contracts and whole life with term insurance riders. Either the policy will lapse (as in Figure 10.2) or the insurance company will demand dramatically higher premiums to maintain the policy in force. If you own an insurance contract that was sold to you with projections in excess of the current market conditions, *you need to review it now* to determine whether it is performing in a manner consistent with your needs and expectations.

The demutualization of insurance companies provides another potentially ugly story. I mentioned earlier that mutual insurance companies that wanted to grow decided to become publicly held in the 1990s, the great era for IPOs. The good news is that the company's then-current policyholders were issued publicly traded stock in these companies and, in many instances, this turned out to be good for the new stockholders. However, there is never a free lunch. After the IPOs, the excess earnings above guarantees needed to be shared with a third party: the common stockholder. So in exchange for stock, policyholders were and are getting a lower-than-projected dividend scale on their existing participating whole life policies. If you own an insurance policy issued by a company that has demutualized, it is imperative to evaluate that contract to determine whether it is performing in a manner consistent with your needs and expectations.

Base your decision on purchasing any form of permanent insurance on the *guarantees*, not the *projections*. The agent shows the projections and not the guarantees; you need to do the opposite. Furthermore, it is essential to buy a policy *you can understand*. Note how much this resembles Norm's advice, elsewhere in this book, to invest your money in strategies you can understand.

At Terra in the early 1990s, when the landscape on investment returns changed, we reviewed the effects on some of the policies we had sold. Where appropriate, we ran in-force projections at the then-current interest rates, and then at rates lower than those currently being projected, to look at the effect on those policies. Then we had to go back and talk to selected clients about the premiums that might be necessary to keep the policies in force.

Borrowing Against Life Insurance

As part of the inducement to purchase a high-premium, cash-value policy, prospective clients would be told that the cash values and dividends would give them the ability to borrow against the policy and thus access a significant net after-tax cash flow to fund retirement. The pitch goes something like this: You pay into your policy until it has a chance to build up some cash value, and then you can borrow some of that cash value tax-free. Because the withdrawals are either loans against the policy and/or part of the dividends paid, they are income-tax-free. But in this case, as always, there is no free lunch.

While that is theoretically true, first of all, in most cases, it takes a long while—maybe many years—with any policy to build up sufficient value to start to take withdrawals. Then when you do get to the point where there is enough built-up value to borrow, you find that, although the money is tax-free, it is not free money: The policy charges an interest rate, which can eat away at the overall cash value of the policy and can end up destroying the policy and leaving a significant tax liability. The more you borrow, the likelier it is that you will end up harming the policy. Borrowing against an insurance policy just does not work very well in most situations, unless carefully monitored—and maybe not even then.

The worst situation can happen to people who bought policies in anticipation of withdrawals via loans. After these loan sequences begin, these policies become at risk of lapsing at some time in the future. When an insurance policy lapses, all of the withdrawals in excess of the tax basis (in excess, essentially, of premiums paid) are considered taxable gains. The interest on the loans, even though that interest was not paid in cash, is also considered withdrawals immediately, at the point of the policy lapse. Because of the compounding of interest on the loans and the deferred recognition of gains on an insurance contract, there are potentially very, very large taxable events that occur on a policy with loans when it lapses or is surrendered for cash. Remember, lapse happens when there are no values in the contract, so just at the point in time when there is no further insurance available or the premium required to keep the contract in force is very large, there are no values to pay this large tax liability. This is very serious.

Any policy on which systematic or ongoing loans are made must be reviewed every several years. If you should surrender or lapse these policies and there is a taxable gain, it is immediately recognized for income tax purposes. Once surrender or lapse happens, the genie is out of the bottle and there is no way to get it back in. However, there are strategies to reform the situation if there is enough time.

Trying to Fund Retirement with Life Insurance

For the vast majority of people, buying whole life as a funding mechanism for retirement benefits is inappropriate. The tax deferral and potential for tax-free withdrawals do not overcome the cost involved with issuing the contract. There may be situations for a minority of people—particularly in some business situations or in extremely large estate planning scenarios—where this extra leverage and structure can be useful to help fund insurance. Unfortunately, insurance salespeople look at whole life and UL policies as the Swiss army knives of financial solutions.

As I outlined elsewhere, there are additional risks when you try to make an insurance policy provide strategies for adding economic value beyond what insurance was created for, which is to provide death benefits when you die. Sadly, there are still many insurance agents devising too-good-to-be-true schemes to sell cash-value products with economic incentives beyond the death benefit.

Common Sense for Cash-value Products

If you are discussing the use of insurance as a cash value/retirement accumulation, here is an overall guideline for planning your retirement finances:

- Make sure you have built up a liquid cash reserve to meet short-term emergencies.
- Optimize all the available programs sanctioned by the tax code: business and government retirement plans, regular and Roth IRAs.
- Before you begin using insurance vehicles for retirement, consider whether you have saved sufficient money in *taxable*, not tax-sheltered, retirement accounts. Almost all tax-sheltered retirement accounts have restrictions or penalties on withdrawals. Having money available to draw on without penalty is important throughout a person's economic life cycle.
- Consider variable annuities with guaranteed retirement provisions and weigh the advantages of them against using life insurance as a deferral vehicle.

Getting the Insurance You Need

It is expensive for an insurance company to issue a policy. The largest expense, of course, is the commission structure and the marketing expense associated with distributing the coverage. Then there is the fact that the company must have sufficient reserves to be able to pay claims in the event an insured passes away soon after the contract is issued. These expenses to issue and reserve for a new policy exceed the initial first-year premium. In fact, the insurance company does not even break even on a policy until many years after a policy is issued. But remember that insurance companies fill a fundamental economic role and provide a product that is unique in the marketplace. Like all businesses, insurance companies are in business to make a profit. Profit is not bad; it is fundamental to capitalism.

While some aspects of the way insurance companies work might sound unfair to the consumer, being able to buy insurance is greatly beneficial for individuals who have to consider the possibility a parent might die while a family is young; that a business might need liquidity to meet its obligations if a shareholder dies; or that an estate might have to write a large check against illiquid assets.

The insurance industry's commission structure is part of the current environment. In the recent past there have been attempts by some carriers to provide products with lower or even no commission structure, but these attempts have pretty much failed. No one wanted to sell those products. Without distribution, the idea pretty much died on the vine.

Guidelines for Purchasing the Appropriate Policy for Your Situation

Life insurance is essential to most people at some time in their lives. Here are four simple steps to use when considering the appropriate product to purchase.

1. Determine how much insurance is needed. Here is a simple formula for people with family obligations:
   - Determine the income needed to maintain the household in the event of an untimely death.
   - Subtract any sources of income (earnings from spouse, Social Security, pension, trust funds, etc.).
   - This equals the amount of income shortage.
   - Divide by 5 percent (which means to divide by 0.05).
   - This equals the amount of capital needed to fund the shortfall (assuming that a portfolio will yield on the order of 5 percent a year).
   - Subtract any liquid investment assets and existing insurance that can be used to offset the shortfall.
   - You now have an indication of the amount of additional insurance needed.

     For businesses and estate planning, working with a qualified insurance professional in conjunction with an attorney and tax professional is essential to determine the insurance need and product choice.
2. Determine the length of time that the insurance need will be in place. For business and estate situations, this time period will certainly be different from that of a family with children.
3. Choose the longest time horizon to determine the product choice. Often some combination of term insurance and permanent insurance products will be appropriate.
4. Cost is the final issue. If you cannot afford to fully fund the appropriate mix and type of insurance as ruled by point 3, then the most important criterion often is getting the appropriate amount of insurance for as long as possible for an affordable price.

Life insurance is not an investment! You buy it for very specific reasons, such as wanting to protect your family from adverse economic consequences in the event of your untimely death. Do not try to use a form of insurance solely to capture equity returns. While that might have seemed like a brilliant strategy in 1999, after the bear market of 2008 it seems like an exceptionally bad idea. Everything you own has gone down in value, and now you might be forced to pay in additional funds to your variable universal life insurance policy because its equity subaccounts are also down in value and are no longer funding your death benefit.

There are situations such as estate or business scenarios where cash-value products and, sometimes, a creative structure of insurance policies need to be employed in order to have the appropriate amount of insurance in place to provide liquidity in the event of death. However, even in normal environments, and especially when the creative use of cash values is employed, policies need to be reviewed every three to five years to see if they are performing as anticipated. You can request an in-force ledger from your carrier and it should be reviewed by competent insurance professionals. Leaving your policies in the desk drawer and just paying the premiums is not sufficient, especially with the structures that were devised in the 1980s to induce you to purchase cash-value products.

Using Life Insurance to Transfer Wealth

Term insurance works very well to protect an income stream. However for protecting an estate and transferring wealth, term insurance just does not work. Insurance must be in force at the point in time that estate taxes are due. Devices such as an irrevocable insurance trust, where you pay premium dollars in the tens of thousands and can transfer wealth and income in the millions of dollars, can become very powerful planning tools. In essence you can prepay taxes with discounted dollars. You might pay $100,000 in premiums to buy life insurance, but that insurance can move and control millions of dollars in inheritance. However, it should usually be some form of permanent insurance.

Sometimes I encounter clients in their 30s and 40s who have already accumulated a substantial amount of wealth that they want to transfer to their children. The dilemma is that no one can predict what their circumstances are going to be over the coming years; they are themselves still early in life. They might need the money themselves. The question then is figuring out how to make a gift to the children that will not affect the parents' financial future.

Using life insurance as a wealth transfer device may be better than giving away, for the sake of estate planning, a financial asset that the couple may need for their own retirement. In other words, keep control of assets you may need and use insurance premiums to leverage the value of the gifts you give. The annual premium for life insurance that has the potential to transfer $1 million dollars of death benefits provides very significant leverage.

Imagine that I have a very large estate and I want to buy some life insurance on myself. If I own it individually or if my wife owns it, the proceeds are going to be in our estate and subject to the potential 42 percent estate tax. Life insurance proceeds are almost always income-tax-free to the beneficiary, but if the beneficiary is not the surviving spouse, the life insurance will be subject to estate taxes. After all, you owned it, even if it did not pay out until after your death. The misconception that life insurance proceeds are tax-free has probably arisen because so few estates, relatively speaking, have to pay the estate tax, and many people are completely unfamiliar with the idea of estate taxes. This is also one of those cases where people think that not having to pay income tax means not paying any tax.

To take the life insurance proceeds out of the estate, you have to set up an irrevocable life insurance trust. If insurance is owned by an irrevocable trust and the grantor does not own or control the life insurance, the proceeds will be not only income-tax-free but estate-tax-free to my children. Let us say that the premium on the life insurance is $10,000 annually. I am 40 years old and buy $1 million worth of life insurance. I am the grantor and I put $10,000 a year into this trust and have no control over it. The trust then pays the premium; this is done to ensure that the grantor has no control over the life insurance policy, even to make the payments on it. If it is not done correctly, the insurance proceeds could be subject to estate taxes.

The trust says that when I die, the life insurance proceeds, $1 million, are paid into the trust, and the trust states that my wife can live off the income during her lifetime. When she dies, the money goes to the kids. At the time of the second spouse's death, the trust may be worth more or less than the original $1 million. The trust document may state specifically that the trust's primary use is for the spouse—to the disadvantage of the children. Most trust documents give the trustee broad discretion on investing those proceeds. So I have given up control of only $10,000 a year but I have transferred $1 million in wealth. There is no income tax and no estate tax on that $1 million when I die. At this point, perhaps you are finding the idea of life insurance a little less distasteful; it can be a necessary and valuable tool for transferring wealth.

The amount of insurance that can be put into the trust is determined by the amount of insurance that can be bought by using the annual gift exclusion. (There is a full discussion of gift taxes and the gift tax exclusion in Chapter 12.) The purchase of insurance for the irrevocable trust starts by the grantor gifting the amount of the annual gift exclusion (or less) to the trust; at the moment, it would be $13,000 for one child. If this life insurance trust will be for the benefit of more than one child, then I can put in additional amounts of $13,000. The trust then uses that money to pay the premium on the insurance. How much insurance it would buy would depend on the age and health of the person the life insurance is for. The premiums that are paid every year are subject to the annual gift exclusion or the lifetime gift exclusion.

There is one extremely important caveat about the irrevocable insurance trust. When the grantor dies and the life insurance proceeds are paid into the trust, those proceeds can never be used to pay the taxes on the estate. The law is worded to say that the insurance trust must not be used to relieve the debts of the estate (which would include the estate taxes); this is just the way the law is written. The insurance proceeds could lend money to the estate to pay the taxes, but they cannot pay the taxes themselves.

If I want to transfer some wealth to my children—wealth my wife does not need to live on—and I want to reimburse them for the liability of the estate taxes my estate will have to pay, there is a kind of insurance policy called a second-to-die policy. As the name implies, the policy pays when the second person of a couple dies. The policy should cost about half of what an insurance policy on one person's life should cost, although that of course also depends on your health. This kind of policy can be valuable and important for closely held businesses or if you own illiquid assets. For example, if you were to own a business worth $5 to $10 million, the estate taxes could be high and your heirs would need liquidity to be able to pay them. Insurance can provide that liquidity and is a way of prefunding the estate-tax liability. The actual product used is irrelevant; the point is to get the proceeds out of the insured's estate (using an irrevocable insurance trust) whether it is a single-life or last-to-die product. Almost any time we use insurance for estate planning, it is accomplished through the mechanism of an insurance trust, which is an important tool for transferring wealth.

Buying Life Insurance

While writing this chapter, I was also reflecting about how I felt about my own selection of insurance products. I have term insurance, interest-sensitive universal life, whole life, and even some variable life. Let me share a most irrational thought about insurance. My children are grown and I hope they will very shortly be able to manage their own financial obligations. Until this most recent market downturn, I was fairly confident that my personal plans to reach retirement were reasonably secure as long as I could continue to work for a period of years. I have a large, 20-year, level term policy that will expire in a few short years. The recent bear market means I will have to work longer than I was planning. If I should die in the interim, I suspect that my wife will be financially secure. However, in the back of my mind, I really do not want to lose that large, level term policy; I really wish it were more permanent.

When you purchase insurance today, you determine the amount based on your current finances. There is no precise answer as to the type and amount of insurance a person should have. As I have often said to clients, "If you can tell me exactly when you are going to die, I will tell you exactly the right amount and type of policy to buy with the best economic value." (The joke of course is that it is impossible to know when a person is going to die and therefore we are stuck with making our best estimates of needs and costs.) When considering your mix of insurance, I urge you to consider the longest time horizon in your purchase decision because this will provide you with the most flexibility for the future.

The Underwriting Process

The underwriting process for an insurance policy should take around 60 days from the time you submit your application to the time you get your policy, but many variables can lengthen or shorten this period. Life and/or health insurance typically require both financial and medical underwriting. The goal of *financial underwriting* is to determine whether the amount of insurance you applied for is appropriate for the overall financial circumstance of the insured.

During *medical underwriting*, you will probably have an exam by a medical professional, and the insurance company will most likely request your medical records from your doctors. When you first start to work with an insurance professional, it is imperative that you fully disclose all of your medical conditions, to allow the agent to provide you with a reasonably accurate quote on what the insurance companies might offer. Your medical condition will help to determine what carriers the agent will submit you to for underwriting. This means, for example, if you are a closet tobacco user, do not try to deny it because it will show up in the exam or records. Without committing intentional deception, you will not be able to escape paying the appropriate premium for your risk category. Deception can cause a policy to be voided by the insurance company (especially during the first two years—the contestable period).

One of our clients neglected to mention his open heart surgery during our interviews. He was not considering that a nurse would set up an EKG and would easily see that history from the scars on his chest. Sometimes we do uncover the unexpected. We have many instances when a simple insurance exam uncovered serious health conditions the insured did not know about. In one memorable case, a medical examiner actually drove the potential insured to the emergency room—resulting in an emergency bypass.

Going Forward from Norm

Over the years, I have strongly encouraged my clients to get life insurance. Insurance for some of these people, in million-dollar amounts, is expensive. In large, complex estate planning it is the kind of expense that a normal, middle-class person is not going to contemplate. For example, some years ago, a friend of mine had a high net worth invested mostly in illiquid real estate. I just about forced him to buy insurance, which was expensive, because he needed $3 million of insurance and had already had a heart attack. So he got the insurance—and then died four years later. Paying the estate taxes would have required his heirs to sell off properties at emergency prices, but instead the estate was well provided for. This kind of insurance costs in the tens of thousands of dollars, but has a million-dollar payoff—and, you might say, a happy ending.

Let me conclude with a thought about life insurance salespeople and those high commissions. It is possible to get some preliminary prices and apply for term insurance online, but then, at some point, you enter into the usual relationship with an insurance company—and a health exam is still required, of course. Because of the low premiums, term policies are not that lucrative for insurance agents and they are happy to let this kind of business go online. There actually have been attempts to create fee-based insurance models in the United States, but they have not worked. I saw an alternative—more evolved—financial system in Australia when I was fortunate enough to visit there a few years ago. The first year that full disclosure of fees was required in Australia, most life insurance agents exited the business. Full disclosure in Australia changed all that, but I just do not see that happening here.

I think we are basically stuck with the current system for the time being. Some new low-load insurance policies have been introduced that build cash values faster. A client can get them only by buying them through a financial adviser. Unfortunately, those policies have been introduced by new, smaller companies, and I do not yet have enough faith in their long-term viability to use them.

Financial advisers have to find insurance agents they can trust. I believe individuals are better off dealing with a financial adviser who has some perspective on the insurance industry, works with a variety of different insurance agents and companies, and can explain the process to the client as well as guide him through it. Dealing directly with the captive agent of an insurance company will lead you inevitably to only one recommendation: more insurance with that company.

If you have a health impairment, you may still be able to get the insurance you need. When I started in the industry, a person who had had a heart bypass had little or no chance of being able to get a policy. That is no longer true. Depending on current health, follow-up and monitoring, exercise, and a sufficient amount of time since the procedure, there is a good chance that person can obtain insurance.

An Insurance Agent's Final Thoughts

Here are some of my final thoughts on the matter:

- Insurance is a complicated financial instrument that is essential in most financial plans.
- Your first task is to determine the proper amount of insurance required, preferably while working with a good insurance professional.
- Determine the time horizon for which the insurance is needed.
- Match your time horizon with what you can afford.
- Fully disclose all medical conditions.
- Expect your insurance adviser to review several quotes from financially sound insurance companies.
- Engage an attorney to ensure that the ownership of the policy is structured to minimize tax implications and coincides with your wishes about the use of the proceeds.
- Review all insurance contracts on a regular basis to make sure that their financial performance is consistent with your original intentions and need.

CHAPTER 11

The Importance of Long-Term-Care Insurance

Protection from Disaster-Level Medical Care

This section is about the financial devastation that can occur when a family member needs nursing care, although, given the way medical costs in general have been rising, basic medical care by itself will soon be out of reach for those without private insurance. I have experienced the stress and expense of nursing home care with my own family members, and it is not a situation you want to live through without prior planning.

Medicare and Medicaid do not and are not meant to provide the solution for the cost of nursing care. As I am writing this book, in the Midwest it costs about $7,000 a month for nursing care. Historically, those costs have increased by 6 percent annually, which means that $7,000 will double to $14,000 in 12 years. If you are now in your 50s, unless there is some major change to this inexorable linear progression of costs, you could be facing costs of $28,000 a month when you reach retirement age and beyond. Furthermore, the average stay is four to five years; once you have reached the age of 65, there is a high probability that you or your spouse is going to need nursing care at some point.

Government programs were designed for those who are impoverished. The joke on all of us as taxpayers is that if we are not impoverished before needing extended nursing care, we will be impoverished by the time the government makes us spend all our money. Although trying to divert assets is a game many people have tried to play in the past, it is not really practical anymore. The government has tools to

(continued)

(Continued)

trace those funds. Besides, most people do not really want to give their money away anyway.

The most practical answer is to buy a form of long-term-care insurance. It is not too early to make this purchase in your 50s, when you can lock in a lower premium. In my capacity as both attorney and financial adviser, I routinely suggest this in the strongest possible terms to my clients. I have already experienced a number of occasions when, 5 or 10 years later, a daughter or granddaughter walks into my office bemoaning the cost of care for a parent or grandparent. They also ask me if I did the right thing by their relative; they are looking for a way to assess some liability against me. I pull out the file to show that I made the recommendation and it was turned down. Long-term-care insurance is one of the most significant factors in protecting assets. There is a greater probability that this type of nursing care cost will wipe out a person's portfolio than there is that a bear market will do that.

It has taken a long time for professional financial advisers to recognize the importance of long-term-care insurance in an individual's financial plan, and individuals have been even slower to understand that essential truth. The need for long-term-care insurance is being driven by the demographic factors that are becoming familiar. We are all living much longer than ever before, and most of us will live many years in retirement. Then add the second important factor: The cost of medical care is rising much faster than the general rate of inflation, partly due to the amazing advances in medical care that offer the possibility of extremely expensive new procedures to treat diseases and prolong life.

In 1900, the global average lifespan was 31 years, and it was below 50 in even the richest countries.[1] Any longer-term nursing that was needed was done by family. By 2005, average life span reached 80 years in some countries, and by 2030, average life expectancy at birth for women in countries like the United States will be 85 years. That is an incredible change in the human condition in a hundred years. The health care that prolongs our lives is expensive now and getting more expensive fast. The longer a person is alive, the more likely that person will need intensive health care at some point. The Centers for Medicare and Medicaid Services estimates that about 9 million individuals in the United States over the age of 65 needed health care in 2006, and 12 million will need it by 2020. A study by the U.S. Department of Health and Human Services predicts that people who reach age 65 have a 40 percent chance of needing a nursing home, and about

10 percent of those who enter a nursing home will stay there five years or more. According to the Health Insurance Association of America, approximately 50 percent of all Americans will need long-term health care at some point during their lives. There have been a number of studies that showed how ignorant most Americans remain about the costs of such care and how they overestimate the amount that government programs like Medicare will pay.

Make no mistake about it, long-term care is expensive. A private room in a nursing home in the United States can cost an average of $217 per day, or over $79,000 annually, and a visit by a home health aide averages $21 per hour.[2]

Long-term-care insurance is not needed simply for an unfortunate possibility; as these few statistics point out, it is very likely that you or your spouse or someone in your immediate family will require long-term care, and it will be devastating to you both personally and financially if you do not plan properly for it.

Long-term care is not just about you—it is about your family above all. The impact of needing care affects family members and retirement goals. While family members are usually willing to help all they can, over time the strain and cost can be overwhelming. Caregivers often experience serious economic losses due to changes in work patterns, including lost wages, loss of health insurance, and other lost job benefits.[3] And the difficulties may be magnified as the costs add up quickly. Savings and assets are often used to pay for the care. Paying the cost out-of-pocket may have other costs associated with it, such as early withdrawal fees, immediate tax liability, capital gains taxation when using low-base assets, and more. A written long-term-care plan can help guide your family as it will outline the appropriate funding options available.

The saddest aspect of the occurrence of a long-term care event happens between a married couple. A typical situation might be that when a long-term-care event happens to the first spouse, a great amount of capital is used up for that person's care. Sadly, the remaining person is left with the unanticipated depletion of assets. Typically, that remaining spouse will need to adjust his or her lifestyle to a new reality. Assets often are depleted enough to compromise the quality of care in the event the remaining spouse requires care. This time the need can result in dependence on other family members for financial support or caregiving.

Nothing is likely to pay for adequate care except long-term-care insurance. It pays for covered custodial care not covered by any health insurance, disability insurance, Medicare, or Medigap plan, and pays for community care, home care, adult day care, and care received in assisted care facilities and in nursing homes. It also helps to protect your financial strategies. Long-term care insurance does not replace the need for care from family members—it builds on it, allowing the caregiver to take care of the patient better and longer.

The financial demands of care for older individuals with functional limitations (often due to unexpected diseases such as Alzheimer's, Parkinson's, multiple sclerosis; or the unfortunate result of an auto, sporting, or farming accident; or other chronic disabling condition due to the natural process of aging) could dramatically accelerate the depletion of your retirement nest egg. As we have discussed in prior chapters, there is an inherent danger in withdrawing a high percentage rate from your portfolio before it collapses. Typically anything above 4 percent can deplete the best plans. Imagine the impact on your portfolio if you accelerated the withdrawal from 4 percent to 8 percent or more to cover unexpected long-term care costs.

In addition to the financial burden, there is a significant emotional and physical burden imposed on the caregiver. We all know someone—a woman more often than not—who has spent years caring for an ailing parent or loved one, often while still responsible for raising her own children. There is little time or energy left for much else in the caregiver's own life.

Long-term health care, as generally defined in terms of insurance, is care needed by those suffering from chronic physical or mental impairment which lasts at least 90 days. Insurance benefits are triggered when the individual is unable to perform two out of six activities of daily living (bathing, dressing, transferring, feeding, toileting, and incontinence), or in the event of cognitive impairments such as Alzheimer's disease or dementia.

The Cost of *Not* Including Long-Term Care in Your Retirement Planning

Long-term-care (LTC) insurance is about your family, and it is also about managing financial risk. A long-term-care event in your life can do as much damage to your portfolio as a bear market. It is very important for a wealth manager to have those discussions about health and the possible need for long-term care and to strongly recommend that his clients buy health care insurance. For myself, I try to discuss it with all of my clients and constantly emphasize the need for it. Some do not want to spend the money. But as clients get older, they can develop the kind of health issues that would make coverage unavailable. Typically, reaching age 50 is a good time to obtain an LTC policy.

Most of us fail to consider the impact long-term-care expenses will have on our retirement incomes. Even abbreviated long-term care can quickly decimate a nest egg. The risk from a long-term-care event is equal to or greater than the risk of a bear market. With a market loss, at least there may be a recovery, while money spent for long-term-care costs is never recovered.

TABLE 11.1 How the Cost of Long-Term Care Erodes a Portfolio

Time	Portfolio Amount $
Beginning of year 1	500,000
End of year 1	418,750
End of year 2	328,814
End of year 3	229,670
End of year 4	120,615
End of year 5	−5,000

Source: Forum Financial Management, LLC.

The consequences of extended long-term care can be catastrophic. Extended health care costs—beyond what are covered by private and government programs—are one of the major causes of personal bankruptcies in the United States.

The costs of such care can rapidly deplete most individuals' retirement portfolios, leaving the stay-at-home partner with an empty nest egg. Consider the impact of long-term-care costs on a retirement portfolio. Starting with a $500,000 retirement nest egg and no debt, at current prices, that entire nest egg would be gone within just five years if either member of the couple required long-term care. (See Table 11.1.)

Table 11.1 is an illustration of the kind of impact a long-term care event can have on a portfolio.[4] It is not intended to indicate a budget or to take into account the myriad of other factors that would influence a real-life situation, but to demonstrate how dramatically the expenses of a long-term-care incident can affect a portfolio. This is much worse than any bear market because at the end you have less than zero—you are in debt.

Table 11.2 shows another way to look at costs. The lowest predicted annual inflation rate for this kind of care that I have ever seen is 4 percent annually. That 4 percent is a best-case scenario that envisions very little

TABLE 11.2 Long-Term Care Cost: Projections for National Averages

Year	Daily Cost	Yearly Cost
2008	$209	$ 76,286
2017	$309	$112,920
2027	$458	$167,150

Source: Genworth Financial 2008 Cost of Care Survey—Nursing Home Private Room; assuming that costs increase 4 percent annually, as stated in the survey.

future inflation—which I think is unlikely. This table is a simple illustration showing costs increasing in a straight line, but health care is rarely that simple. I hope that seeing numbers like these makes you get the message about the importance of planning.

The Medicare Fallacy

Many persons facing retirement mistakenly assume that Medicare will pay for long-term health care costs; nothing could be further from the truth. Like many Americans, the couple in the preceding $500,000 nest egg example assumed that long-term health care expenses—just like other types of health care expenses—would be covered by Medicare after retirement.

In fact, the government has sent a clear message to us in our Social Security statements on page 4 by stating: "Medicare does not pay for long-term care, so you may want to consider options for private insurance."

Limitations and restrictions in Medicare eligibility are such that very few, if any, long-term health care services are covered. Medicare was designed for short-term acute care, and short-term rehabilitative stays in a rehabilitation center or long-term-care facility.

Even if you did receive benefits from Medicare, how will you pay for long-term health care costs after 100 days? Chronic diseases such as Alzheimer's, Parkinson's, or multiple sclerosis require custodial care—which is not covered by Medicare. Custodial care is personal care, to help you meet personal needs such as bathing, dressing, eating, transferring from the bed to a chair, and toileting. This type of care can be administered in your own home, around-the-clock, or in an assisted living facility, adult day-care center, or nursing home. Please note, however, that each type of care has various costs associated with it.

Most people would rather receive care in their home as long as possible. At a current cost of approximately $18.75 per hour, it would add up to $450 per day for 24/7 coverage or $164,250 per year. In 20 years, using a 5 percent inflation factor, this amount grows to a staggering $709,560 per year. (We use a cost of $18.75 per hour as a typical cost in Chicago, but you can substitute any number you want for your own area and it will still multiply over the number of hours in a week to become a very large number.) Even the strongest retirement portfolio will suffer under the weight of these costs unless steps are taken beforehand to help mitigate some of these expenses.

For these reasons, purchase of long-term health care insurance is essential to retirement portfolio planning for most Americans. As you age, the cost of such care, and the likelihood that it will be unavailable for you, increases dramatically. For most persons planning their retirement portfolios, the purchase of long-term health care insurance—the sooner the better—is highly advisable.

Insurance is *essential* to eliminating or mitigating the consequences of long-term health care costs. It is not just for nursing home assistance. It includes settings such as:

- Your own home.
- Assisted living facility.
- Adult day-care facility.
- Hospice care.
- Nursing home.

We get more information than we want or need about these topics every day: the aging of America, the overburdened state of Social Security, the health care cost explosion, and other equally depressing, related stories. I find it odd that although many individuals do a reasonable job of trying to plan for the future and accumulating enough wealth to live on for the rest of their lives, the ostrich syndrome is in full force when confronting the very great likelihood of needing long-term care at some point in their lives; we put our heads in the sand and leave our assets exposed. Very few Americans can afford to do this without impacting their retirement portfolio. The sooner we accept the likelihood of long-term health care costs depleting our assets, the more affordably we can deal with it.

Why is it important to purchase now, versus waiting? Not only will it cost more if you wait, changes in your health could impact your ability to even *purchase* a plan.

The Cost of Waiting

Currently, purchasing a long-term-care insurance plan at age 65 would cost $62,640 over 20 years. As Table 11.3 shows, had you purchased it at age 55, you would have paid only $28,800. This represents a 46 percent increase in the cost of premiums just for waiting 10 years.

For illustrative purposes we are using $100/day as the cost of care, so you can adjust the premiums based on your geographic area. Double the premiums to determine what $200/day would cost. Triple the premiums for $300/day.

Table 11.3 provides an example of one particular plan design. There are a variety of plan designs available in the marketplace today to fit the budget of every person who considers this program.

These include different elimination periods (60 days, 90 days, and 180 days), shorter benefit periods (from 2 to 20 years), and the ability

TABLE 11.3   Cost of Waiting to Purchase a
Long-Term-Care Policy

Age	Annual Premium
50	$ 2,976
55	$ 3,434
60	$ 4,120
65	$ 5,101
70	$ 6,965
75	$10,104

Based on $100/day benefit, nonsmoker, standard health, lifetime benefit, 90-day elimination period, 5 percent compound benefit rider.
Source: Forum Financial Management, LLC.

Why Car Insurance Is Like Long-Term-Care Insurance

I find that my clients confuse long-term-care insurance and life insurance. I have had clients tell me, "I have paid tens of thousands of dollars into my policy and never gotten any benefit." You need to think of long-term-care insurance in terms of car insurance, not in terms of life insurance. It is not a cash-value policy that will build value over time, although there are policies that do provide a refund of premium but you need a large initial cash deposit of something like $100,000. Long-term-care insurance is in force only for the time you pay for it.

So I ask you, how many dollars have you paid into car insurance over your lifetime? And yet if you have a safe driving record and have rarely or never needed to access that insurance, would you drive your car into a wall or cause a wreck so you could realize some value from all the amounts you have paid in over the years?

You also understand and accept without question the fact that your car insurance is good for a year, and if you do not pay for the next year, you no longer have insurance—no matter how many years you have been buying it. While long-term-care insurance is much more expensive than car insurance—and getting more expensive all the time, due to the rapidly rising cost of medical care—it still works on the same principle as car insurance: It is in effect for the period of time for which you have bought it and does not build up residual value. It is not cash-value life insurance!

to adjust the daily benefit to reflect the cost of care in the local retirement community. One new and interesting plan design several carriers have introduced is called *shared care*. Under this plan, one policy is issued for a couple which allows that couple to share in the same *pool of money*.

Note that the elimination period, or number of days that you are in care before the policy begins to pay out, is like a deductible on your car or house insurance. You have some choice about what you want this period to be, and your cost will reflect this. A 90-day elimination period means that your policy begins to pay when you are really sick enough to need it and are probably going to need it for some time. It means the insurance company does not have to worry about whether you are really sick or start to pay out for only a short period of time. Your plan design also has to take into account which state you retire in, because costs vary dramatically. Even within individual states or regions, cost can vary depending upon specific locales.

In my mind, the only thing more expensive than buying long-term-care insurance is not buying it. Yes, it is expensive—and if and when you or your loved one needs to draw on it, you will realize what a good decision you made.

Final Thoughts: Pay Now or Pay Later

Doesn't it make sense to pay a little now to protect your future? The pennies-on-the-dollar approach shows us that in many situations you can take less than 1 percent of your portfolio to protect 99 percent by putting together a written plan of long-term-care insurance. The dollars that are paid out to you in the future are, generally speaking, deemed to be tax-free. Hence the pennies-on-the-dollar approach in action.

Long-term health care costs are more than a financial issue. They are really a family issue that every family should address. When the unexpected happens to you and your family, will you be prepared? Long-term health insurance planning provides a safety net to protect you, your family, and your retirement dreams and goals. It is a plan to be included in every retirement planning strategy. It affords you the freedom to make choices that fit your health care needs. Don't leave your retirement-planning strategies exposed to this crisis as you reach retirement. Planning ahead for long-term health care expenses has never been more important than it is today.

Preserving a family's dignity and providing peace of mind are truly priceless commodities that should be included in every retirement plan in America today. What's in your family's plan?

PART V

Transferring Wealth and the Next Generation

CHAPTER 12

Transferring Wealth
with Estate Planning

A ship without a planned route is unlikely to make its port. Just as you need to plan for your investment and retirement strategies, you need professionally advised planning to ensure that the estate you leave behind ends up where you want it. Once you figure out your philosophy about passing money to the next generation, you are ready to start looking at the tools that lawyers and financial planners use to accomplish your wishes.

In my years of experience helping couples and individuals plan estates, I have been witness to every kind of behavior. I have met sensible, caring couples with several children—of which only one is troubled, difficult, or otherwise behaviorally challenged. I routinely see the problems that stem from second marriages and stepchildren. I have met the millionaire-next-door types, driving 10-year-old cars, who don't want to own up to being

Don't Try This at Home

If you think the U.S. income tax system is complex, wait until you start to learn about estate planning! If you have any property at all, even a car and a 32-inch TV, you should be (but probably are not) aware of the implications of estate planning. Those with more assets have to take a greater interest in estate planning, unless they like the idea of the state arranging their affairs after their death. The truly affluent probably have estate-planning attorneys on permanent retainer. In my experience, however, there is one group of people who should take a much greater interest in estate planning and often do not: entrepreneurs with family businesses. For that reason, I have devoted a separate chapter

(continued)

(Continued)

(Chapter 13) to their concerns; the issues are somewhat different when the family business is central to the family estate.

Yet many individuals mistakenly believe that they do not have enough assets to justify doing any estate planning. If you have children, it does not matter what you own—above all, you need estate planning for the sake of your children. If you or your spouse has been married before, and especially if there are children by one or both of those marriages, it is essential that you work with an attorney on estate planning. If you own a home, you need to specify what you want to happen to it in the event of your death. Furthermore, the value of a home can put the overall value of the estate at a high enough level really to need estate planning. Even small estates need a living trust. You certainly need a living trust if you own property in more than one state. A childless couple might or might not have strong feelings about bequeathing wealth to the next generation—nieces and nephews, and so on—or they might be charitably motivated in a way that calls for careful planning. One thing I am absolutely sure about: There are a great many people who ought to be much more concerned than they are about their estates and their heirs.

In this chapter, I introduce some of estate-planning's most important concepts. If I only awaken you to the critical importance of having a will, a living trust, and the other essential documents, it will have been a good use of this space in my book. But do not imagine that you can complete any of this yourself, without the help of an attorney. The best-laid plans can go awry when documents are not crafted and executed precisely correctly; the last thing you want is a defective document, which can be extremely expensive when it causes millions of dollars to be returned to a taxable estate. A defective document can also cause your heirs to waste thousands of dollars fighting about your assets in court. One of the most important things you will learn is that title holding and beneficiary designation are both critically important in the transfer of wealth.

worth millions of dollars—and who, therefore, keep me from being able to deliver the kind of estate planning they need because they are secretive about their assets. I see grandparents who are not happy with the way their children have turned out, and want me to work with them to design generation-skipping trusts; I always warn them to give it time, because soon enough they will find themselves disapproving of their grandchildren's behavior as well. I worked with a man in a second marriage who was torn by the provisions in his will and thus kept asking me to draft one complicated amendment to his will after another, because he just could not bring himself to sign the document, and waiting for another amendment was a good tactic to stall some more.

Although the topic is complex and the strategies appear to be arcane beyond belief, there are ways to mitigate the effects of taxation and to offer families ways to pass financial security down the generations.

In this chapter, I provide a brief overview of the types of property ownership and the rules associated with those types. Next, I discuss the impact the types of ownership and the associated rules have on the way ownership is transferred. Later in the chapter, I introduce you to the essential documents and structures of estate planning as well as a few of the more sophisticated devices available.

This chapter is not intended to be a comprehensive overview of the area of estate planning, for two reasons: limited space and pending legislation that may date anything I write on this topic at this time. That said, there remain two themes in reducing estate taxes:

1. Transfer highly appreciated assets.
2. Use trust or legal entities to discount and fractionalize the value of the gift for gift and estate-tax purposes.

The devices most commonly used include family limited partnerships, grantor annuity trusts (GRATs), life insurance trusts, defective grantor trusts (discussed in Chapter 13), and grantor trusts. For the charitably disposed, the most common devices include charitable remainder trusts and charitable lead trusts. I have used all of these devices, which may still be viable in the future. However, the first challenge in estate planning is usually getting the clients to the table to do just the basics, which are what I discuss in this chapter.

Property Ownership

There are three basic ways to own property. Within these three categories, there are additional choices:

1. *Sole ownership.* In sole ownership, property is owned in the name of an individual and can be used, transferred, or disposed of only by the owner alone or by the owner's agent during the owner's lifetime.
2. *Joint ownership.* In joint ownership, two or more individuals own an undivided fractional interest in property. There are three kinds of joint ownership:

a. *Tenants in common.* Owning property as tenants in common means that each owner has an undivided, fractional interest in the property. The same rules that apply to sole ownership apply to the interest of each tenant in common. For illustration, Charlene and Bill could own 40 percent and 60 percent (respectively) of a piece of property. If Bill passed away, his 60 percent interest in the property would be treated in the same way as if it were sole ownership: not a happy situation for Charlene, who now finds 60 percent of the property— in which she has an interest— tied up in probate.

b. *Joint tenancy.* Joint tenants are owners of an undivided interest in property. In other words, they share equal control over the same piece of property. Although joint tenants are often married, that is not a requirement. In terms of the estate, though, there is an added benefit to this type of ownership: The surviving joint tenant automatically becomes the owner of the deceased joint tenant's interest. No probate is required.

Holding assets in joint tenancy is often viewed as an efficient way to designate an heir without having to go through a big legal process to create a will or a living trust. Assets that spouses share or own together, such as bank and brokerage accounts or a house, are routinely titled *joint tenants in common with rights of survivorship* (and often abbreviated JTWROS in, for example, account names on brokerage or bank accounts). You will also see this with an aging parent whose grown-up child is helping to pay bills or manage money; the parent's bank account also has the child's name on it. At the parent's death, the account then belongs to the child.

Joint tenancies can pose problems, however. The elderly parent with the grown-up child on the account to facilitate bill paying during his waning years might not intend to have that one child inherit the whole account at the parent's death; the parent might intend, rather, that the joint tenant would divide the account among the siblings after death. However, in most states, the courts would assume that the surviving joint tenant is now the owner of the account. There is more on this topic below.

c. *Tenants by the entirety.* Tenants by the entirety is a form of joint tenancy for married couples and, in most states, is available only for ownership of the married couple's primary residence. Each tenant owns the entire property and neither tenant can transfer his or her interest in the property independently of the other. The property is not severable.

The added feature of tenancy by the entirety is that a creditor of one spouse cannot attach or secure a lien on the marital home in the event a judgment is obtained against only one spouse. This is a very useful type of joint tenancy used for asset protection if one or both spouses have creditor issues or are in a profession with personal liability exposure.

3. *Trust ownership.* There are many types of trust and trust ownership. All trusts must have a *grantor*, a *trustee*, and a *beneficiary*. The *grantor* is the one who creates the trust. The *trustee* holds and manages the assets for the benefit of the named *beneficiary*. A trust can be revocable or irrevocable; it can be created while you are alive or created at death. Trusts are highly flexible devices for managing a person's estate.

A Sneak Peak into Title Holding

There are also some techniques that are less obvious. I have had situations where Grandma has only one child or grandchild and cannot see any reason to pay for the expense of a will or trust. She tells me just to put her house into joint tenancy with the grandchild so that when she dies the assets will transfer to grandchild without a will or probate. While this does make sense, it does not really take the big picture into account. But the biggest problems can occur from something that seems too simple. What if the grandchild is in an auto accident? Grandma could potentially lose the house she still lives in due to the judgment of a plaintiff if the grandchild did not have enough insurance. Title holding becomes very important in protecting assets. We discuss this at greater length in this chapter.

Main Goals of Estate Planning

The goals of estate planning can be realized in a variety of ways, but always depend on the way property is owned. You might say that how you own property is the foundation of your estate planning. You cannot transfer property or even minimize the tax bill without understanding who owns the property and how it is owned and held.

There are two main aspects to estate planning:

1. Transferring property when you die.
2. Minimizing the tax bill.

What happens when you die? If you hold property in your name, in any state, your property goes through probate. *Probate* is the formal judicial proceeding to prove or confirm the validity of a will, appoint an executor, and settle an estate. It is a procedure to transfer assets after death, in an orderly way, to protect the beneficiaries, heirs, and any creditors of the estate. If you own any assets in your own name, then your estate will have to go to probate. Probate is a public process and can be very costly in some states. People often do not understand that probate has nothing to do with federal estate taxes, which have to be paid no matter how an estate is settled.

In a larger sense, *probate* has come to be recognized as the legal process whereby a dead person's estate is administered and distributed. The court *proves up* the will, meaning that the court finds that the will is valid, and appoints the executor. The executor's job is to collect all the assets, pay off all the debts, and distribute all the money.

Even though a will nominates an executor, an executor is not appointed until the court orders it. Every state has a probate code which will require individually owned assets to be *probated* if their total value exceeds the state limit or minimum. Some states have a probate limit as low as $10,000, while others vary from $10,000 to $100,000.

If the total assets in the decedent's name are less than the probate limit, the executor can avoid probate proceedings and transfer the assets of the decedent to the beneficiaries of the will using a *small estate affidavit*. If the total assets equal or exceed the probate limit, the executor must petition the court for *letters of office* in order to transfer or deal with assets.

If you die without having a will, you die *intestate* (pronounced "in-TESS-tate") and the state—not you—will presume the order of how the assets from your estate should be distributed. Remember, the rule of intestate succession applies only to assets held in the decedent's name (and not to assets held in trusts, for example). Your estate will be divided among your spouse, your parents, your children and grandchildren, and so on, according to certain preset rules. Those rules vary from state to state and have a certain logic, but are unlikely to be what you had in mind.

Ensuring a smooth transfer of assets in the event of death or incompetency means trying to minimize the whole probate experience. Probate can take a long time—a year or two or more—and can be very expensive, whereas the cost of setting up your estate to avoid probate is usually considerably cheaper than the cost of probate.

In some circumstances, it is possible to avoid probate using some fairly simple methods, as I mention in the next section, and it all depends on the complexity of the estate. As your estate becomes more complicated and includes real estate as well as financial assets—and especially if you own property in more than one state—then a living trust becomes a necessity. The cost of having a trust document drawn up can be a fraction of the cost of probate. I discuss living trusts later in this chapter.

Protection from Tort Liability

You might wonder why I am discussing this topic in the chapter on estate planning. I wanted to give at least a short introduction to the topic in this book, and given the highly litigious society we are living in, without understanding the basics of tort liability, you could find yourself with no estate to plan for. Thus I am including it here.

You do not need me to tell you stories about people getting sued for all kinds of innocuous activities, including selling coffee that is too hot. Whether you are a business owner or an employee or a neighbor or a dog owner, the fact of the matter is that you always have to look out for the potential of getting sued.

The simplest kind of protection is an umbrella insurance policy, which can cover your home, cars, property, and anything that might result in injury to a third party. These umbrella policies can be part of your normal homeowner's policy. You have to figure out how much is enough, and there is no good answer to that. The bar is constantly being raised on how much liability a person is considered to have. You have to let yourself be guided by common sense. For example, if you are a professional person, you are going to have increased potential to be the object of a lawsuit. The level of malpractice insurance a doctor has to carry is beyond the scope of this discussion. As you get older, you become more likely to have assets that are worth protecting or that need to be protected.

If you are a professional, you might want to have your assets held in the name of your spouse because the spouse will not have the same kind of professional exposure for litigation. Of course you absolutely have to keep in mind the state of your marriage and your sense of security with your spouse, but the fact of the matter is that, for most professionals, a lawsuit is a greater threat than divorce. Some states recognize a technique like holding your house as "tenants in its entirety." This special kind of registration, not available in all states and restricted to spouses, gives each owner full interest in the account. The account passes to the survivor upon the death of one owner. This kind of ownership makes it very difficult to exercise a judgment against a husband and wife holding their primary residence this way. In many instances, with the exception of inherited property, gifted property, or a prenuptial agreement, title-holding by the spouse may not mean anything in the event of a divorce anyway.

(continued)

(*Continued*)

(Obviously your legal counsel needs to review how you decide to title your property.)

Your potential liability increases geometrically if you are a business owner. You need to take this potential liability into account when making the most basic decisions about your business, such as how the business is structured. You may want to structure your business as a corporation or limited liability corporation or a limited partnership, to prevent litigation affecting your business from spilling over to your personal assets. The following chapter provides more details about some of these important topics. These commonsense techniques offer protection at the lowest level. As your level of assets rises, you have to work with your attorney and tax adviser to figure out which of the more sophisticated techniques will be appropriate for your situation.

In summary, you can say that, in a litigious society, protecting your assets requires you to have an umbrella policy first and then to be aware of how you hold title to your assets and how you structure the business entity you operate.

Simple Ways to Avoid Probate—and Why They Are Not Enough

Probate is the default way that property passes after death. You need to understand its basic principles so you can understand why you need to do more specialized planning to achieve your own wishes for your property after your death. You should also understand why these simple ways to avoid probate are generally not sufficient in most circumstances.

Although everyone should have a will, people also want to avoid probate. (Please keep in mind that having a will does not mean you avoid probate.) They view it, correctly, as time-consuming and expensive. There are a number of ways to avoid probate, such as joint tenancy, as mentioned earlier. If one person dies, the survivor gets the money; that's very clear. But what if the two joint tenants die in a car crash and you do not know who died first? Those two individuals might share property but have different arrangements for how it should be distributed.

Joint tenancy is not flexible and has only one general outcome if one joint tenant dies: The asset goes to the surviving joint tenant. There can be other disadvantages to using joint tenancy as a shortcut method of asset transfer. On page 257, I mentioned how this simple and inexpensive title-holding can have unintended results while both joint tenants are still alive. In this example, Grandma and grandchild share title on her house so she does not have to make a will, and now the house belongs to both of them. While she might still think of it as her house, from a legal point of view it also belongs to the grandchild and can be deemed an asset that plaintiffs in a lawsuit can seize to settle their claim against the grandchild.

Transfer on death (TOD) is another way to transfer property without going through probate. You can use it for a brokerage account, CDs, and other securities. You register the account as TOD or *POD* (*payable on death*) and designate the person you want it transferred to at your death; that person is essentially a beneficiary. At your death, the property gets transferred without going through probate. The disadvantage is that this very simple and cheap form of transferring property anticipates only one set of circumstances. If the circumstances have changed since the time the action was first taken, the unforeseen consequences could be undesirable. What if the person to whom the transfer was directed has passed on in the meantime? Or suppose your mother really wanted the CD to be paid to you to split with your siblings, but you decide not to?

There are other kinds of assets that do not go through probate because they use the beneficiary designation. Such assets include IRAs, insurance policies, and annuities. It is extremely important for all such assets to include both a primary and a secondary beneficiary because you never want them to end up in the estate. There can be devastating consequences to incorrect beneficiary designation on IRA accounts and pension accounts; typically you name an individual as the beneficiary. The worst thing you could do is to name your estate as the beneficiary of a pension or IRA. You never, ever want to do that. (There is more information on this topic in Chapter 9.)

There are three main ways that property passes to a person's heirs:

1. Operation of law.
2. Contract.
3. Will.

The precedence is the order given. Listing a beneficiary on an IRA is an operation by law. If a person lists his spouse as his beneficiary in his will but lists a sibling as the beneficiary of an IRA, the sibling will inherit, not the spouse. If the IRA did not have a beneficiary listed, then the IRA would be added to the estate and would have to go through probate. In the case of joint tenants, when the share of the first to die transfers to the surviving tenant after the first one has died, that is also an operation by law. A prenuptial agreement is a contract. If the prenuptial agreement differs from the will, the prenup will have precedence. If that were not so, then either party to the prenuptial agreement could void its provisions by writing a will that changed them.

In the popular understanding of estate planning, the first thing that comes to mind is a will, and for good reason, since every person should have a will, regardless of property or circumstances affected by operation of law or contract. I spend much of the rest of this chapter talking about wills.

The Basics of Estate Planning

No matter how simple you think your estate might be—and if you have any property or relatives at all, it is likely to be more complicated than you think—everyone needs a living trust, a will, and a durable power of attorney. I describe the basics in this section.

Living Trusts

I was ahead of my time in understanding the importance of having a living trust, and I have been an advocate of living trusts starting with my first clients. A living trust gives you the ability to transfer assets without going through probate and also provides the means of dealing with your affairs efficiently if you become incompetent to manage your own assets. Maybe a will is enough; maybe joint tenancy is enough; but for many people a living trust becomes extremely important in ensuring a smooth transfer of wealth and the proper funding for estate taxes.

What is a trust? Trusts have been used for hundreds of years. A *trust* is an agreement that allows one person (the *grantor*) to transfer the title to property formally to another person (the *trustee*), who manages it exclusively for the benefit of whoever is named in the trust agreement (the *beneficiary*). A will passes property directly to someone after the death of the person who wrote the will. A trust, by contrast, holds the property for the benefit of someone else during the lifetime of the grantor, or after death, or both. Another important distinction is that a will is a public document; you can look it up and see what was in it. A trust, however, is a private document and the provisions of the trust will not be available for others to see.

Thus, a trust has three parties: the grantor, the trustee, and the beneficiary or beneficiaries. When I create a living trust, I am the grantor. I am also the trustee of the trust, meaning that I manage it, and I am my own beneficiary. I am all three parties until I become incapacitated or until I die. When creating the trust, I also name a *successor trustee,* who becomes trustee of the trust if I become incapacitated or die. In either case, the successor trustee, usually my spouse, manages the trust.

Trusts come in many different flavors. Since these trusts can be changed, they are called *revocable living trusts*, and they are very powerful devices.

There are also *irrevocable trusts*, where I have to give up all control. One of the most-used kinds of irrevocable trust is an irrevocable insurance trust, which I discuss later in this chapter; this topic was also covered in Chapter 10 under the section, "Using Life Insurance to Transfer Wealth." This living trust or self-declaration trust provides an easy way to eliminate probate and can also deal with more complicated things. For example, if you do not want your money to go to your children when they are minors, you would set up a trust within your living trust that says that at your death the money goes to your wife; at her death, the money is held in trust for your children. You can designate that you do not want the money divided equally among your heirs. You can design any kind of plan you want within the living trust. It is much more flexible than merely having a joint account.

The living trust is a document that reads, "I, Norm Mindel, create this trust. While I am alive I can do anything I want with this trust and when I die I name my wife the successor trustee." Writing this document and creating this entity does not incur income taxes or taxes of any kind. It is a legal document. I can change it as much as I want while I am alive. My wife also creates a living trust and it contains the assets that belong to her.

Once the trusts have been created, you retitle the assets so they are in the names of the trusts. For example, the house will not be held in joint tenancy. Instead, the title will read "Judy Mindel, as trustee of the Judy Mindel trust date 00/00/00." My bank accounts will be titled, "Norm Mindel, as trustee of the Norm Mindel trust date 00/00/00." If we divide all our assets this way, when we die, there is nothing to go through probate. Living trusts can hold any kind of property. Most estate planners would recommend that a person establishing a living trust transfer all of his or her nonretirement assets to the trust. In some cases, retirement assets are also transferred to a trust.

Living trusts are the most flexible estate-planning vehicles for holding property. Each living trust can be carefully drafted to fit the needs of the grantor who establishes the trust. The trust is effective as soon as it is executed. It can be freely amended, restated, and revoked during the grantor's lifetime. It can provide for management of assets in the event of disability. At death, it can help achieve estate tax goals and dispose of the grantor's property as he or she desired. If proper planning is done, a living trust can avoid both an expensive guardianship during the grantor's lifetime and probate proceedings at his or her death.

During the grantor's lifetime, a living trust is merely a way to title property. Accounts titled in a living trust use the grantor's Social Security number as the tax identification number. All interest, dividends, and capital gains from such accounts are reported on the grantor's personal income tax returns. It is not until death that the trust becomes a separate taxpayer. As long as the grantor is alive and well, the living trust is revocable; at the grantor's death or permanent disability, it becomes irrevocable.

Usually it is not until permanent disability or death that the successor trustee steps into the shoes of the grantor to act as trustee. The mechanism to become successor trustee is private and simple; usually, the trust document designs a system wherein the trustee automatically becomes successor trustee (1) upon written determination of disability, or (2) upon death. Determination of disability is normally made in writing by the grantor's physician and a family member chosen by the grantor.

In theory, the probate court will not have to administer the distribution of the assets. Instead, the trustee of my trust or my wife's trust will hold and/or distribute the assets according to the terms of our respective trusts. Under normal circumstances, I would name my wife as successor trustee of my trust and vice versa. However, the trust document should also name other trustees in case there is no surviving spouse. The issue of who should be trustee can be complicated in certain situations, such as in the case of a second marriage where the relationship between the new spouse and the stepchildren is not warm and fuzzy.

Why You Need a Will

Even with a trust, an estate plan needs a will. If a person dies with assets in his or her name alone (as opposed to joint tenancy or trust), the property is frozen. It cannot be accessed or used without the appointment of an executor. When you have a living trust, your will is called a *pour-over will* because it states that, in the event you die with property still in your own name (and not in the trust), that property shall be added to or "poured into" the trust created during your life. Even those clients who have transferred most of their assets to a trust will often have one bank account, such as a checking account, in their own name. The will transfers such assets to the trust.

If you have minor children, you must have a will to name the guardian for your children in the event of your premature death. Even though you make a will, if minor children lose both of their parents, they become temporary wards of the state until the guardians have been appointed by a court of law. In most cases, the courts will honor the wishes of the parents and appoint the guardians nominated by the parents in the will. There are two types of guardians. The *guardian of the person* takes physical care of the children and the *guardian of the estate* administers the children's financial affairs. If you have minor children, I cannot overemphasize the importance of having a will and naming guardians.

In my situation, my wife and I struggled to figure out which of our relatives was best-suited to be the guardian of our children. I will not tell you what we finally decided, but I will stress to you that deciding who you will trust with the upbringing of your children is one of the most important decisions you will make in your life, even though you hope with all your heart that it never has to be implemented. It is essential to think long and hard about who you would trust with this responsibility.

Durable Powers and a Living Will

In addition to a will and trust, a complete estate plan will always include durable powers of attorney (all attorneys use this expression, *durable power* or *durable powers*, but it is short for *durable power of attorney*) for health care and property, as well as a living will. These terms are very confusing, but the durable powers and the living will are separate and distinct from the living trust and the will. You will need two kinds of durable powers: One is for property and one is for medical issues. Both kinds designate someone to make decisions on your behalf if you become incapacitated. A person normally names the spouse or a grown-up child.

This form of power of attorney—a durable power—is unique because, under common law, a power of attorney terminates when the person granting the power becomes incompetent. But both these powers of attorney work in the opposite way. It is only when we become incompetent that we need someone else to act for us, and this kind of power of attorney becomes effective when we become incompetent; hence the term *durable*. This type of power survives our incompetency. Each state has its own statute describing how the document needs to be drafted to be valid in that state. It is a form of power of attorney that is specifically designated in the statutes of each state to allow someone to act on your behalf. These documents vary from state to state.

The durable power of attorney for property is an important estate planning tool, even if you have a trust in place. The property power of attorney document designates a person to manage your assets and sign your documents if you become incapacitated. A durable power of attorney will aid in gaining access to a safe deposit box and handling tax matters and Social Security issues. If specific language is included in the power of attorney, it can also assist in handling asset transfers to a trust, gifting from a trust, taking required minimum distributions from an IRA, and other specialized tasks. Talk to your lawyer before making your decision, and think very carefully about whom you trust. If you do not have a living trust, it is even more important to have the durable powers for property; everyone should have that document.

Generally, a durable health care power of attorney permits you to appoint someone to make health care decisions for you in the event of a disability or if you are not competent to make those decisions. Health care

decisions covered by the power of attorney can include the use of medi-
cations, surgery elections, and the withdrawal of life-sustaining procedures.
With the passing of the federal HIPPA laws, it is important to update your
powers of attorney for health care to specifically authorize your agents to
review and have access to all of your medical records. Sometimes when
you check into a hospital—if you are extremely ill—the hospital will ask
you to sign a durable power of health and a living will, because if you
become incapacitated while you are in the hospital, then it will be too late
to execute such documents.

Under the terms of the durable power, a physician will determine if you
are incapacitated. In most situations I have been involved in, the spouse or
children receive a letter from a physician saying that the spouse or parent
has become incapacitated and is no longer capable of making his or her own
decisions. For children—or anyone—the determination about the capacity
or incapacity of a loved one is very emotional; it is heart-breaking trying to
figure out when your parent, for example, can no longer write his or her
own checks.

Finally, a living will—which in some jurisdictions can be combined in
the durable health power of attorney—is your statement about how you
want your relatives or doctors to handle your situation when you approach
the end of your life. This living will is different from the will that directs
your entire estate and also different from the living trust that you put your
property into. Some states have living-will acts that authorize you to direct
those responsible for your medical care not to use extraordinary means to
keep you alive in the event death is imminent with no chance for survival.
It can be as simple as *DNR*: do not resuscitate. It can state that you do not
want extraordinary means, such as a feeding tube, to be used to sustain
your life. Although these directives are useful for the end-of-life decisions,
they are very narrow in scope and should not be your only health care
directive. Naming an agent for health care decisions under a health care
power of attorney covers more health care issues and rests the burden of
such decisions with family members or close friends who would be in the
best position to make decisions for you if needed. Once again, each state
has its own statutory requirements.

Anyone with even a minimal amount of money needs a will and durable
health and property powers of attorney. Whether you need a living trust
depends on the size of your estate, whether you own property in more than
one state, and whether you are in a first or second marriage. When property
is in your name individually in any state, when you die, you have to have a
probate estate in that state. For example, if you own property in both Illinois
and Florida, you would have probate proceedings in both states. Although
not everyone may need a living trust, everyone should have durable powers
(i.e., both health and property powers) and a living will.

A Complicated Caveat about Community Property States

In the United States, there are common law states and community property states. The community property states use principles derived from Spanish law; they include Arizona, California, Idaho, Louisiana, Nevada, New Mexico, Texas, Washington, and Wisconsin. If you live now or have lived in a community property state while married, your will and estate provisions will have to be somewhat different from what I am outlining in this chapter. Due to the space limitations of this book, I urge you to consult your own attorney for estate planning.

The Next Generation

Now that you know the basics of protecting your assets at your death, you have to think about how you would like to distribute your assets. There are many more things to consider besides the legal mechanisms for your estate. You have to take a step back and look at the potential effects receiving your wealth might have on your potential heirs.

Estate taxes and state inheritance taxes have an essential effect on what your heirs receive, and there are ways to manage those taxes. But before you even start to look at the legal process and procedure of managing your estate and planning how to disburse your property, you should stop and ask yourself how you feel about the money you are transferring to your children. I have seen many instances where large transfers of wealth to the next generation do not seem to have yielded much benefit to the heirs, although, again, that depends on your definition of benefit. Some people want to leave their money to charity. You have to decide for yourself what you think is the best way to manage your money and your children.

Is there a middle ground where you want your children to inherit a certain amount of money and then have the rest of the estate held in trust for your children and grandchildren and further descendants? I had one wealthy client—let's call him Bob—who came up with a clever scheme for his dad. Almost all estates of any size get audited, and the IRS will expend a great amount of energy trying to prove that your estate is worth more rather than less, to maximize the amount of estate taxes that you have to pay. Bob's dad had a fairly large estate worth in excess of $20 million. In order to avoid the endless negotiation with the IRS, Bob's dad wrote his will so that anything in the estate in excess of $20 million would go to charity, thus cutting short the IRS audit of valuation. The IRS might want to disagree about valuation, but the more the IRS says the estate is worth, the more goes to charity; the government does not collect anything more in taxes no matter how high the valuation.

Is your goal to transfer $5 million, $10 million, or $20 million to your children or grandchildren? Is that a good thing? Each of us has to make our own decisions. I urge you to think about these issues carefully.

Planning with Living Trusts

The first part of an estate plan is designed to fully use a person's applicable federal estate tax exclusion amount as well as the applicable exclusion of the spouse. The next stage of estate planning could be considered advanced planning, and it can be separated into three parts:

1. Providing liquidity to pay estate taxes.
2. Fully using annual exclusion-amount gifting.
3. Maximizing the lifetime use of the applicable exclusion amounts.

But before you get to advanced planning, there is one essential principle that you must not lose sight of: *Estate planning has to be balanced with your lifetime goals.* Just trying to give money away because you do not want it in your estate is not balanced. The first goal of planning is to make sure *you* have enough money for retirement. You have to take care of yourself first. Estate planning has to take a secondary role. While there are many strategies available for giving away money, you might or might not be in a position to do that.

Using Living Trusts to Maximum Effectiveness

A living trust can be structured in a number of different ways. You need to work with a specialized estate-planning attorney to know which kind best suits your circumstances. A living trust needs to be flexible enough to deal with the uncertainty of health and life as well as with the changing circumstances of children, but of course it has to comply with certain strict legal requirements.

There is another very important point to keep in mind: Between you and your spouse, you cannot possibly know who is going to die first. Of course there are mortality probabilities, but those probabilities are true across millions of lives and not when looking at the two lives of my wife and me. So whatever estate planning we do must be efficient for both of us, regardless of which of us dies first.

When you die, you can always leave an unlimited amount of money to your surviving spouse using the spousal exemption. It has been that way for a long time and is not a problem or an issue. This means if you die and you have a surviving spouse, there is no estate tax. However if you die and you do not have a surviving spouse, all amounts in the estate over the value of $3,500,000 (as of 2009) are taxed at a rate that starts at 42 percent. It is very important to note that the value of your estate for estate tax purposes means all the assets you owned or controlled and has nothing to do with whether wealth was transferred through probate or a trust.

Let's say I die and my spouse and I together have an estate of $7 million. I might have property in my own name, but when property is held in joint tenancy with my wife, half of it is deemed to belong to me. If property is held in joint tenancy between nonspouses, then ownership belonging to each of the two joint tenants will depend on the specific contribution each one made. There is a principle called *incidents of ownership* that determines what belongs in my estate: anything that I control, that I can change, modify, or benefit from. This is extremely important for estate planning, because if, for example, I give something away but still retain some right or control over it (which means that I still retain some incidents of ownership), then it still belongs to me and stays in my estate for the purpose of valuation.

In my hypothetical example, I leave all $7 million of my property to my surviving spouse, who pays no estate taxes because I can leave as much as I want to a spouse without paying taxes, according to the spousal exemption. I could have an estate of $20 million and leave it all to my spouse and there would be no estate taxes owed. The problem for estate planning is not what spouses leave each other; the problem comes when the second spouse dies and now estate taxes become very important in figuring out how assets are bequeathed. However, by the time the second spouse dies, the time for planning that estate is long gone; planning for the death of the second spouse must happen before the first spouse dies.

Because of the annual change in the estate tax qualified exemption (there is more about this topic under "Introducing Estate Taxation"), I have to make this a weird example, because the numbers work only if this all happens in 2009. So in my example, my wife lives for a few months more than I do, and at her death probably has pretty much the same $7 million she inherited from me to bequeath to our children. (Under normal circumstances, the amount the surviving spouse still has would depend on his or her spending habits and the growth of the assets during the time he or she had them.) In this case, she has a qualified estate tax exemption of only $3.5 million and everything over that will be subject to the 42 percent estate tax. So the total amount she is able to leave to our children (and any other heirs) is $2,030,000 ($3.5 million minus 42 percent) plus the exemption, so $5,530,000.

The problem with this example is that I had a $3.5 million federal estate tax exemption of my own that I never got a chance to use because I used the unlimited spousal exemption to transfer my whole estate to my wife. So now I am going to try this again, using a different method, because if I use my exemption when I die and I add that to my wife's exemption, together we can increase the amount of wealth we can transfer without incurring estate taxes.

My spouse and I have an estate of $7 million between us, and again, say I die first—in 2009 (when the estate tax exemption is $3.5 million). Rather than transfer all our assets, the full $7 million, outright to my spouse, I will give her only $3.5 million using the spousal exemption. I take the other half of my estate, also worth $3.5 million, and give it to a trust—called a family trust—using my federal estate tax exemption, which at the moment, unfortunately, is changing every year.

This trust is going to be for my children, but before they get the money, my wife will have—for her lifetime—the income from the trust as well as access to the principal under certain conditions, primarily for health and welfare maintenance. She cannot have this money outright and does not have absolute control. This trust does not qualify for the spousal exemption because of the limitations—the strings limiting access—put on the trust, but it pays no estate taxes at my death because of the federal estate tax exemption. So my wife gets $3.5 million outright and the income from another $3.5 million in a trust. If our estate together was $7 million and it was held in joint tenancy, then you could say that half of it was hers anyway. If I had a larger estate, say $10 million, and somehow we determined

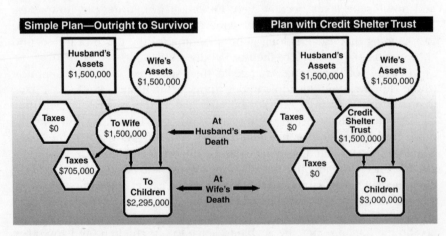

FIGURE 12.1   Advantages of Using a Family Trust

Source: Forum Financial Management, LLC.

that her portion was only $3.5 million, then I would fund the family trust with $3.5 million, she would have her part that was $3.5 million, and the remaining $3 million I would bequest to her tax-free as part of the spousal exemption. That amount, however, would get taxed when she died and it passed to the next generation.

The trust that is created by using my federal estate-tax exemption is known by a number of different terms. It can be called a *family trust*, a *unified credit shelter trust* because of the use of the $3.5 million exemption, or a *B trust*. This is very arcane: When you die, your living trust is divided into two trusts. The A trust goes to your wife and the B trust is the family trust. At my wife's death, the trust will transfer to our descendants with no estate taxes. During my wife's lifetime, this trust could grow to $10 million and no more estate taxes will have to be paid, although the trust probably has to pay income taxes on the income it generates. Whatever the family trust has grown to is not in her estate and is not subject to estate taxes.

Figure 12.1 illustrates how a credit shelter trust works. First, I have to explain that the amount of this exemption has changed dramatically in recent years and, at this moment, it is impossible to predict what it is going to be even in the near future. Table 12.1 shows how it has changed since 2005. Since I have to use some value to be able to demonstrate the impact that this kind of trust might have on an estate, I have used a sample exemption of $1.5 million.

In Figure 12.1 on the left, there is an outright disposition to the surviving spouse. This means you did not utilize the deceased spouse's credit-shelter exemption and thus have increased the size of the surviving spouse estate by the $1.5 million bequest. The resulting taxes are $705,000. If you look at the right side of the diagram, rather than giving the money outright to the spouse, the maximum exemption—which in this case is $1.5 million—is transferred into a family trust. As a result, at the death of the wife, the family trust is not included in the estate of the surviving spouse and no estate

TABLE 12.1   Estate Tax Exclusion Amounts, by Year

Year	Applicable Exclusion Amount
2005	$1,500,000
2006	$2,000,000
2007	$2,000,000
2008	$2,000,000
2009	$3,500,000
2010	No estate tax
2011	$1,000,000

Source: Forum Financial Management, LLC.

taxes will be owed. It is not included in the estate of the surviving spouse because there are restrictions on its use and access to the funds, but these restrictions are typically not onerous. A typical family trust might have the following language: "The trustee shall distribute income to my wife at least quarterly and principal for her health welfare and maintenance."

In fact, to assuage the surviving spouse's concern about these restrictions, the surviving spouse can be made the trustee.

Second Marriages and a QTIP Trust

"Second marriage" always raises a red flag for me, especially when there are children involved. Some of the most challenging circumstances I have encountered in my practice stemmed from second marriages and stepchildren; I guess those old fairy tales were expressing something fundamental in human nature.

So a man marries for a second time, but he already has children. He wants to ensure that his assets ultimately go to his children (and not to the relatives of the second wife), but he also wants to provide for his second wife. He can accomplish all that by using a *qualified terminal interest property (QTIP) trust*. The QTIP trust offers increased control over where your property ends up.

If I am the person getting married for the second time, I set up a QTIP trust and put money in it. I can fund it to whatever level I want, because it is subject only to the unlimited spousal exemption. The funds put into a QTIP trust qualify for the unlimited estate tax spousal exemption but my surviving (second) wife gets only income from the trust, not control of it. In fact, the QTIP requires the trust to distribute income. The principal will ultimately go to my children. When the spouse—who now has the QTIP trust—dies, the estate tax will be due.

This is all I am going to say about this type of trust. The most important thing is that affluent individuals entering into a second marriage know that it exists. The documents must be drafted with extreme care because even a small mistake could end up voiding the trust and causing estate taxes to be due on the death of the first spouse rather than on the death of the second.

Generation-Skipping Trusts

Sometimes grandparents just do not like their own children that much, and have a better feeling about their grandchildren (although as I said before, I always figure that, soon enough, the grandchildren will annoy them, too). In other circumstances, families with great wealth want to use every mechanism possible to transfer wealth to later generations.

Affluent individuals need to know only that this device exists. If you were going to use it, your estate-planning attorney would explain it to you and draft the documents. But the principle is this: There is a generation-skipping transfer tax (GST tax) on transfers of property to individuals, such as grandchildren, who are more than one generation below you. The tax is in addition to the estate tax and the gift tax and is at a flat rate of 45 percent in 2009. (See Table 12.2.) Each person is also entitled to an exemption from the GST tax that uses the same schedule as the federal estate tax exemption. This exemption allows some trusts to be created for the grandchildren which will also permit assets to be available for a child without being included in the child's estate. This can significantly reduce the transfer taxes over time.

The alternative to the generation-skipping strategy is to have money go from parent to child, and get taxed, and then from child to grandchild, and get taxed again. While generation-skipping trusts in excess of the exemption are certainly taxed, it is not as much as the double taxation incurred by passing through two generations rather than one.

Introducing Estate Taxation

I said earlier that estate planning is fundamentally concerned with transfer-ring property at your death in the way you want it transferred. We have spent much of this chapter so far discussing this. Now we come to the second fundamental issue of estate planning, which is minimizing the tax bill on your estate using techniques beyond the basic documents and trusts.

No one likes to pay taxes. We all want to leave as much of our property as possible to our heirs and minimize the tax bite of how we do that. Unless you plan carefully, the money and property that you leave to your heirs could potentially subject them to taxation they were not expecting.

The U.S. government has a number of methods for extracting money from us. There are three main systems of taxation in the United States, plus a fourth system that is used less often. All of these taxes are designed to tax the transfer of wealth.

1. *Income tax.* We are all aware of the income tax system that requires us to file our taxes—or an extension—on April 15 every year.
2. *Gift tax.* This is potentially a tax on gifts you give to your children during your lifetime.
3. *Estate tax.* This is the tax your children pay on what they inherit upon your death.
4. *Generation-skipping tax.* If at death or during your life you want to transfer wealth to your grandchildren, there could also be a generation-skipping tax, in addition to the other taxes.

The interaction of these different taxing schemes is very confusing. The estate tax is separate and distinct from the gift tax, and both are different from income taxes. As I write this book at the beginning of 2009, the estate tax system is in an uproar because of the changes that have been legislated into the system. We are already hearing a great amount of discussion about the estate tax, due to the government's need for money to finance the various financial and economic stimulus methods that have been put into place in 2009.

The Economic Growth and Tax Relief Reconciliation Act of 2001 (EGTRRA) increased the amount that you can leave to others after you die without having to pay estate taxes; this amount is called your personal federal estate tax exemption. For those who died in the years 2001–2002, the amount of money and assets they could leave in their estates without paying federal estate taxes was $1 million. You can see in Table 12.1 how the personal estate tax exemption increases every year until 2010, when the entire estate of anyone who dies in that year will be exempt from federal estate tax. The uproar comes from the idea that anyone who dies in 2010, no matter how wealthy, will not have to pay estate taxes.

What were they thinking in 2001, since federal estate taxes have been a centerpiece of U.S. tax policy for a long time? At the very least, our legislators were not contemplating the kind of vicious down markets and the collapse of housing prices that have characterized 2008 and will probably continue for some time in the future. Given the massive amount of government spending that has already gone into trying to prop up our economy, one has to doubt that that year of no estate tax is really going to happen. And then 2011 arrives. The way the system is now set, the estate tax exemption will go back to its 2003 level and everyone with a total estate greater than $1 million will be subject to the estate tax. Here is the best advice I can offer you if you are getting on in years and have a substantial estate: Beware of who serves you food in 2010!

You have no doubt heard about the supposed trillions of dollars that are expected to transfer from the "greatest generation" to the baby boomers over the next few years. That transfer might or might not take place, but only a small percentage of wealth owners are going to be paying the wealth tax on it. My personal feeling is that the federal estate tax exemption will probably continue to be high, but the government could recoup what it loses in tax revenues from the high exemption by legislating carryover basis rather than stepped-up basis for most inherited assets (see "A Note about Tax Basis" on page 277). The problem is that we have no idea what is going to happen and how the legislation will go. No one knows. It makes all aspects of estate planning extremely difficult.

A person's gross estate for estate tax purposes includes the value of all assets owned by that person at the time of death, including proceeds of life insurance, annuities, IRAs, 401(k) accounts, pension and profit-sharing accounts, real estate, tangible personal property, bank accounts, and investments of all kinds. But you are taxed only when your estate is greater than a certain dollar amount. Instead of just saying that, the law is worded to state that the *applicable exclusion amount* is the amount of property which will be excluded from the taxable estate for federal estate tax purposes. As I mentioned before, Table 12.1 shows the schedule for the applicable exclusion amount as it now stands.

The phase-in of the current law is making planning very difficult. For younger people with modest estates, it may be difficult to figure out how much planning and preparation are necessary. To be conservative, any single person or married couple with assets over $1 million should consider trust planning for estate taxes. Most people at or beyond retirement age should seriously consider trust planning, taking into consideration lifetime disability and the possibility that trust documents may not be able to be amended if the grantor becomes permanently disabled.

Transferring Wealth Using Gifts

The preceding section introduced the subject of estate taxes, and I said that aside from income taxes and estate taxes, there is a whole system for taxing gifts, to keep wealthy people from simply giving wealth to the next generation without paying taxes on it. The gift tax system is separate from the other two tax systems—income taxes and estate taxes—and has its own separate set of rules and complexities.

According to gift tax rules, you can give away a certain amount of money without tax consequences every year. At the time I am writing this book, that amount is $13,000 annually, but this amount is adjusted by the IRS every year using an inflation factor. That means that you and your spouse together can give $26,000 a year to each of your children. If you have five children, you can transfer $130,000 annually to the children. The person receiving the gift does not have to report it. People always talk about this exclusion in terms of children, but you can actually give $13,000 away annually to as many people as you want to give it to, relative or not. The person to whom you give a gift is called the *donee*. The person making the gift is called the *grantor*. Technically, it is the *tax-free transfer of wealth using the annual exclusion*.

Each person is allowed to give away a total of $1 million in gifts in his or her lifetime; that means a total of $1 million, not $1 million to each of your children. Once you have given away $1 million in your lifetime, you have to pay a federal gift tax on all subsequent gifts. You by yourself (without involving your spouse) could give away $20,000 to one person in a year. The excess $7,000 (the amount over the annual gift tax exclusion) would not be taxable at this time to either you or the recipient. Rather, the excess $7,000 starts to count against your lifetime exemption of $1 million. There is an important distinction between gifts made during your lifetime and those made at death. Once you die, gifts become subject to the estate tax and its rules, not to the gift tax and its rules.

The funny thing is that this $13,000 annual gift is exempt from the $1 million lifetime limit. You can give away $13,000 annually to 100 people and it still does not count against your $1 million lifetime limit.

If the transfers of money or property are made at death, you are now talking about estate taxes, so the amount you can give in 2009 is $3.5 million, transferred or bequeathed, as we have mentioned many times, before you have to pay federal estate taxes. However, if you have made gifts above the gift tax exclusion during your lifetime, the amount you have given away as gifts gets subtracted from the estate tax exemption. For example, if I am a very generous person and have given away $1 million in my life and then I die in 2009, I will have only $2.5 million left of my federal estate tax exemption.

Seen in this light, the $13,000 annual exclusion offers the opportunity to give away much more than the $1 million without having to pay taxes—as long as it is given in these annual $13,000 amounts. The term *exclusion* refers only to the fact that it is excluded from my lifetime limit of $1 million of gifts that I do not have to pay tax on.

To reiterate this important point: If a person uses a portion or all of this lifetime gift exemption during his lifetime, it will reduce the amount of the estate tax exemption at death. So, for example, a single dad gives his only child a gift of stock valued at $250,000. The results would be as follows. First, the annual exclusion would apply, $13,000. The $237,000 balance would reduce the $1 million lifetime exclusion down to $763,000. If the dad makes no more lifetime gifts, at his death that $237,000 excess gift will reduce the federal estate tax exclusion at death. Say the dad makes only this one gift during his lifetime, and then dies in 2009, when the estate tax exemption is $3.5 million. At his death, his estate tax exemption will be reduced by $237,000, so it will be only $3,263,000. Say this dad has an estate that is valued precisely at $3,500,000. That means that the only part of his estate that will be taxable at the current estate tax rate of 42 percent is $237,000.

There is one more highly technical point to be made about gifts you make during your lifetime and gifts made from your estate, meaning that you leave them to someone in your will; that point concerns tax basis. (See Table 12.2). There is one more caveat here. Individual states also levy transfer or estate taxes, and the levels of exemption might not match the federal exemption, especially over the past few years which have seen so many changes in the federal level. This is yet another reason to work with a professional for this kind of planning.

TABLE 12.2   Estate and Gift Tax Rates and Exemptions

Year	Top Estate Tax Rate	Estate Tax Exemption	Top Gift Tax Rate	Gift Tax Exemption
2002	50%	$1 million	50%	$1 million
2003	49%	$1 million	49%	$1 million
2004	48%	$1.5 million	48%	$1 million
2005	47%	$1.5 million	47%	$1 million
2006	46%	$2 million	46%	$1 million
2007	45%	$2 million	45%	$1 million
2008	45%	$2 million	45%	$1 million
2009	45%	$3.5 million	45%	$1 million
2010	0%	Repealed	35%	$1 million
2011*	55%	$1 million	35%	$1 million

*Estate tax reform of 2001 sunsets in 2011. At that time the law reverts back to rules in place in 2001.
Source: Forum Financial Management, LLC.

A Note about Tax Basis

I have to believe that every single person who reads this book knows about income taxes. If I buy a stock at $1 and it goes to $101, and then I sell it, I owe income tax on $100. If I own this stock for at least a year before I sell it, I will pay the long-term capital gains tax, which is currently 15 percent for most taxpayers (for those in the 25 percent tax bracket and higher). I can never escape the fact that I bought it for $1 and have to pay tax on all the appreciation above that amount when I sell it. That $1 price is my *basis* in the stock, the price that the tax system says I paid for it. This is a simple example, but pay attention, because there will be a twist.

Pretend that the price went to $101 and has been there ever since. Now say that instead of selling it for myself, I decide to leave it to my son in my will. If I do that, he gets what is called a *stepped-up basis* for tax purposes. The new basis takes a *step up* to the value of the stock—or any property—on the date of my death.

Now let me say that this stock that I bought for $1 has taken half my lifetime to increase 100 times in value. If I sell it myself, I will owe a huge amount of tax. But by giving it to my son through my will, he inherits it with a basis of $101. If he sells it at that price, he will not owe any income tax at all on it! If it increases in price to $110 before he sells it, he will owe tax on only $9 of appreciation, not on $109. This

(continued)

(Continued)

is a huge break for my son and me because it saves me from paying a very large amount of tax on a lifetime of appreciation. He inherits much more value by getting this stock, in essence, tax-free than if I had sold the stock, paid the capital gains tax, and then given him the money that was left over. This part of the estate tax law could well change after 2009, but right now it is one of the most important breaks you can get in this system.

Now say I want to give my son this stock now, as a gift, rather than waiting for my death. The gift tax works differently from the estate tax. Property that is given as a lifetime gift—while the grantor is alive—keeps a *carryover basis*. So if I give this stock to my son while I am alive, his tax basis in the stock is the same as mine was, $1. If the stock goes to $110 and he then sells it, he will owe tax on $109 of appreciation.

The implications of this difference in how basis is treated may not make a great deal of difference to many of my readers, but it can be extremely important for the really wealthy. It means that if parents want to make gifts during their lifetimes, they should choose property that has not yet appreciated in value. If the parents have property that has greatly appreciated in value while they have owned it, they should bequeath that property through their estate. Think about a family home that might be considered a landed estate. Dad bought it for $100,000 when he made his first million in 1950. Now it is worth millions. It would be foolish for dad to use his lifetime gift tax exclusion of $1 million to give this home to his son, because the gift tax exclusion would not cover its value anyway, and the son would get it with the same highly appreciated tax basis his father has. It would be better to bequeath it to the son as part of the estate at dad's death, so the son inherits it with a tax basis at its current value.

Life, Death, Taxes, Revocable Trusts and Irrevocable Trusts

As I discussed earlier in this chapter, living trusts are revocable; during my lifetime, I can change them as much as I want to. As the name implies, an irrevocable trust is one that you cannot change. The issue is control. Remember that I mentioned incidents of ownership; if I am able to control an asset, then it belongs to me. Even if I act like I wanted to give the asset as a gift or otherwise to remove it from my estate, if I can still change it or affect it, then it still belongs to me. If I put an asset into an irrevocable trust that means it is beyond my control. Only then can I count it as having been removed from my estate.

Irrevocable trusts are important to using life insurance to transfer wealth, which I discussed in Chapter 10. They can also be used when you do not want your child to have access to money for a certain amount of time. You move it definitively out of your estate by moving it into an irrevocable trust that you do not control. The child or grandchild then inherits the money

Common Sense versus Estate Principles

The client of an adviser I work with was a widow in her eighties who was shocked to discover that she was worth $1.5 million. Her father had given her many shares of Standard Oil stock over her lifetime, and she had kept it without paying much attention to it. She discovered the value of her holdings as she was doing some advanced estate planning.

Assume now that she has children. Holding that much stock in one company is simply a terrible idea any way you look at it—a completely undiversified holding that relies on the fortunes of one company. But if she starts to sell out some of the position, she will incur huge tax costs, because she has had some of that stock for most of her lifetime; diversifying will be extremely expensive. Furthermore, if she is able to give the stock as an estate bequest, the heirs she gives it to will get a stepped-up basis and the taxes owed on those old shares will never have to be paid. Her estate will be much larger if she can keep those shares and leave them to her heirs, rather than having to sell them. She cannot even give those shares as gifts to avoid the tax bill, because a gift during one's lifetime results in a carryover basis and the recipients would have to pay the large tax bill when they sold the shares. What should she do?

This is a real quandary. I think you would have to consider her health, and if she seems to be relatively healthy and expects to live many more years, you would want to diversify her holdings. If she appeared to be in bad health, you might take the chance of holding on to those shares. Sometimes you have to rely on common sense. You might also take into account whether she was otherwise well off or if she was going to have to depend on those shares to pay her expenses for the rest of her life, which might indicate the need to diversify, despite the tax bill.

at the time you have specified. In a way it is like a prenuptial agreement for your children, especially when it is held separately but according to the wishes of the grantor. A prenuptial agreement specifies that certain property will never be part of what you might call the marital property. The assets in an irrevocable trust, since it was not created by the child or grandchild, cannot be attached by a creditor (including a spouse in a divorce). Again, the definition of *marital property* and the requirements of a valid prenuptial agreement vary from state to state. To achieve optimal asset protection, you and your attorney must plan carefully.

Final Thoughts

If you want to make a large gift, one of the best ways to do that is to give an asset that you believe is going to grow in the future. You make a gift of it both because you want the recipient to have it and to remove the growing asset from your estate; you want it to grow after it leaves your possession. So the best gifts are stocks, life insurance, and real estate. I give away assets that I believe have value and that I essentially want to keep within the family. Maybe I have some real estate that I think will do well in the future, or a stock I like. Even if this is a gift (using carryover basis) rather than a bequest, my son could well be in a lower income tax bracket than I am, if he wanted to sell the asset. The worst thing to give away is money. It is highly preferable to give a gift of $13,000 worth of stock, for example, than to give money that the recipient then uses to buy stock.

Transferring Wealth within the Family: Inheritance Issues for Family Businesses

F amily businesses are a powerhouse for the economy of the United States and have a massive impact on the economy as a whole. Using the broadest definition of family business, the 2000 census showed that 62 percent of the U.S. workforce was employed in a family businesses; this translates to some 82 million individuals.[1] The idea of owning your own business and being your own boss is a deeply entrenched part of the American dream. But family businesses have issues that are very different from those of larger or publicly owned firms, and one of the most important of those issues is figuring out how to take the success of the first generation of entrepreneurs and safeguard and institutionalize it so that the children can inherit a thriving concern. You have to navigate family politics, inheritance law, and IRS regulations to accomplish it. It requires careful planning and a realistic understanding of family characteristics and roles. It really is different from the kind of estate planning a corporate executive would do, because the value of the inheritance lies overwhelmingly in keeping the business alive. It also differs from other kinds of business or estate planning because the family members are tied together in a business such that family relationships are also business relationships, and the level of emotions involved is often very high.

Try to imagine yourself being in business with your parents and siblings. Instead of arguing about who is going to have Thanksgiving or who did not give a good Christmas present, you are in business with these people and your entire livelihood and the ongoing family fortune are wound up in these long-term family emotions. Family members can have long memories for slights and grudges.

Family Inheritance 101

Before I start to discuss the particular circumstances of family businesses and inheritance, I want to state an important principle that might seem obvious: The goal of almost all inheritance is to minimize the amount of taxes that have to be paid to state and federal governments when the original owners of the assets die. One of the best ways to do that is to make the estate seem to be as low in value as possible. Again, stating the obvious: An estate that is worth less pays lower taxes. While the principle seems simple, putting it into actual practice can occupy an estate attorney's entire life.

So in the case of a family, you want to get discounts on the stock given to children, meaning make the stock seem as low in value as possible (more on this later). Then you want to take advantage of the current maximum lifetime gift that an individual can make tax-free, which is $1 million. You want to lower the value of the business as much as possible to use each parent's $1 million gift. If the business is growing, you want to transfer as much stock or ownership as you can today because then, at the time of the parents' death, the value has already been passed and is not in the estate. (You will have read much more on this topic in Chapter 12.)

There are always choices in transferring wealth. For example, the parents can *sell* the business to the kids. In that case we say that they are using the income tax system to transfer ownership and wealth. The parents will pay gains on the sale and the kids will use after-tax dollars to pay back Mom and Dad. The parents can *give* the business to the kids, using the gift exemptions to transfer ownership. Each method has benefits and disadvantages. A successful business working with a skilled and experienced estate attorney might well use both methods for maximum efficiency of wealth transfer.

Mom and Dad almost always want to treat kids equally. Many times the nonworking kids look at the business as being an unfair gift to the working child—which, in my opinion, it is not. The business can be a burden, or it can be nothing more than a job. Whether the family is working with a financial adviser or an estate lawyer, that person often has to become the family mediator, and might be the only person in the room who is neutral. This mediator tries to reach a solution that is a compromise all family members can live with, even though no one is completely happy. These situations do not lend themselves to easy mathematical formulas.

Meet the Family

Let's take an example where Mom and Dad own a thriving business and they are reaching retirement age. Estate planning has become essential. There are four children: One is a leader in the business, one works part-time in the business, one is a starving artist in Seattle, and one lives nearby and occasionally helps out at Christmas. Dad and especially Mom are vocal in expressing that they love their children equally and therefore want to divide the assets equally. But what can *equally* mean in this scenario? The essence of family business inheritance is figuring out how to divide assets that do not divide, among children who work in the business, do not work in the business, work occasionally in the business, or participate in family life in some other way.

This type of scenario is common for a family business but any variation is possible. Generally you will find that, among several children, only one or two will have taken a real leadership role in the business. The leadership role is gender-neutral. Since the parents take the position that they love their kids equally, the first thing they tell their attorney or financial adviser is that they plan to divide everything equally.

The role of the adviser is to do some comprehensive fact-finding about the family and the business. Sometimes the business is really just a job where the kid works hard and gets a paycheck. As an adviser, you have to figure out how much value there really is in the business, or is this shackling a person to 80-hour weeks? If it is necessary to work 80 hours a week to make a good living, you can see where that is headed: If you give the business equally to all the kids, the nonworking kids will want to get paid the same amount as the working kid, and the working kid says, hey, I'm working 80 hours a week and you aren't. That's where the problems begin.

My objective as an adviser is to get the family to focus on the succession and estate planning while everyone is still alive. The first thing to do is to delve as deeply as possible into the facts of the family and family personalities. In my experience, there is almost always real estate associated with the business, and one approach is to separate the real estate from the business itself. This allows you to split the income streams. You set up a limited partnership for the real estate while Mom and Dad are alive. (A limited partnership is a legal structure that has at least one general partner, who manages the business and assumes legal debts and obligations; and at least one limited partner, who has liability only to the extent of his or her investments. Limited partners also enjoy rights to the partnership's cash flow, but are not liable for company obligations.) The limited partnership then signs a lease with the family members who will inherit the business. The child who inherits control of the business will be running it, but he will have to lease the real estate for a reasonable amount. Meanwhile, the nonworking children will get compensated by rental payments. This is a fairly common situation.

The reason for signing a lease now is because Mom and Dad are still alive and everyone is rational; we want to establish a situation that takes away most of the things that would cause friction at the death of the parents.

I have worked with this solution for family businesses a number of times and it can work very well. If the business alone is not worth as much as the real estate, the working child can also be a partner in the limited partnership. In fact, many times the working child will get an equal share in the limited partnership because, although the business pays a reasonable salary, it could easily have significantly more risk. In addition, the rent to the limited partnership may be soaking up much of the business's cash flow.

As far as the estate plan and estate taxes, the deal has to pass an IRS reasonable test for the rent and other factors but, even more importantly, the deal has to pass what you might call the family reasonable test. Do all family members believe this to be fair? Does this placate the nonworking children? You want to build in an inflation clause so that both parties feel they have been reasonably compensated if the succession plan has been designed far in advance. The resulting fights are almost predictable if you do not do this while the first generation is alive.

The next issue is figuring out how to pay the estate taxes on the business. The parents want the child to get the business and also want to ensure that he can pay the federal estate tax debts which will certainly be owed, but even a thriving business might not have the liquidity necessary to pay them. The overlay on this arrangement is to set up an irrevocable insurance trust so the working child who gets the business will have enough cash to pay the estate taxes attributable to the business, while the nonworking kids get family cash and real estate.

One small note about one kind of business that is easier to divide: If the majority of the business is real estate, inheritance issues are much easier because there is rental income coming in that can be divided. Most of the inheritance issues emanate from active businesses.

When There Is No Family Leader

Families of course come in every size and flavor, and sometimes it is not clear if there is a family leader in the second generation, even if all the kids do work in the business to some degree. This gets to be more complicated. The family will need to set up a buy-sell agreement. You have to recapitalize the company and create voting and nonvoting stock. There are various ways to get the nonvoting stock over to the children but you have them sign a binding buy-sell agreement while everyone is alive. The buy-sell could have provisions specifying how the kids who do not work in the business can get bought out, or different types or levels of compensation for nonworking children.

A *buy-sell agreement*, in case you are not familiar with it, is a contract between business partners that acts like a kind of prenuptial agreement between the partners: It spells out the how business interests may be transferred among the partners (or the partners' estates) if certain triggering events occur. It provides for the future sale of the business interest of one partner to another partner under certain circumstances. Buy-sell agreements may also be known as *business continuation agreements* or *buyout agreements*. In the family situation, a buy-sell agreement ensures business continuity in the event of the death, disability, or retirement of one of the children, and also avoids the situation where the remaining children have to be in business with the survivors or estate of the one who has passed away. A buy-sell agreement that includes appropriate amounts of insurance on the lives of the participants can ensure that the buy-sell is funded and that there will be enough liquidity to effect the buyout should a triggering event occur. Typical provisions of the buy-sell agreement include who may buy out the departing child's share, what events will trigger a buyout, and what the price will be.

A note about nonvoting stock: This is where the family can recognize IRS discounts on the value of the business. When a family member is issued nonvoting stock, what does that family member really get? In the eyes of the IRS, not a lot. What is the value of a business? What a willing buyer is willing to pay to a willing seller. Nonvoting stock does not have a market, does not have control, and maybe cannot even be sold at all. So the IRS values it at a discount.

There are two important issues for the buy-sell agreement. First, the children have to buy in contractually; second, you have to ensure that there is enough liquidity actually to pay the buyout price.

Creating the buy-sell agreement and arrangement requires company recapitalization. The lawyer might draft an agreement that says each child will get 100 shares of stock in the company, subject to the provisions of the agreement that they have all signed. For example, if one of the kids dies, the buy-sell will say that the three surviving children can buy out the estate of the deceased child. If one of the kids becomes disabled and can no longer work in the business, the others can buy him or her out; the same if one of them retires. There might be a provision stating that if one of the children does not work in the business, the others can buy out that child. The agreement binds the family members to a policy that prevents three of the children from teaming up against one of the other children.

The point of that buy-sell is really almost giving the family the rules of engagement for dealing with each other from an ownership perspective. It can be challenging to write this agreement if one child really does not work in the business, but maybe you include a provision that says that child is not entitled to compensation from the business and that the others who work in the business have the right to buy him out. This might not be easily resolved because one child might not have skills or the right skills for the business.

This child can say, I want to work in the business but you won't give me a job. All around, this can be very complicated to work out. But your chances of being able to help the family resolve these issues are much better if the parents are alive and mediating and expressing their own wishes. Once the parents have passed on, family fights can get bitter.

I have observed these situations for years, and in my experience there are usually one or two children who have become established and deeply involved in the business. It really makes the most sense for the parents to give the business disproportionally to those children and compensate the remaining children with other assets.

However, I have also experienced situations where Mom and Dad are just determined to give all the stock to all the kids equally. In this case, you have to help the family develop a succession plan that has to be more than just legal arrangements; there has to be a business plan everybody agrees to. It is absolutely essential that Mom and Dad sit down with the kids and tell them firmly what their wishes are. There is a limit on what a financial adviser or lawyer or both together can do: The kids ultimately have to get along to some degree. You can only do so much. You can set them on them right path and then try to get them to deal with the liquidity issues.

Thinking a Generation Ahead

The parents should consider putting the stock for the children into some kind of trust. Problems arise when one of the children goes through a divorce and you want to at least put some limitations on the accessibility of the actual stock by the divorced spouse. The parents need to think a generation ahead, because you do not want to foist a spouse—let alone an ex-spouse—onto the children or possibly grandchildren. If you think it is challenging to try to transfer a business from one generation to the next, the challenge increases geometrically trying to transfer it two generations down.

Many family businesses are built on the dynamics of a unique entrepreneur—either Mom or Dad—with skills that are not transferable. The best guarantee of the transferability of the business is having the entrepreneur with the talent spend time while alive building a succession plan, which may or may not include the children. An important part of that succession plan might be working with the children to help them develop some of those unique skills.

Using Insurance

It is very common—and relatively simple—to use life insurance as a way to get cash to the children who are not working in the business, although this will not work in every circumstance because not everyone is insurable or the insurance might not be realistically affordable. Furthermore, the insurance is needed not only to equalize the value of the inheritance to the children who are not working in the business, but, as I mentioned earlier, insurance is also needed for the child who is inheriting the business, to have liquidity to pay inheritance taxes. A valuable business could easily owe, for example, $5 million in estate taxes—a sum the business might or might not be able to generate. There are provisions under the tax code where you can pay that over a multiyear period, but that means you are basically borrowing from the IRS, which is not an ideal business proposition.

Insurance can be a valuable tool but it does not fit every picture. How to best use insurance is a big debate because some planners and advisers love it and others hate it. Some say the business should use insurance only as a last resort. Some clients do not like it on principle alone. The job of the financial adviser is to take the emotion out of the issue by doing an analysis. Sometimes the numbers do not work all that well and the appropriate use of insurance becomes a tough call. But then it winds up being a necessity because insurance offers liquidity and might be the only way to get that liquidity. In the end, it is difficult to generalize any more than I already have, except to say that insurance is one of many tools to use to ensure a smooth and effective transition of a family business to the next generation.

Using Assets in Novel Ways to Solve Problems

Now imagine a successful family business where Mom and Dad are trying to do the right thing by planning for the business beyond their own lives, but one of them does not want to give up control. Dad will sit with you and nod his head. While he does understand that there are important issues at stake, he is just not going to give up control. The adviser's job now is to figure out a way to pass on the value of the business in a tax-efficient way while retaining current control.

An S corporation is one way to do that. Like a C corporation, an S corporation is a separate legal entity that offers liability protection but, according to IRS rules, the S corporation elects to be taxed like a partnership, meaning that the income, deductions, and tax credits of an S corporation flow through to shareholders annually, regardless of whether distributions are made. This means that income is taxed at the shareholder level and not at the corporate level. There are a number of requirements that determine whether a corporation is eligible to be an S corporation, including having no more than 100 shareholders.

The family business decides to recapitalize as an S corporation and creates voting and nonvoting stock. The children get the nonvoting stock, so although some value has been passed, Mom and Dad retain the voting stock and control. And now you have a way to shift off value to the children along with the possibility of getting those IRS discounts (for nonmarketability, etc.) that I mentioned earlier.

Specialized Inheritance Techniques

By the time you have a successful family business and a number of children, you have moved beyond using simple estate techniques and you certainly have to work with a specialized attorney. One of the complex and sophisticated techniques an attorney might recommend is a type of *grantor trust* called a *defective grantor trust* that is generally established to look like a sale to the children, but is set up under the tax code to be a sale where the seller does not recognize any gain. The trust is created to take advantage of the fact that rules governing the income tax system and the estate tax system are not always exactly the same.

A *grantor trust* is created when someone, the grantor or trustee, initiates a contract because he or she owns valuable assets or property. The trust is created during the grantor's lifetime and is generally used to plan a person's will and distribution of an estate. It is a specific type of trust that allows the person who creates the trust, the grantor, to control the assets in the trust and recognize income generated by the trust. It can be terminated or changed during the grantor's lifetime. The trust agreement is a contract that specifies all of the circumstances of the trust, which is for the benefit of someone or something, such as the wife, children, or grandchildren. The trust can be revocable or irrevocable. Each such trust has a great many variables that need to be taken into account when creating the trust; the trust can be used to satisfy a great many different estate needs.

A *defective grantor trust* is one type of irrevocable (unchangeable) trust, offering an opportunity to transfer family wealth to successor generations using asset valuation discounting techniques to significantly reduce the current gift tax which will be paid when the parents *gift* their property into the grantor trust for the benefit of their heirs. Normally, income of an irrevocable trust is taxable to the trust or to the beneficiaries of the trust (in this case, the children). In a grantor trust, however, the trust income is taxed to the creator of the trust, the grantor.

Using a defective grantor trust allows you to basically freeze the value of the business. For example, I sell my son $1 million worth of stock in my business company; for income tax purposes the sale is neutral, meaning that I do not recognize any capital gains on it. This situation is complicated, but essentially there is a technique under the tax law where the sale is ignored for income tax purposes, as though the seller were selling it to himself.

This is one of those oddities of the tax code that, from one point of view, might not make total sense except to take advantage of it. The value of the business remains at the value of the note the seller takes back. The business has essentially been transferred at that price although it may continue to grow during the parents' lifetimes. Over the next 10 years, my son will pay me $1 million on the note using money generated by the business. If that company grows to be worth $2 million or $3 million in the next 10 to 15 years, that growth has already been transferred to my son. Meantime he is paying me back and I walk away with the cash. I can still retain control of the business, however, because I still have the voting stock.

One of my clients is a very wealthy family that used this method with a business valued at about $15 million. They set up the deal some seven or eight years ago and were able to transfer about $10 million of appreciation to the next generation.

This technique is very sophisticated; you need counsel and tax advisers to get it done. It is not cheap from an advisory point of view, but it works extremely well if you have an estate large enough to justify it. An estate worth that kind of sophistication also requires advisers who have spent a great deal of time with the family learning about the business and the family dynamics well enough to know this kind of technique is appropriate. I have explained it in a fairly simple way but the nuances are complicated.

As I have mentioned, the objective of estate planning is to get those IRS discounts on the value of the assets to be transferred to the children by creating limited partnerships or nonvoting stock. If you use a sale, you can freeze the value of the business, although selling to kids can be expensive. The seller (the parents) has to pay tax on the profits, and the buyer has to use after-tax dollars from the business to pay you back, so running this through the income-tax system means getting taxed at two levels.

Making a sale to a defective grantor trust eliminates one level of taxes. The seller does not pay taxes on the sale because there is no profit through that quirk in the IRS code I mentioned earlier. In the right set of circumstances, you have achieved the goal of locking in the value of a business that is appreciating. Once again, these are just tools. You have to figure out what is appropriate in your case.

One final thought is using an employee stock ownership plan (commonly called an ESOP) as a technique to create liquidity in the business. An ESOP is an employee benefit plan that makes the employees of a company owners of stock in that company. When compared to other employee benefit plans, there are several features that make ESOPs unique as compared to other employee benefit plans. First, an ESOP is required by law to invest primarily in the securities of the sponsoring employer. Second, it may borrow money, which makes it unique among qualified employee benefit plans. As a result, *leveraged ESOPs* may be used as a technique of corporate finance.

Especially in the case where there is no dominant child, the parents may sell the business to an ESOP. An ESOP is a complicated device that essentially permits an owner to sell his business to an ERISA-qualified plan. The plan might be in existence already and be converted to become an ESOP or it may be a new plan. Since the plan has most of the employees as participants, it is essentially a sale to the employees. There are potentially significant tax advantages to the seller such as tax deferral to the owner. In addition, the plan can borrow money from a bank to pay for the stock. In this scenario, the bank may get a tax break on the interest it charges. Additionally, the loan is paid back through deductible contributions to the plan each year. These types of plans are very complex and need counsel and a tax professional who specializes in this area.

Vacation Homes

The family vacation home can offer another conundrum. The parents brought up the kids in the house or at least spent summers there, it is on a lake, and it is associated with many years of happy memories. The parents want to give the home to all the kids and they want the kids and grandkids to use it for generations.

But guess what? There is a cost associated with it, and some of the children might have the money to contribute to its maintenance while others might not. This can become problematic as the years go by and the house needs maintenance and repair. The parents want everyone to enjoy it and yet it is not an easily dividable asset. The parents might even set up trusts or set cash aside to maintain the home, but once it is in a trust or partnership, the parents have to be very specific in spelling out how to handle all the ownership issues that go with it. Making it work depends on the reasonableness of the family.

In fact, taking a home and trying to divide it among three or more children, and maybe put it into a trust, could be a recipe for disaster. One child might not be able to contribute to upkeep; another child might live too far away to take advantage of the home and figures he should not be on the hook for maintaining it; and a third child might need money and want to sell his share but cannot do that because of the trust.

You can of course draft language in the will so that if a majority of the owners want to sell, the home can be sold. You can draft to offer a right of first refusal to the other beneficiaries. You have to be aware that a lot of that comes from talking out the issues and then having a skilled tax or estate lawyer draft the will or trust, someone who is aware of the things you can draft to.

Heirlooms and Jewelry

I have been working with families, wills, and estates for more than 25 years. I have seen complicated inheritance transactions within complex family businesses, and I have to tell you that the worst and most bitter fights are over heirlooms and, above all, jewelry. Honest to God, it just throws you. There have been more family fights about jewelry than about the division of the estate—I see siblings bitterly alienated from one another, and it is about jewelry!

This kind of personal property is never just property: It has symbolism, meaning, memories, and an incredible amount of emotion attached to it—and jewelry is the worst. Although I do not want to be sexist, it is above all moms and daughters who become very emotional about jewelry because of course that is where the associations are. I have also seen it—to a lesser extent—with sons and dads about cars or a gun collection, or whatever the children associate with memories of the parents.

There are two main ways of dealing with these things from the family. One is to use a will provision that says that if the children and family cannot agree on how to divide up the possessions, the executor will sell everything and divide the cash. The other way to deal with this is not binding from a legal point of view but helps the process. You tell Mom and Dad to write down how they want the heirlooms split up and then talk it through with the children while everyone is alive so the children know what their parents' wishes are. This goes far towards resolving the issues that would otherwise come up later

And occasionally you come upon a rational family group with kids who get along. The children will tell me that when their mom was sick, she sat down with them and told them how she wanted the jewelry split. "And my sisters and I are okay with that." I hear that more today than I used to.

Some Concluding Thoughts

Dad made a good living running the business, which, as far as the kids can see, provided an incredible accumulation of wealth. Sometimes the kids assume that the business is a machine that sheds money, and the nonworking kids give very little credit to the working children who are running the business.

There are no easy answers. Much of how the estate and business are structured depends on the advisers doing a good job of delving deeply into the facts to understand the family and the business. And while everyone is alive, it is possible to resolve all or almost all of the issues. With the help of the adviser or attorney, the whole family has to think through the consequences of the arrangements they make. Even signing a lease can create bitter feelings. The child who receives the rent may think it is unfair, and the child who is running the business may think it is unfair. So even though the parents try very hard to equalize everything, everyone could still wind up unhappy. Aside from that, the outcomes also depend greatly on unpredictable family dynamics.

I enjoy working with entrepreneurs, people who have worked hard and established a successful business that provides a good living for a family. I am always available to sit down with them to go through the issues of estate planning and passing the business to the children, but I encourage Mom and Dad to talk to their children even before they talk to me. They call me to make an appointment, and I say to them, "Did you talk to the kids?" There is often this funny reluctance to face the issues with their children. They say, "No, we were kind of waiting to talk to you." And I say, "You have to talk to your children. You have to have a family meeting. You have to express directly to them what your wishes are."

Reluctance can come from a wide variety of sources. For one thing, many people just do not want to face the fact of their own mortality, or do not want to contemplate losing control of their business. Parents are sometimes afraid their children will be upset with them, or they are worried that their children will not value what they have accomplished with the business. Despite their rational understanding of the way the tax code and inheritance laws work, some parents might find themselves just unable to give away their business, their wealth, or their control. Furthermore, like all of us, they procrastinate and see no urgency at all in making decisions that are important but painful—they would rather defer those to another day, but then they find they have run out of time. They might even have an all-too-human reason for not acting because they do not like the in-laws or some other factor about the way the children have led their lives.

Elsewhere in this book I have told the joke about the family business: Dad comes home every night for years and complains about the unions, the payroll, the customers, the employees, and so on, and then turns to the children and says, "Someday this will all be yours." The point of the joke is, when you give somebody a business, what are you really giving them? And yet this has been the parents' whole life—it is the legacy they have to pass on. A financial adviser can help to smooth the transition.

Epilogue

It has taken me 30 years to write this book. It took bull and bear markets, building and selling financial service firms, and trying every failed strategy of the Really Smart Guys. This book relates the years I spent learning these expensive lessons. My goal in this book has been to share these 10 lessons with you and keep you from having to make the same mistakes I did.

1. Don't believe cable TV, magazines, or books on how to make a quick buck in investing. The members of the financial media have no particular insight into what makes a great investment. If they did, why are they working for a living?
2. Equities do offer a risk premium and do outperform bonds in the long term. This means we need to own equities to maintain or create wealth.
3. Capitalism is a harsh mistress in a deep bear market. Massive diversification is essential. There is risk in investing in stocks but there is also risk in not investing in stocks: inflation and taxes. Keep separate buckets of money to weather these tough times. Do not fall in love with your stocks or hold concentrated positions for any reason.
4. Make sure your asset allocation accounts for both your risk and your goals.
5. Do not be fooled by track records and hot managers. Chasing returns is a waste of time. Stock markets work and are efficient. Avoid active stock managers; use a passive strategy and execute it with index funds or, better yet, with asset-class mutual funds.
6. Creating retirement income to last a lifetime requires a change in attitude from accumulating wealth. Use the EAGR system and consider an income annuity to deal with point-in-time risk and mortality risk.
7. Use insurance where it makes sense to protect against certain kinds of risk. Specifically, maintain an umbrella policy for asset protection; use life insurance to provide replacement income in the event of untimely death or to provide estate tax liquidity; and use long-term-care insurance to protect against devastating medical costs.
8. Capitalism works because it is the only system that has created wealth in the past 3,500 years.

9. Don't stay on the sidelines waiting for a good time to invest. You cannot time the market since just a very few days in a 25-year period provide most of the market's return for the whole period. Additionally, geopolitical turmoil may or may not have a positive or negative effect on markets. War and turmoil are simply a fact of human history: In the past 3,500 years, there have been fewer than 300 years of peace. It is essential to keep your wills, trust, and powers up to date. Also keep the named beneficiaries for all your various accounts up to date.
10. Maintain updated wills, trusts, and durable powers.
11. Work with a trusted independent adviser to keep the emotion out of these decisions. Being successful in a profession or business does not mean you can be successful in rationally implementing these rules. You can't!

In 2002, I started a new wealth management firm, Forum Financial Management, LLC, the goal of which is to implement these lessons. Forum represents the culmination of more than 25 years of my experience. The principals of Forum represent over 150 years of experience and have backgrounds in tax, accounting, and law. This is the ultimate culmination of my business career, to have dedicated partners and associates providing fee-based wealth management services alongside some of the most talented advisers in the industry. To provide credible financial advice, you need two things: experience and talented associates. I am lucky to have both.

Notes

Chapter 1   Starting Out

1. *Due diligence*: If you are not part of the financial industry, you are going to find the phrase "doing due diligence" quite weird. *Due diligence* is a precise, technical term for the way any financial entity is supposed to investigate and understand its partners, vendors, or anything it sells. Then you are left with the term, *doing due diligence* for that process of performing the due diligence. It is industry jargon for an important principle.

2. *Front-end-loaded* refers to the way fees and commissions were paid out of the capital raised for the deal. Salespeople might get 7 to 10 percent commission, and the general partner would get paid for forming the group, and you would have to pay the lawyers and accountants. By the time you were done with all that, there might be 10 to 20 percent of the money raised that did not actually become part of the investment into which the investor had thought he was putting his money.

3. *Passive losses* is a term we hardly hear any more, but it was an important concept during the time I am referring to here, the late 1970s and very early 1980s. The tax law for partnerships now says that you cannot deduct losses (from the partnership) from your income taxes unless you are active in the business as a general, active partner to take the losses. The way it worked at that time is that you could be a limited partner and not active in the business but could still deduct these losses from your income taxes. The limited partner was said to have *passive losses*.

4. The 500 in 1980 increased to over 3,500 in 1992, according to Jerry W. Markham, *A Financial History of the United States* Vol. III (M.E. Sharpe, 2002), 186.

5. Stan Luxenberg, "From Complexity to Simplicity and Back," August 1, 2006, http://registeredrep.com/mag/finance_complexity_simplicity_back/.

6. This is the front-end commission (called a front-end load) for investing in a mutual fund. It is discussed at greater length later in this chapter. The percentage amount of the load is subtracted from the investment

amount to pay the registered rep and the broker-dealer for whom he works.

7. A *real estate investment trust*, or REIT, is a company that owns and often manages a portfolio or group of real estate properties such as office or apartment buildings, shopping centers, warehouses, hotels, or golf courses. REITs may be publicly listed on an exchange, or be unlisted or private. They may have equity positions in properties or they may just own the mortgages on these properties. A REIT has the advantage of being a pass-through entity, meaning it is exempt from taxation at the corporate level. In order to gain this advantage, the company must meet certain requirements. The most important requirement is that the company must derive at least 75 percent of its gross income from real estate–related income such as rents and mortgage interest; at least 75 percent of a REIT's assets must consist of real estate assets; and the REIT must distribute at least 90 percent of its taxable income.

Chapter 2   A Decade of Active Management

1. *Alpha* is one of those complex financial ideas that I could spend all day talking about in terms that no one would understand. So here is an example, using the term rather informally. Say that, in a given year, the large-cap asset class provides a 10 percent return. If a large-cap manager has a fund that returns 11 or 12 percent or more, he would be said to have achieved a high alpha—something in excess of the return on the basic asset class return. The formal definition: the abnormal rate of return on a security or portfolio in excess of what would be predicted by an equilibrium model like the capital asset pricing model (CAPM). I could provide equations but I do not believe they would help clarify the concept.

2. Black Monday is the name given to Monday, October 19, 1987, when the Dow Jones Industrial Average (DJIA) dropped by 508 points to 1,739 (22.6 percent), and similar enormous drops occurred around the world. It was the largest one-day percentage decline in stock market history. During that October, there were similar declines in stock markets around the world. Interestingly, the DJIA was positive for the 1987 calendar year, but would not regain its August 25, 1987, closing high of 2,722 points until almost two years later.

3. Thomas M. Anderson, "What Do Morningstar's Stars Really Tell Us?" *Fund Watch*, September 14, 2006, http://kiplinger.com.

4. Dagen McDowell, TheStreet.com, "Dear Dagen: Morningstar Revamps Its Star System," April 29, 2002, http://TheStreet.com.

Chapter 3   Working with Individual Investors

1. Much of the industry information on overconfidence and investor trading originates with Dr. Odean's research. After the first study, the rest were done with Professor Brad M. Barber, from the University of California at Davis. More information about Odean's studies can be found on his web site, www.odean.us. The data I am discussing here comes from a presentation and paper presented at the Legg Mason Funds Management Investment Conference in Las Vegas, November 2003, "What I Know about How You Invest."
2. Brad M. Barber and Terrance Odean, "Why Do Investors Trade Too Much?" Research Summary, Graduate School of Management, UC Davis, 2006, p. 4.
3. Brad M. Barber and Terrance Odean, "Trading Is Hazardous to Your Wealth: The Common Stock Investment Performance of Individual Investors," *Journal of Finance* 55, no. 2 (April 2000): 773.
4. Shlomo Benartzi and Richard H. Thaler, "Heuristics and Biases in Retirement Savings Behavior," *Journal of Economic Perspectives* 21, no. 3 (Summer 2007): 90.
5. Thomas J. Stanley and William D. Danko, *The Millionaire Next Door: The Surprising Secrets of America's Wealthy* (Atlanta: Longstreet Press, 1996).
6. Jennifer Levitz, "When 401(k) Investing Goes Bad," *Wall Street Journal*, August 4, 2008, R1.
7. We discuss this at greater length later in the book, especially Chapters 7 and 8. The 4 percent rule says your money is most likely to last you for your entire retired life if you withdraw not more than 4 percent annually from your overall portfolio to live on. If $140,000 represented 4 percent of your overall portfolio, then your portfolio would be $3.5 million. The actual calculation: $140,000 ÷ 0.04.
8. PBGC is a federal corporation created by the Employee Retirement Income Security Act (ERISA) of 1974. It currently protects the pensions of nearly 44 million American workers and retirees in 30,330 private single-employer and multiemployer defined-benefit pension plans. PBGC receives no funds from general tax revenues. Operations are financed by insurance premiums set by Congress and paid by sponsors of defined-benefit plans, investment income, assets from pension plans trusteed by PBGC, and recoveries from the companies formerly responsible for the plans.
9. General Motors, "GM Statement on Additional Cost Cuts," press release, July 15, 2008, Detroit.
10. Vanessa Fuhrman and Theo Francis, "Retiree Benefits Take Another Hit," *Wall Street Journal Online*, "Careers" section, July 16, 2008.

11. Nicholas Barberis and Richard Thaler, Chapter 18, "A Survey of Behavioral Finance," in *Handbook of the Economics of Finance*, ed. G.M. Constantinides, M. Harris, and R. Stulz (Elsevier Science B.V., 2003), 1071.

12. Gary Belsky and Thomas Gilovich, *Why Smart People Make Big Money Mistakes* (New York: Simon and Schuster Paperbacks, 1999), 56.

13. Douglas A. George, "Behavioral Finance," *Risks and Rewards,* published by the Society of Actuaries, no. 43 (October 2003): 5.

14. Terrance Odean, "Are Investors Reluctant to Realize Their Losses?" *Journal of Finance* 53, no. 5 (October 1998): 1797.

15. George, "Behavioral Finance."

16. Brad M. Barber and Terrance Odean, "Boys Will Be Boys: Gender, Overconfidence, and Common Stock Investment," *Quarterly Journal of Economics*, February 2001, 261–262.

17. Ibid., 289.

18. Shlomo Benartzi and Richard H. Thaler, "Heuristics and Biases in Retirement Savings Behavior," *Journal of Economic Perspectives* 21, no. 3 (Summer 2007): 86.

19. George, "Behavioral Finance." p. 5.

Chapter 4   The Futility of Active Management

1. Tom Lauricella, "The Stock Picker's Defeat," *Wall Street Journal*, December 11, 2008.

2. Scott Woolley, "Bad Buys," *Forbes*, April 13, 2009, 44.

3. Peter L. Bernstein, *Capital Ideas: The Improbable Origins of Modern Wall Street* (New York: Free Press, 1992), 141.

4. Charles D. Ellis, "The Loser's Game," *Financial Analysts Journal* 31, no. 4 (July/August 1975): 19–26.

5. Thomas P. McGuigan, CFP, "The Difficulty of Selecting Superior Mutual Fund Performance, *Journal of Financial Planning,* February 2006.

6. Eugene F. Fama and Kenneth R. French, "Luck versus Skill in the Cross Section of Mutual Fund Alpha Estimates," March 9, 2009. Tuck School of Business Working Paper No. 2009-56; Chicago Booth School of Business Research Paper. Available at SSRN: http://ssrn.com/abstract=1356021

7. Zero Alpha Group, "Study: Investors in Broker-Sold Mutual Funds Miss Published Performancer Numbers by Wide Margin, Timing Is Culprit," press release, December 6, 2007, http://www.zeroalphagroup.com/news/120607_release.cfm.

8. Scott Woolley, "Bad Buys," *Forbes*, April 13, 2009, 45.

9. Ibid.

10. Jason Zweig, "Why Market Forecasts Keep Missing the Mark," *Wall Street Journal*, January 24, 2009; citing research by Javier Estrada, a finance professor at IESE Business School in Barcelona, Spain.

Chapter 5   The Academic Background

1. Bernstein, *Capital Ideas*, 41.
2. *Journal of Finance* interview at http://www.afajof.org/association/historyfinance.asp.
3. Ibid.
4. Bernstein, *Capital Ideas,* 54
5. Harry Markowitz, "Portfolio Selection," *Journal of Finance* 7, no. 1 (March 1952): 89.
6. Bernstein, *Capital Ideas,* 43.
7. Ibid., 48.
8. Precisely why and how he approached this subject in this way would require 10 more pages of text and a lot of equations. If you want to know more about this subject, you should refer to a book with in-depth information about the CAPM and its origins. Almost any advanced finance textbook will treat this subject.
9. An interesting side note is that Sharpe identified systematic risk with the letter *b*, and others also adopted that identification. Somehow Wall Street began to refer to it using the Greek letter *beta*, and that is how it has been designated ever since; even Sharpe adopted that designation. Sharpe must have liked the beginning of the alphabet, because the other financial theory he is known for—developed many years after beta—has alpha as its important component.
10. Bernstein, *Capital Ideas,* 191
11. Ibid., 199.
12. Ibid.
13. Ibid., citing Frederick L. A. Grauer, "On the Occasion of the 25th Anniversary of the Capital Asset Pricing Model," *Currents*, Wells Fargo Investment Advisors, July 1989.
14. Ibid., 107
15. According to his bio on the University of Chicago Graduate School of Business web site.
16. Bernstein, *Capital Ideas,* 132.
17. Ibid., 141.
18. Ibid., 139.
19. Ibid., 234
20. Burton G. Malkiel, *A Random Walk down Wall Street* (New York: W. W. Norton & Company, 2003), 356, citing the first edition of the book.

21. Bernstein, *Capital Ideas*, 249.

22. Joanna L. Ossinger, "The Dimensions of a Pioneering Strategy," *Wall Street Journal*, November 6, 2006.

23. Shawn Tully, "How the Really Smart Money Invests," *Fortune*, July 6, 1998.

24. John C. Bogle, *Common Sense on Mutual Funds: New Imperatives for the Intelligent Investor* (New York: John Wiley & Sons, 2000), 403.

25. John C. Bogle, "The First Index Mutual Fund: A History of Vanguard Index Trust and the Vanguard Index Strategy," Bogle Financial Markets Research Center online, www.vanguard.com/bogle_site/lib/sp19970401.html.

26. Investment Company Institute, *2009 Investment Company Fact Book*, 33.

27. Ibid., 154–155.

28. Gary P. Brinson, L. Randolph Hood, and Gilbert L. Beebower, "Determinants of Portfolio Performance," *Financial Analysts Journal,* July/August 1986, 39.

29. Gary P. Brinson, L. Randolph Hood, and Gilbert L. Beebower, "Determinants of Portfolio Performance II: An Update," *Financial Analysts Journal,* May/June 1991, 40–48.

30. Ibid., 40.

31. Bogle, *Common Sense,* 68.

32. Brinson et al., "Determinants of Portfolio Performance II," 44.

Chapter 6   Implementing the Strategy

1. Zero Alpha Group, "Portfolio Transactions Costs at U.S. Equity Mutual Funds," November 2004. http://www.zeroalphagroup.com/news/Execution_CostsPaper_Nov_15_2004.pdf.

2. John C. Bogle, *Bogle on Mutual Funds: New Perspectives for Intelligent Investors* (Burr Ridge, IL: Irwin Professional, 1994), 204.

3. Nick Murray, "The Four Essential Characteristics of All Bear Markets," Nick Murray Interactive online, Sample Issue 2009 from October 2008, http://nickmurrayinteractive.com/articles/sample2009_four.html.

4. Ned Davis Research, December 31, 2007; stocks are represented by the Dow Jones Industrial Average, a widely used indicator of the overall U.S. stock market, without considering income, transactions costs, or taxes. These statistics on bear markets have been widely quoted in the financial press.

5. Jeremy J. Siegel, *Stocks for the Long Run: The Definitive Guide to Financial Market Returns and Long-Term Investment Strategies* (New York: McGraw-Hill, 2008), 69.

Chapter 7   Planning for Your Retirement and Creating Income for Life

1. John Ameriks, PhD, Robert Veres, and Mark J. Warshawsky, PhD, "Making Retirement Income Last a Lifetime," *Journal of Financial Planning*, December 2001, Table 6.

Chapter 8   Using Annuities as an Income Tool

1. Terri Cullen, "Change Annuities or Not," *Wall Street Journal*, April 26, 2007.

Chapter 11   The Importance of Long-Term-Care Insurance

1. World Health Organization, "Health, History and Hard Choices: Funding Dilemmas in a Fast-Changing World," Thomson Prentice Global Health Histories, University of Indiana, August 2006, 7.
2. "Long-term Care Facility Costs: A Nationwide Quantitative Evaluation of U.S. Facilities," Prudential Financial Global Market Research, March 2008, http://www.prudential.com/view/page/13951.
3. AARP Public Policy Institute, "Valuing the Invaluable: A New Look at the Economic Value of Family Caregiving," *In Brief*, no. 142 (June 2007).
4. Assumptions: $500,000 savings earning 5 percent net of expenses; current long-term care costs $76,285 per year in private room in a nursing home, according to a Genworth Financial 2008 Cost of Care Survey (April 2008), with 4 percent simple inflation increase annually; spouse requires $30,000 annual withdrawal with a 5 percent simple inflation increase each year. All earnings and withdrawals occur at the beginning of each year. This scenario does not take into account any other additions or subtractions that may occur with this account. The assumptions used are only for illustrative purposes. Geographic locations, return on investments, individual circumstances, and medical and financial inflation rates will impact these results accordingly.

Chapter 13   Transferring Wealth within the Family: Inheritance Issues for Family Businesses

1. Panikkos Zata Poutziouris and Kosmas Smyrnios, *Handbook of Research on Family Business* (Edward Elgar Publishing, 2007), 63–64.

About the Authors

Norbert M. Mindel, JD, CPA, CFP®, PFS

Born and raised in Brooklyn, Norm Mindel was accepted into the elite Brooklyn Technical High School after passing a rigorous exam. He received a scholarship to Illinois Institute of Technology (IIT) in Chicago, and graduated with honors with a degree in accounting in 1973. He then graduated from the Chicago-Kent Law School in 1978 in the top 10 percent of his class, and had also passed the CPA exam by the time he got his law degree.

He and a law school colleague started a law firm in 1978, and his practice concentrated on taxes, estate planning, business succession, and real estate. During that time, he also served as a lecturer in accounting at Benedictine College and then as a full-time lecturer of accounting at the Stuart School of Business at IIT.

In the early 1980s, he teamed up with Dave Reedy and Tom King to found the Terra Financial Companies, which included Terra Securities Corporation, a broker-dealer. The partners quickly discovered that they could grow the company much more quickly if they expanded beyond personal production. Terra focused on providing licensing and training for accountants and tax professionals so they themselves could become financial professionals. Norm was instrumental in helping Terra grow into a national, multidisciplinary, financial services organization.

Norm always took the lead in company strategy and products. In 1994, he led the development of a fee-based, investment advisory platform which eventually grew to $3.4 billion in assets. This program quickly emerged as one of the fastest-growing financial segments of the business, and had a strategy that fit extremely well with the part-time accountant advisers who worked with Terra.

In 1997, recognizing the need to grow the business aggressively, Norm led the effort to analyze how best to do that. He developed a business and growth strategy that eventually resulted in the sale of the broker-dealer in

1998 to GE, then one of the largest companies in the world. While at GE, Norm worked on business development and strategic acquisitions.

It became apparent to Norm that his first love was advising clients personally, and he decided to reduce his role at GE to devote more time to working with his long-time personal clients as an Investment Advisor Representative. In 2001, Norm and two of his former partners from Terra, Marcus Heinrich and Brian Savage, co-founded Forum Financial Management, LLC, a wealth management firm located in Lombard, Illinois. Norm's service and personal attention to his clients have served as the foundation for the substantial and consistent growth of the firm's national clientele.

In 2004, GE decided to divest itself of its insurance and other financial holdings, and Genworth Financial, based in Richmond, Virginia, was formed through an IPO. Terra Securities, in Schaumburg, Illinois, became Genworth Financial Investment Services. In 2008, Norm decided to devote himself full-time to Forum Financial.

Norm's natural abilities as a speaker were honed during his early years in business, when giving speeches, presentations, and seminars was one of the best ways to build his law business and, later, Terra Securities. He has become a noted national speaker on many topics, specializing in asset management and practice management for financial advisers, and often addresses large groups of financial planners and accounting professionals. Norm has a rare ability to involve and engage his audience while still imparting critical teaching points along the way. His high-energy, compelling keynotes and seminars are derived from his own 25 years in the financial services business.

Norm's many speaking engagements have included being a frequent guest of CNBC's *Power Lunch* and CNNfn's *Your Money* show. He has been quoted in the *Chicago Tribune*, *L.A. Times*, *Smart Money*, the *New York Times*, *Crain's Chicago Business*, the *Financial Times*, and a great many other industry publications.

In addition to being an attorney, he is a member of the American Institute of Certified Public Accountants, and the Financial Planning Association.

In his spare time, Norm belongs to the Autobahn Club in Joliet, Illinois, where he races sports cars, and he regularly participates in Bikram yoga.

Norm lives with his wife, Judy, in the southwestern suburbs of Chicago and is the proud father of Rachel, Ariel, Talia, and Zachary.

You may contact Norm at Forum Financial Management, LLC, 1900 S. Highland Avenue, Suite 100, Lombard, IL 60148; 630-873-8520. His direct e-mail address is nmindel@forumfin.com. Learn more about Forum Financial at www.forumfin.com.

Sarah E. Sleight

Sarah E. Sleight was born and grew up in California, but has lived in Chicago for more than 30 years. Her undergraduate degree is a BA with honors in history from Bucknell University (1972) and she earned a master's in management with a major in finance, granted with distinction, from the Kellogg School of Management at Northwestern University (1982).

Before starting in business, she spent two years living and working in Europe: a year in Stuttgart and a year in Paris. She says that learning those two foreign languages contributed to her command of the English language.

She began her career at the World Bank, in Washington, D.C., and moved to Chicago in 1978. She worked at a major money center bank, and then spent seven years as a salesperson in institutional sales on the trading floor of a large bank broker-dealer. She worked for a start-up third-party provider of securities services to banks. She served as director of marketing for a money management firm and then for a clearing firm. She also worked for a well-known provider of asset allocation and other financial consulting, and for a private association of family offices.

She first met Norm Mindel when she was hired by Genworth Financial as a member of the marketing team; her responsibilities included working with the passive investment program Norm founded.

She is co-author of another book, *Reinventing the Retail Bank*, published by Probus Publishing in 1993. She ghost-wrote a book on a specialized securities strategy as part of her responsibilities at the money management firm, and edited a number of financial books for Probus Publishing. She has written many articles for publications in the financial services world.

She and her husband, Peter K. Muecke, have been married for more than 20 years and live in Chicago with their various pets. She has been an enthusiastic participant in a book club for more than 25 years. She thanks Pete for tolerating almost two years of spending all of her time outside of her job working on this book.

Index